OPTIMIZATION IN MICROECONOMICS

Revised Edition

By Christopher Curran
and Skip Garibaldi

Bassim Hamadeh, CEO and Publisher
Michael Simpson, Vice President of Acquisitions and Sales
Jamie Giganti, Senior Managing Editor
Miguel Macias, Graphic Designer
Seidy Cruz, Senior Field Acquisitions Editor
Natalie Lakosil, Licensing Manager

First published in the United States of America in 2016 by Cognella, Inc.

Printed in the United States of America

ISBN: 978-1-5165-0551-7 (pbk) / 978-1-5165-0552-4 (br)

www.cognella.com   800-200-3908

CONTENTS

CHAPTER 1 | Memories of Calculus   1

CHAPTER 2 | Optimizing Functions with One   15
            Control Variable

CHAPTER 3 | Matrices   41

CHAPTER 4 | Optimizing Functions with   51
            Two Control Variables

CHAPTER 5 | Optimizing Functions with Several   79
            Control Variables

CHAPTER 6 | Constrained Optimization   89

CHAPTER 7 | Quasi-Convexity   115

CHAPTER 8 | Homogeneity and Duality   121

❦ PREFACE

This text is the product of teaching a course on mathematical economics for almost 35 years. Throughout the time that this course has been taught we have maintained the position that a course in mathematical economics is an opportunity to examine how two disciplines analyze an issue—optimization. In their models economists generally assume that some agent is either maximizing or minimizing some function in order to attain an objective. Economists use the mathematics of optimization to derive implications of the models in order to set up ways to test these models. Indeed, the testable implications of the models are what makes this sort of economic theory scientific: to be useful, an economic model must yield some implications that are potentially testable. By "testable" we mean that there exist potential outcomes to an economic experiment that would contradict the model. This is the approach that informs every part of this text.

The textbook describes in detail the mathematical tools necessary to analyze the optimization models used by economists. We move from the simple model of unconstrained optimization with one control variable through unconstrained optimization with multiple control variables to optimization models with equality constraints. In each case we develop all the tools needed to derive the comparative static implications of the model. Moreover, we emphasize the importance of the Envelope Theorem throughout the text. We end with a discussion of duality theory.

The main material of this book is contained in the even-numbered chapters, 2, 4, 6, and 8. The odd-numbered chapters 1 and 3 review the mathematics needed in the even chapters, whereas chapters 5 and 7 extend the mathematics used in the even chapters. In the review chapters, we present only the material needed in the subsequent chapters or that we have found our undergraduates to have not remembered from earlier mathematics classes. Thus, unlike many other mathematical economics texts, we do not present encyclopedic discussions of topics like matrix algebra. The chapters cover the minimum mathematics necessary for later material.

We believe that the key material in this textbook are the problems included in the various exercise sets. Many of these problems begin with a verbal description of a model that the student has to translate into a mathematical form that he or she can use optimization theory to analyze. Then the student is asked to translate the results of their mathematical analysis in to words that a non-mathematician can understand. Our students have found these problems to be the main way that they learn the material. The exercises are so indispensable to the learning process that we have had our students present their answers in class. While this is a time-consuming process, it has proved to have the additional benefit of providing the students with an opportunity to improve their communication skills.

We end this brief introduction with a brief note about the numbering convention used in this text. The system we use, while intended to making finding numbered material in the text easier to locate, may not be familiar to economics students, so it is worth taking a moment to explain it. All of the chapters and their sections are identified with Arabic numbers, e.g., section 7 of chapter 4, etc. We identify all examples, figures, tables, theorems, lemmas, and propositions sequentially. Thus, Figure 2.5.1 is the first item in Chapter 2, section 5. If the next item is an example, it will have the label Example 2.5.2. This numbering system should make it easier to find these items when they are referenced in the text. The numbered equations follow a similar rule, except that all equation numbers are in parentheses. Exercises have their own, albeit similar, numbering system. Exercise 3.3.5 is the fifth exercise in the third section of Chapter 3.

We end this brief introduction with a few acknowledgements and thanks. First, we acknowledge the silent contributions of David Ford of the Emory Mathematics Department (now retired) to the development of this book. Professor Ford co-taught the Mathematical Economics course with Dr. Curran for over thirty years and during that time patiently corrected his many misunderstandings of the subtleties of mathematical reasoning. Second, it is often said that teaching is the best way to learn a subject. This adage certainly is true for us. Thus, we would also like to acknowledge our debt to the many mathematical economics students we have taught. Fourth, we appreciate the contributions to the editing and content of this text made by our colleagues Steve Batterson (Mathematics Department) and Christina DePasquale (Economics Department); their contributions have added substantially to quality of the final product. Finally, we would like to thank our wives, Nannette and Julia, for their unwavering support while we completed this project.

Christopher Curran & Skip Garibaldi
Emory University
Atlanta, Georgia

CHAPTER 1
MEMORIES OF CALCULUS

T o follow along with this book, you will need to use some of the things you learned in calculus. Some things we will recall along the way, but some are too tangential. The purpose of this chapter is to recall the latter material.

1.1 FUNCTIONS OF ONE VARIABLE: POSITIVE, INCREASING, CONVEX/ CONCAVE UP

Examine the graph of a function $f(x)$ given in Figure 1.1.1. The function has the properties listed in Table 1.1.2.

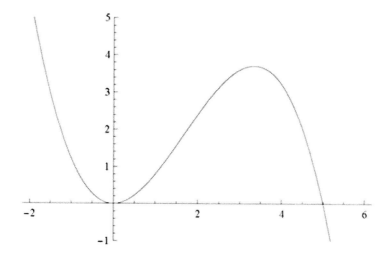

Figure 1.1.1 Graph of a function $f(x)$.

Table 1.1.2 Properties of the function $f(x)$ graphed in Figure 1.1.1

Interval	$f(x)$	$f'(x)$	$f''(x)$
$x < 0$	decreasing, concave up	negative, increasing	positive
$0 < x < 1.7$	increasing, concave up	positive, increasing	positive
$1.7 < x < 3.3$	increasing, concave down	positive, decreasing	negative
$3.3 < x$	decreasing, concave down	negative, decreasing	negative

Sometimes economists talk about functions being "convex" or "concave" instead of "concave up" or "concave down." These terms are not exactly the same. See Chapter 5 for details.

Example 1.1.3

A utility function $U(x)$ says how much utility a particular individual (say, Alice) derives from having income x. We assume that having money is good, so $U(x)$ is positive. We also assume that more money makes Alice happier, i.e., $U(x)$ is increasing. (This is called non satiety, meaning that Alice is never satiated and always wants more money.) In terms of derivatives, this means that $U'(x)$ is positive.

Finally, we assume that a poor Alice would appreciate receiving a million extra dollars much more than would multi-billionaire Alice, i.e., we assume that $U(x)$ is increasing at a decreasing rate. This means that $U(x)$ is concave down, equivalently, that $U''(x)$ is negative.

Exercises

1.1.1 The graph of the first derivative $f'(x)$ of a function $f(x)$ is shown in Figure 1.1.4.

    (a) On what intervals is f increasing? Explain.
    (b) On what intervals is f concave up? Explain.

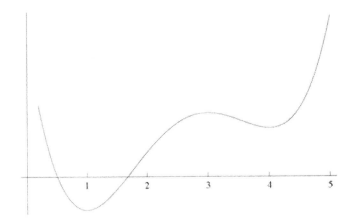

Figure 1.1.4 Graph of the derivative, $f'(x)$.

A critical point x^* of a function $f(x)$ is a point such that $f'(x^*)=0$. How can you tell if x^* is a maximum of $f(x)$? From calculus, you remember: If $f''(x^*)<0$, then x^* is a local maximum, $f(x) \leq f(x^*)$ that is, $f(x) \leq f(x^*)$ for x near x^*. This is known as the second-order condition for a local maximum; if $f''(x^*)<0$, we say that the second-order condition (for x^* to be a local maximum) holds. (To remember the second-order condition, it can be helpful to think about parabolas. The downward-opening parabola $y=-x^2$ has a maximum

at $x=0$ and the second-derivative $d^2y \big/ dx^2 = -2$ is negative. In contrast, the upward-opening

parabola $y=x^2$ has a minimum at $x=0$ and the second-derivative $d^2y \big/ dx^2 = 2$ is positive.)

In many cases, we want to know if a critical point x^* is a global maximum, that is, if $f(x^*) \geq f(x)$ for all x. The second-order condition for a global maximum is:

Theorem 1.2.1 (Global SOC Theorem). *Suppose that x^* is a critical point for $f(x)$. If $f''(x)<0$ for all x, then x^* is the unique critical point and it is a global maximum for $f(x)$.*

The theorem makes sense: If $f''(x)$ is always negative, then the graph of the function is concave down, so any local maximum is a global maximum. We give a more rigorous proof for those who want one.

PROOF. For sake of contradiction, suppose that there is another critical point *c*. That is, $c \neq x^*$ and $f'(x)=f'(x^*)=0$. Then by the Mean Value Theorem there is some *b* lying between x^* and *c* such that $f''(b)=0$. This is a contradiction, so x^* is the unique critical point.

Again, for sake of contradiction, suppose that there is some point e $> x^*$ such that $f(e) > f(x^*)$. Then

$$0 < \frac{f(e)-f(x^*)}{e-x^*}.$$

But the Mean Value Theorem says there is some *d* such that $x^* < d < e$ and

$$\frac{f(e)-f(x^*)}{e-x^*} = f'(d) = \int_{x^*}^{d} f''(x)\,dx < 0.$$

This is a contradiction, so no such *e* can exist. An analogous argument shows that there is no e $< x^*$ with $f(e)>f(x^*)$. This shows that x^* is a global maximum.

This argument also proves the second-order condition for a local maximum that you remember from calculus.

In the statement of the theorem, we implicitly assumed that $f(x)$ is defined and twice differentiable for all real numbers x, as you can see in the phrase "for all *x*". Economists often consider functions $f(x)$ that are only defined for positive *x*; for such a function we could replace "for all *x*" with "for all positive *x*". Such a replacement is harmless.[*]

If we are a little more clever, we can get the same conclusion while assuming less about $f(x)$.

Alternate proof of Theorem 1.2.1 (Global SOC Theorem). Suppose that we only know the following: If $f'(c)=0$, then $f''(c)<0$, i.e., every critical point of $f(x)$ is a local maximum. Obviously this assumption is weaker

---

[*] For the mathematically inclined reader: The important thing is that we are only considering values of *x* in some *open interval* of the *x*-axis. In the language of economics, we only look for "interior solutions", and not "corner solutions".

than the assumption "$f''(c)<0$ for all x" from the earlier proof of the Global SOC Theorem. We assume that there is a critical point x^* of $f(x)$ and we will show that it is the unique critical point and is a global maximum for $f(x)$.

Because $f'(x^*)=0$ and $f''(x^*)<0$, the derivative $f'(x)$ is positive just left of x^* and negative just to the right. If we zoom in on the point $(x^*, f(x^*))$ on the graph of $f(x)$, we see what looks like an upside-down parabola with its apex at x^*.

For sake of contradiction, suppose there is another critical point c. By our hypothesis on $f(x)$, c is also a local maximum, and when we zoom in on the point $(c, f(c))$ on the graph of $f(x)$, we again see an upside-down parabola. In order to connect these two sections of graph, there must be a point b between c and x^* where there is a local minimum. But this is impossible, because every critical point of $f(x)$ is a local maximum. Therefore, x^* is the unique critical point of $f(x)$.

Finally, $f(x) < f(x^*)$ for all $x \neq x^*$. Otherwise, there is some d such that $d \neq x^*$ and $f(d) = f(x^*)$. By the Mean Value Theorem, there is some c properly between d and x^* with $f'(c) = 0$, but this is impossible because x^* is the unique critical point.

1.3 CLOSED INTERVALS AND CORNER MAXIMA

So far we have been implicitly assuming that the function $f(x)$ is defined on an open interval, say for all x or for all $x > 0$. Then maxima and minima for such a function will occur at critical points. This is the typical situation we fill consider in this book.

However, sometimes it is more natural for $f(x)$ to be defined on some closed interval, say for $a \leq x \leq b$. One natural example is when $f(x)$ measures the utility Alice derives from consuming x dollars worth of some good. It is reasonable to imagine that this function may only be defined for $0 \leq x \leq I$, where I is Alice's total income. In terms of the story, this would say that Alice can spend nothing on the good, can spend everything she has on the good, or can spend something in between.

In this case, we have a recipe for a solution. First, find all the critical points of $f(x)$ in the interval $a < x < b$. Plug these and a and b into $f(x)$. Whichever gives the biggest value is the location of the global maximum. If the maximum is at one of the critical points (lying properly between a and b), we say it is an *interior* maximum. If the maximum is at one of the endpoints a or b, then we say it is a *corner* maximum.

Of course, a similar recipe and similar words apply to finding a global minimum of the function.

Example 1.3.1

Let us return to the example where $f(x)$ is Alice's utility from spending x dollars on some good. As in Example 1.1.3, $f'(x)$ is positive for $0 < x < I$, so there are no critical points. We are left with comparing the value of $f(x)$ at the endpoints 0 and I. As $f(x)$ is increasing and $I > 0$, $f(I) > f(0)$, and I is the location of the global maximum for $f(x)$.

Exercises

    1.3.1 Look back at the graph of $f'(x)$ in Figure 1.1.4. At what values of x does f have a local maximum? A local minimum? Explain.

    1.3.2 Give an example of a continuous function that is defined for all $x > 0$ and such that $x = 1$ is a local maximum but not a global maximum. [This question has two parts: You have to find such a function, and then you have to explain why the function you found has the desired properties.]

1.3.3 The function $f(x) = \ln(x)$ is defined for $x > 0$. Show that $f''(x) < 0$ and that $f(x)$ has no critical points for $x = 1$. [This problem shows why the Global SOC Theorem starts by assuming that $f(x)$ has a critical point x^*. Here we have a function where $f''(x) < 0$ and there is no global maximum.]

1.3.4 Give an alternative proof of the Global SOC Theorem using the Fundamental Theorem of Calculus. [One possible approach is to use the Fundamental Theorem to show that $f'(x)$ is positive for $x < x^*$ and $f'(x)$ is negative for $x < x^*$. Then use the Fundamental Theorem again to prove the theorem.]

1.3.5 Give an alternative proof of the Global SOC Theorem using Taylor's Theorem. [For a precise statement of Taylor's Theorem, see any advanced calculus or real analysis text, such as W. Rudin, *Principles of Mathematical Analysis*, McGraw-Hill, 1976.]

1.3.6 A man stands on a beach at point A (see Figure 1.3.2) and throws a stick into the water to point D.[*] His dog, a time-minimizing animal, then fetches the stick by taking one of three routes: (1) swim the whole way to point D, (2) run to point C and swim to point D, or (3) run along the beach to point B and then swim from point B to point D. The speed of the dog on the beach is r and the speed of the dog in the water is s.

Figure 1.3.2 What's the fastest way to the stick?

a. How long will it take the dog to reach point D if he swims the entire way (following route 1)?

b. How long will it take the dog to reach point D if he runs to point C and then swims out to point D (following route 2)?

c. How long will it take the dog to reach point D if he runs to point B and then swims to point D (route 3)?

d. Looking back at your answer for part (c), if you plug in numbers such that $y > z$, your formula probably says something that does not make sense physically. That's okay because we do not care about that case. But why doesn't your formula from (c) model reality in this case?

e. If $r \leq s$, what route does the dog take, and why?

---

[*] This problem is based on T.J. Pennings, Do dogs know calculus?, *College Math. Journal*, vol. 34 (2003), pp. 178–182.

f. Suppose that $r > s$ and $\dfrac{x}{\sqrt{\left(\dfrac{r}{s}\right)^2 - 1}} \le z$. Find the value y^* of y that minimizes the time for the dog to

cover route 3. Check the SOC to verify that y^* is a local minimum. Write y^* as a function of x and r/s. Verify that y^* is between 0 and z, i.e., is in the range where your answer for (c) makes sense.

g. Suppose that $r > s$ and $\dfrac{x}{\sqrt{\left(\dfrac{r}{s}\right)^2 - 1}} > z$. (This is the only case we have not covered yet, and

corresponds to the man throwing the stick much farther into the water than along the beach.) Verify that the derivative of the time t that it takes the dog to run route 3 with respect to y is negative for $0 < y < z$. What route does the dog take in this case?

h. Suppose that you have a particular dog, so that r/s is fixed. Use the results of this problem to describe a way to test if dogs choose the time-minimizing path to a stick thrown into the water (i.e., to test if dogs are "rational"). There is no single "correct answer to this question since each scientist might design the experiment differently. There are descriptions, however, that provide a more thorough description of an experiment that is likely to produce convincing results.

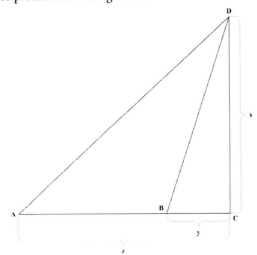

Figure 1.3.3 Graph to accompany Exercise 1.3.6.

1.4 THE CHAIN RULE

Chain rule for functions of one variable

In calculus, you learned the chain rule for functions of one variable:

$$\frac{d}{dx} f\big(g(x)\big) = f'\big(g(x)\big) g'(x). \tag{1.4.1}$$

Example 1.4.1

If we want to find the derivative of $\sin\left(x^2+1\right)$ with respect to x, we can write

$$f\left(y\right) := \sin\left(y\right) \text{ and } y = g\left(x\right) := x^2+1.$$

Then

$$f'\left(y\right) = \frac{d}{dy}\sin\left(y\right) = \cos\left(y\right) \text{ and } g'\left(x\right) = 2x.$$

So

$$\frac{d}{dx}\sin(x^2+1) = 2x\cos(x^2+1).$$

The chain rule (1.4.1) can be written differently. Put $z := f\left(y\right)$ and $y := g\left(x\right)$. Then[*],

$$\frac{d}{dx}f\left(g\left(x\right)\right) = \frac{dz}{dx}, \quad f'\left(g\left(x\right)\right) = \frac{dz}{dy}, \text{ and } g'\left(x\right) = \frac{dy}{dx}. \tag{1.4.2}$$

So:

$$\frac{dz}{dx} = \frac{dz}{dy}\frac{dy}{dx}.$$

You used this version of the chain rule many times when you did related rates problems.

Chain rule for functions of several variables

Consider the example:

Example 1.4.2

For $z := x_1 x_2^{\,2}$ with $x_1 := t^3$ and $x_2 := t+1$, we have:

$$\frac{dz}{dt} = x_2^2 \frac{dx_1}{dt} + x_1 \frac{d}{dt}x_2^2 \text{ by the product rule,}$$

$$\frac{dz}{dt} = x_2^2 \frac{dx_1}{dt} + 2x_1 x_2 \frac{dx_2}{dt} \text{ by the chain rule, and} \tag{1.4.3}$$

$$\frac{dz}{dt} = (t+1)^2(3t^2) + 2t^3(t+1) = 5t^4 + 8t^3 + 3t^2.$$

Notice that the formula for $\dfrac{dz}{dt}$ has no x_1's or x_2's in it. So far, we have just used the chain rule for functions of one variable. We can re-write this as follows. Suppose that $z = f\left(x_1, x_2\right)$, $x_1 = g\left(t\right)$, and $x_2 = h\left(t\right)$ for some functions f, g, and h. Then the chain rule says:

$$\frac{dz}{dt} = \frac{\partial z}{\partial x_1}\frac{dx_1}{dt} + \frac{\partial z}{\partial x_2}\frac{dx_2}{dt}. \tag{1.4.4}$$

---

[*] Properly speaking, we also have to require that f and g are differentiable. But when dealing with economic problems—i.e., everywhere in this course—we assume that all functions appearing are smooth, as explained in the preface. We can do this because all the functions we deal with appear as part of a mathematical model of some real-world situation. Such functions are found by guessing at a formula and making some measurements to fill in some parameters. Obviously there is some error in that process. Within your error bounds, you can find a smooth function that adequately approximates the data.

We now re-do Example 1.4.2 We have:

$$\frac{\partial z}{\partial x_1} = x_2^2 \text{ and } \frac{\partial z}{\partial x_2} = 2x_1 x_2.$$

So applying equation (1.4.4), we get:

$$\frac{dz}{dt} = x_2^2 \frac{dx_1}{dt} + 2x_1 x_2 \frac{dx_2}{dt},$$

and we can finish as in Example 1.4.2.

We can re-write equation (1.4.4) as:

$$\frac{d}{dt} f(x_1, x_2) = f_{x_1}(x_1, x_2) x_1'(t) + f_{x_2}(x_1, x_2) x_2'(t),$$

where f_{x_1} is shorthand for $\dfrac{\partial f}{\partial x_1}$. (Sometimes we will abbreviate this partial derivative still further as f_1.) There is a useful mnemonic in this re-writing of (1.4.4): *for every comma on the left side, there is a plus on the right side.*

In a typical economic problem, there is not just one parameter t; there are more. For example, suppose that $z = f(x_1, x_2)$, where $x_1 = g(p, q)$ and $x_2 = h(p, q)$ for some functions f, g, and h. Then,

$$\frac{\partial z}{\partial p} = \frac{\partial z}{\partial x_1} \frac{\partial x_1}{\partial p} + \frac{\partial z}{\partial x_2} \frac{\partial x_2}{\partial p}$$

$$\frac{\partial z}{\partial q} = \frac{\partial z}{\partial x_1} \frac{\partial x_1}{\partial q} + \frac{\partial z}{\partial x_2} \frac{\partial x_2}{\partial q}. \qquad (1.4.5)$$

Exercises

1.4.1 Using the chain rule (1.4.1) or (1.4.2), find:

(a) $\dfrac{d}{dx} x^2 \sin(\cos x)$.

(b) $\dfrac{d}{dx} \left(1 - (x+1)^{1000}\right)^{99}$.

1.4.2 For $z = x_1 - 3x_1 x_2 + x_2^2$, and $x_1 = \sin(t)$ and $x_2 = \cos(t)$, find dz/dt using the chain rule (1.4.4).

1.4.3 For $z = x_1^2 - x_1 x_2$ with $x_1 = p\cos q$ and $x_2 = q\sin p$, find $\partial z/\partial p$ and $\partial z/\partial q$ using the chain rule 1.4.5.

1.5 EXPONENTIALS AND LOGARITHMS

You remember the Laws of Exponents that you learned in pre-calculus:

$$a^b a^c = a^{b+c}, \ (a^b)^c = a^{bc}, \text{ and } a^b/a^c = a^{b-c}. \qquad (1.5.1)$$

You also know how to take a derivative

$$\frac{d}{dx}x^b = bx^{b-1} \text{ if } b \neq 0.$$

This is the Power Rule.

The similar-looking but different derivative $\frac{d}{dx}b^x$ requires a different approach. Amongst all positive numbers, there is a unique one, e, such that

$$\frac{d}{dx}e^x = e^x.$$

You might remember that e is about* 2.7.

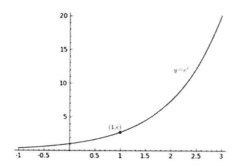

Figure 1.5.1 Graph of e^x.

You can see a graph of e^x in Figure 1.5.1. Note that the function is increasing, that is, as you move to the right along the x-axis, the value of e^x goes up. This means that has an inverse function, which we call *natural log* and denote by ln. The statement that $\ln(x)$ and are inverse functions means that

$$\ln e^x = x \text{ for all } x \quad \text{and} \quad e^{\ln(x)} = x \text{ for } x > 0. \tag{1.5.2}$$

Figure 1.5.2 shows the graph of $\ln(x)$.

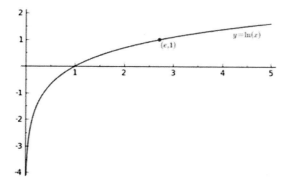

---

* Careful! e cannot be written as a finite decimal or a ratio of two integers; it is a decimal that goes on forever and never settles into a repeating pattern; it is an *irrational* number. For a proof of this, see Aigner, Ziegler, *Proofs from THE BOOK*, Springer, 1998.

Figure 1.5.2 Graph of ln(x)

Laws of logarithms

Because $\ln(x)$ and e^x are inverses of each other, the Laws of Exponents (1.5.1) induce similar rules for logarithms:

$$\ln(bc) = \ln(b) + \ln(c), \quad \ln(a^b) = b\ln(a), \quad \text{and} \quad \ln\left(a\!\big/\!b\right) = \ln(a) - \ln(b).$$

Exponentials, logarithms, and the chain rule

Combining equation (1.5.2) with the chain rule (1.4.1) from the previous section gives:

$$\frac{d}{dx}e^{f(x)} = e^{f(x)}f'(x) \quad \text{and} \quad \frac{d}{dx}\ln f(x) = \frac{f'(x)}{f(x)}. \tag{1.5.3}$$

We can use the first of these rules to evaluate $\dfrac{d}{dx}b^x$ where b is a positive number. We rewrite b as $e^{\ln(b)}$, so

$$\frac{d}{dx}b^x = \frac{d}{dx}(e^{\ln(b)})^x = \frac{d}{dx}e^{x\ln(b)} = e^{x\ln(b)}\ln(b) = b^x\ln(b).$$

The second rule in (1.5.3) can be rewritten as

$$f'(x) = f(x)\frac{d}{dx}\ln f(x).$$

This rule is sometimes known as *logarithmic differentiation*. Applying it to the case where $f(x) = b^x$, we find:

$$\frac{d}{dx}b^x = b^x\frac{d}{dx}\ln(b^x) = b^x\frac{d}{dx}x\ln(b) = b^x\ln(b).$$

This is the same answer we found before.

Exercises

1.5.1 Use logarithmic differentiation to write down a formula for $\dfrac{d}{dx}f(x)^{g(x)}$. Use it to calculate $\dfrac{d}{dx}x^x$.

1.5.2 Let $g(n) = 1 - (1-p)^n$ for some p such that $0 < p < 1$. (Perhaps p is a probability.) Calculate $g'(n)$ and $g''(n)$ and determine their signs for $n > 0$.

1.6 IMPLICIT DIFFERENTIATION

Example 1.6.1

The equation for the unit circle is

$$x^2 + y^2 = 1. \tag{1.6.1}$$

Suppose we want to find a formula for $dy\big/dx$. The naive approach is to solve the equation for y and then take the derivative. That works great for this example, but will not work for the problems below or anywhere else in this text. So we use another approach: we take the derivative of both sides of the equation with respect to x:

$$\frac{d}{dx}\left(x^2 + y^2\right) = \frac{d}{dx}1$$

$$\frac{d}{dx}\left(x^2\right)+\frac{d}{dx}\left(y^2\right)=0 \quad \text{because 1 is a constant}$$

$$2x\frac{dx}{dx}+2y\frac{dy}{dx}=0 \quad \text{using the Chain Rule}$$

$$2x+2y\frac{dy}{dx}=0 \quad \text{because} \quad \frac{dx}{dx}=1$$

$$2y\frac{dy}{dx}=-2x$$

$$\frac{dy}{dx}=-\frac{x}{y}.$$

Note that both x and y appear on the right side of this equation; that is okay.

This technique is known as *implicit differentiation*, because of the following reason: Thanks to the Implicit Function Theorem (discussed in section 2.7), equation 1.6.1 implicitly defines y as a function of x.

Exercises

1.6.1 Find $\frac{dy}{dx}$ by implicit differentiation:

   (a) $y^5 + x^2 y = 1 - x^3 y.$

   (b) $\cos(x) + \sin(y) = 1.$

1.7 INEQUALITIES

Rules for inequalities

Let's remember way back to before calculus, to solving equations involving inequalities. You learned the following five rules:

1. If $a < b$, then $a + c < b + c$. ("You can add to both sides.")

2. If $a < b$ and $c < d$, then $a + c < b + d$.

3. If $a < b$ and $c > 0$, then $ac < bc$. ("You can multiply or divide by a positive number.")

4. If $a < b$ and $c < 0$, then $ac > bc$. ("If you multiply or divide by a negative number, you have to flip the inequality.")

5. If $0 < a < b$, then $\frac{1}{a} > \frac{1}{b}$. ("If both sides are positive, you can take 1 over each side, but you have to flip the inequality.")

Example 1.7.1

Suppose we want to solve the equation $-3x + 2 < 8$. Applying Rule 1 with $c = -2$, we can subtract 2 from both sides to get $-3x < 6$. Applying Rule 3 with $c = -\frac{1}{3}$, we can divide both sides by -3 and find $x > -2$. (For readers who have had a course on mathematical logic, it looks like this argument only shows: "If $-3x + 2 < 8$, then $x > -2$." But Rules 1 through 5 are reversible, so we can do all the steps in the opposite order. Starting with $x > -2$, we apply Rule 3 with $c = -3$ to get $-3x < 6$. Applying Rule 1 with $c = 2$ gives $-3x + 2 < 8$. This shows that the statements $-3x + 2 < 8$ and $x > -2$ are equivalent, i.e., $-3x + 2 < 8$ if and only if $x > -2$.)

Exponentials and logarithms

We can add two more rules for inequalities:

6. If $a < b$, then $e^a < e^b$.

7. If $0 < a < b$, then $\ln(a) < \ln(b)$.

These rules say that the functions e^x and $\ln(x)$ are increasing. Comparing Rules 6 and 7, Rule 7 has an additional "$0 < a$"; this is just to ensure that $\ln(a)$ and $\ln(b)$ are defined.

Exercises

1.7.1 Let a and b be nonzero numbers. For each of the four possibilities for the signs of a and b, either determine the sign of $a - b$ or give explicit examples of numbers a and b to show that you cannot determine the sign of $a - b$.

1.7.2 For which values of x do each of the following inequalities hold? Indicate which rule you used at each step of your solution.

(a) $1 < 3 - 2x \le 9$.

(b) $x < 5 + x$.

(c) $x^2 < x(5 + x)$.

(d) $2^x > 1$.

(e) $2^x \ln 2 < 1$.

(f) $\ln(3x) > \ln(x+2)$.

1.7.3 Show that $e^x \ge x + 1$ for all $x \ge 0$. [Hint: Examine $f(x) := e^x - (x+1)$. Obviously $f(0) = 0$. Show that $f'(x) > 0$ for all $x > 0$.] For which positive numbers b is it true that $b^x \ge x + 1$ for all $x \ge 0$?

Recall from intermediate microeconomics the inverse demand function $p(q)$. It tells you the price at which consumers will demand the quantity q of some good. The price elasticity of demand

$$\varepsilon = \frac{p(q)/q}{dp/dq}$$

measures the relative sensitivity of demand to a change in price.

Since p and q are both positive, ε has the same sign as $p'(q)$. For an ordinary good, demand and price move in opposite directions (the Law of Demand), so $p'(q)$ and ε are both negative. Demand is *elastic* if ε is less than -1 and is *inelastic* if ε is between -1 and 0. (A good is called a *Giffen good* if demand and price move in the same direction, i.e., higher price leads to higher demand. So far, no one has ever presented a clear-cut, well-accepted example of a Giffen good in the real world.)

Given any function $f(x)$, one can talk about its elasticity, which is defined to be

$$\frac{f(x)/x}{f'(x)}.$$

To name this quantity in words, you would say something like "f elasticity of x".

Exercises

1.8.1 A monopolist can sell q units of a product at a price $p(q)$, so that his revenue function is $R(q) = p(q)q$.

(a) Find $R'(q)$.

(b) Write $R'(q)$ in terms of the price, $p(q)$, and the price elasticity of demand.

(c) Show that marginal revenue $R'(q)$ is positive if demand is elastic, and that $R'(q)$ is negative if demand is inelastic.

(d) Suppose now that that p is a linear function of y. (This might be the only type you saw in your microeconomics course.) Show that $R''(q)$ is negative if and only if the good is a normal good.

1.8.2 The Cobb-Douglas function $f(x_1, x_2) = Ax_1^\alpha x_2^\beta$ appears often enough in this and other texts that it seems appropriate to mention a few shortcuts that will make computation of the derivatives easier. This problem takes you through some of these shortcuts.

(a) Find $f_1(x_1, x_2)$. [The notation f_1 is shorthand for $\frac{\partial f}{\partial x_1}$. Your calculus book may have used the alternative shorthand "f_{x_1}".]

(b) Show that $f_1(x_1, x_2) = \frac{\alpha f(x_1, x_2)}{x_1}$.

(c) Show that $f_{11}(x_1,x_2) = \dfrac{\alpha(\alpha-1)f(x_1,x_2)}{x_1^2}$.

(d) Calculate $f_{11}(x_1,x_2)f_{22}(x_1,x_2) - f_{12}^2(x_1,x_2)$ in terms of α, β, and $f(x_1,x_2)$.

(e) Use the answer to (b) to derive an economic interpretation of α assuming that $f(x_1,x_2)$ is output and x_1 and x_2 are two inputs (that is, assume that $f(x_1,x_2)$ is a production function).

1.9 APPENDIX: REFRESHER ON "IF AND THEN"

"If-then" statements are the foundation of deduction. Consider the statements:

If you are from California, then you are from the United States. (1.9.1)

as opposed to:

If you are from the United States, then you are from California. (1.9.2)

The first statement is true, because California is part of the United States, and the second statement is false because many people are from other places in the US. This illustrates the difference between the two general forms:

If A, then B. (1.9.3)

and its converse

If B, then A. (1.9.4)

Comparing (1.9.1) and (1.9.2), we see that if we know whether an "if-then" statement is true or false, we don't necessarily know anything regarding the truth or falsity of the *converse*. (Incidentally, in everyday speech and writing, people often interchange a statement and its converse. Nonetheless, as we illustrated above, the meanings are completely different.)

If you want to give an argument to support an if-then statement like (1.9.3), one way is to start by asserting that A is true, and then try to deduce that B is true. An alternative approach that we will use sometimes in this book is to instead prove:

If not B, then not A. (1.9.5)

This is called the *contrapositive* of (1.9.3); the two statements are logically equivalent. The strategy here is to assume that B is false, and then argue that also A must be false.

Sometimes in this book, we will make a statement like "A if and only if B." This is a shorthand for saying that both of the statements "if A, then B" and "if B, then A" are true. That is, A and B are both true or they are both false.[*]

---

[*] In particular, "if and only if" is different than just "if" or just "only if". This is something that rarely comes up in everyday speech, but nonetheless can be a source of confusion (see, e.g., the entry for "if, and only if" in the otherwise excellent *A Dictionary of Modern American Usage* by Bryan A. Garner, Oxford University Press, 1998).

CHAPTER 2

 ## OPTIMIZING FUNCTIONS WITH ONE CONTROL VARIABLE

I n this chapter we focus on a problem that is familiar to anyone who has completed one course in calculus—optimization of functions with a single control variable. We begin our discussion with an example of the profit maximization problem that specifies the functional form of the cost function. We then generalize the problem by repeating the analysis with a general cost function. Finally, we repeat the analysis for the type of model that describes the structure of most economic models. We call this last form the "prototypical economic model."

The ideas and methods in this chapter will be revisited again and again throughout the book in more complicated mathematical settings. The reader who masters the material here will be well prepared for what comes later.

2.1 PROFIT OPTIMIZATION

The general problem

Consider a firm that sells its output in a perfectly competitive market. Because this firm sells its output in a perfectly competitive market, there is nothing the firm can do that will affect the selling price. Thus, from the point of view of the firm forces external to the firm determine the selling price[*]; the firm only controls the quantity of what it produces. To emphasize this distinction, we call variables whose levels are determined externally to the model under consideration (here, the price) *parameters*, and those variables controlled by the economic actor (here, the quantity) *control variables*.

Example 2.1.1

Consider a firm whose cost $C(q)$ to produce q widgets is given by equation (2.1.1):

$$C(q) = q^2. \qquad (2.1.1)$$

Notice that this cost function fits what economists normally assume about costs—that they increase at an increasing rate as output goes up. The usual assumption that costs increase as output increases is equivalent to assuming that the first-derivative of the cost function is positive. The statement that costs increase at an

---

[*] Sometimes such a firm is called a *price-taker*.

increasing rate as output goes up is equivalent to assuming that the second-derivative is positive. For the cost function given by equation we have:

$$C'(q) = 2q > 0 \text{ and } C''(q) = 2 > 0. \tag{2.1.2}$$

The firm's profits are given by:

$$\Pi(q,p) = pq - q^2. \tag{2.1.3}$$

Obviously, the firm owners want to maximize the firm's profits. But the firm only controls the level of output, q. Therefore, the firm owners must determine the q that maximizes Π for a given price p. The shorthand for this problem is:

$$\underset{q}{Max} \ \Pi(q,p) = pq - q^2. \tag{2.1.4}$$

The function Π is sometimes called the *objective function*, meaning that it is the thing the decision-maker wants to maximize by choosing the level of a *control variable*. In this problem the output, q, is the control variable. The variable price, p, takes on a different role in this problem. We assume that the profit-maximizer treats price as if it were a constant. Later we will ask what happens to the profit-maximizing output, q^*, when the price level changes. We call variables that are held constant in an optimization problem *parameters*.

Viewing p as a constant, we can use calculus of a single variable to find the *profit-maximizing level of output, q^**. We take the derivative of $\Pi(q,p)$ with respect to q and set it equal to zero:

$$\frac{\partial \Pi(q,p)}{\partial q} = p - 2q = 0.$$

We define q^* to be the thing you plug in for q to solve this equation, i.e.,

$$q^* = \frac{p}{2}. \tag{2.1.5}$$

Note that q^* depends on p, i.e., q^* is a function of p. If we want to emphasize this point, we write $q^*(p)$ instead of just q^*.

But does q^* really give the maximum profit? So far, we have just checked that q^* is a "critical point" (in the language of calculus). We compute the second derivative of Π:

$$\frac{\partial^2 \Pi}{\partial q^2} = \frac{\partial}{\partial q}(p - 2q) = -2 < 0. \tag{2.1.6}$$

Since it is negative for all values of q, the critical point q^* is a global maximum by Theorem 1.2.1. That is, q^* does indeed maximize profits.

We can illustrate all this graphically. We can write Π as an accountant might, meaning as revenue ($R(p,q) = pq$) minus costs ($C(q) = q^2$), so $\Pi(q,p) = R(q,p) - C(q)$. For a fixed value of p, we can graph R and C as functions of q as in Figure 2.12, where price is assumed to be \$40. Note that you can see the value of $\Pi(q,p)$ for a given q as the distance between the graphs of R and C. The profit-maximizing quantity q^* occurs where the two curves are farthest apart. Unfortunately, this is not so easy to detect with the eye.

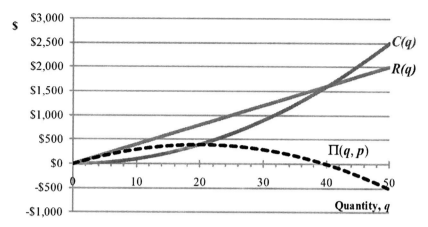

Figure 2.1.2 Example of profit maximization in the "total" space. The curve labeled $R(q)$ represents total revenue and the curve labeled $C(q)$ represents total costs. The dashed line represents net profits.

To make q^* more obvious, we prefer to graph not R and C but rather their derivatives, the marginal revenue[*]

$$MR := \frac{dR}{dq} = p \tag{2.1.7}$$

and the marginal cost

$$MC := \frac{dC}{dq} = 2q \tag{2.1.8}$$

as shown in Figure 2.1.3 (where, as before, we assume the price is $40). Note that the horizontal axis is still labeled q, but the label on the vertical axis is now $\$/q$; that is because the units on R and C are measured in dollars ($), and we are graphing their derivatives with respect to q. On this new graph, q^* is the value of q where the curves MR and MC intersect; it is easy to see.

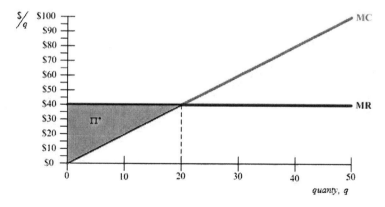

Figure 2.1.3 Profit maximization in the "marginal" space. Marginal revenue, MR, is fixed at the selling price of $40. Marginal cost, MC, is the positively sloped line. The intersection of these two curves occurs at the profit maximizing output of $q^* = 20$. Total profits, $\prod^*$, (assuming no fixed costs of production) are equal to the shaded area.

---

[*] We use the symbol $:=$ to mean "is defined to be." Thus, here $MR := \frac{dR}{dq} = p$ means "MR is defined to be $\frac{dR}{dq}$, which in this case equals p."

We can also see the second-order condition in Figure 2.1.3. To the left of q^*, the marginal benefits curve lies above the marginal cost curve (meaning $\frac{\partial \Pi}{\partial q}$ is positive), whereas to the right of q^*, the marginal benefits curve lies below the marginal cost curve (meaning $\frac{\partial \Pi}{\partial q}$ is negative). This shows that $\frac{\partial^2 \Pi}{\partial q^2}$ is negative at q^*, the second-order condition for q^* to be a local maximum.

This graph also shows profits, Π, as the shaded area in Figure 2.1.3. Indeed, $\Pi(q^*, p) = R(q^*, p) - C(q^*)$, which by the Fundamental Theorem of Calculus is the same as $\int_0^{q^*}(MR(q) - MC(q))dq$, is equal to the area of the shaded region. To distinguish the different graphs, we refer to the graph in Figure 2.1.2 as being in the *total* space and the graph in Figure 2.1.3 as being in the *marginal* space.

We can study more subtle questions. For a given price p, the firm will produce $q^*(p)$ and, hence, will have profit $\Pi(q^*(p), p)$, a function of just p. We call this function Π^*; i.e., we define:

$$\Pi^*(p) := \Pi(q^*(p), p). \tag{2.1.9}$$

Here we have:

$$\Pi^*(p) = p\left(\frac{p}{2}\right) - \left(\frac{p}{2}\right)^2 = \frac{p^2}{4}. \tag{2.1.10}$$

We call Π^* the *indirect profit function*. In math terms, Π (the *direct* profit function) is a function of both p and q, whereas Π^* is a function of just p. In economic terms, Π is an accounting definition that tells you the profit for every quantity q and every price p, whereas Π^* tells you the profit earned when the firm produces the *profit-maximizing* quantity q^* for any given price p.

We can also take derivatives of q^* and Π^* with respect to p:

$$\frac{dq^*(p)}{dp} = \frac{1}{2} \tag{2.1.11}$$

and

$$\frac{d\Pi^*(p)}{dp} = \frac{2p}{4} = \frac{p}{2}. \tag{2.1.12}$$

Both of these derivatives are positive. This result tells us: *If the selling price rises, the firm will produce more and earn a higher profit.* Economists refer to results given in (2.1.11) and (2.1.12) as *comparative statics; testable hypotheses* result when the comparative statics can be given a sign.

We can also see the signs of $\frac{dq^*}{dp}$ and $\frac{d\Pi^*}{dp}$ in the marginal space. Suppose that the price increases from $p_0 = \$40$ to $p_1 = \$50$. The marginal revenue MR will increase from \$40 to \$50, but the marginal cost MC does not involve p and so will not change. In Figure 2.1.4 we redraw Figure 2.1.3, adding another marginal revenue curve for the new price \$50. The intersection of the new marginal revenue curve and the marginal cost curve gives a profit-maximizing quantity $q^*(p_1)$ that is bigger than $q^*(p_0)$. (This increase in output is as it should be, because calculus told us that $\frac{dq^*}{dp}$ is positive.) The total profit, seen as the area between the marginal revenue and marginal cost curves, has also increased by the amount shown with cross-hatching, which agrees with our calculation that $\frac{d\Pi^*}{dp}$ is positive.

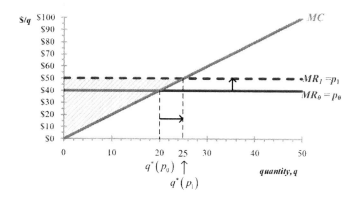

Figure 2.1.4 The impact of an increase of the price from \$40 to \$50 as shown in the marginal space. As a result of the price increase, output increases from 20 to 25 and profits increase by the amount shown by the cross-hatched area.

Exercises

2.1.1 A firm produces wine that gets better with age logarithmically. The firm, of course, has to pay for the cost of storing the wine while it ages. We model this problem as follows: let t be the length of time the firm allows the wine to age before bottling it and taking it to market. Assume that the cost of holding the wine is fixed at c per unit time and that the firm expects to sell the wine at a price of p per bottle. The firm wants to take the wine to market at the time t that maximizes its profits per unit bottle of wine, where profits are given by:

$$\Pi(t,c,p) = p\ln(1+t) - ct.$$

(a) Find the first-order condition. Draw a sketch in the marginal space illustrating the first-order condition. Label the axes and the equilibrium output.

(b) Show that the solution, t^*, of the first-order condition is a global maximum for Π.

(c) Calculate and find the sign of $\frac{\partial t^*(p,c)}{\partial p}$. Illustrate this result graphically in the marginal space.

2.1.2 In this problem a monopolist faces the demand curve: $p = a - bq$, where a and b are positive parameters. Suppose that the monopolist faces a constant marginal cost, c, must pay a per unit ouput tax, t, and that fixed costs are equal to zero.

(a) Find the profit-maximizing levels of output (q^*) and price (p^*). Find the maximum profit function, $\Pi^*(t)$. What impact will an increase in the tax rate have on the price, output, and profit? Illustrate these results graphically where the horizontal axis has the label q and the vertical axis is $\$/q$. Indicate $q^*, p^*,$ and Π^* on your graph.

(b) Find the tax rate t that maximizes the total tax paid to the government. Illustrate your answer graphically in the marginal space, building on your answer to part (a). Include the total tax in your illustration.

2.2 PROFIT MAXIMIZATION IN GENERAL

In the previous section, we worked an example where we had an explicit formula for the cost function $C(q)$. But that's not very realistic. So let's forget about this explicit formula and try to do all the same things we did before but with the intention of deriving a more general result, one that is not dependent on the particular cost function chosen. We assume that the economic problem facing the firm's owner is to choose the level of output, q, that maximizes its profit, Π, given the price level, p:

$$\underset{q}{Max}\ \Pi(q,p) = pq - C(q), \tag{2.2.1}$$

where $C(q)$ is the firm's cost function. Following the traditional assumption of diminishing marginal product, we assume the cost function is such that $C'(q)$ and $C''(q)$ are positive for all relevant values of q.*

In these types of optimization problems, we refer to the variables that the optimizer can control as the control variables. It is traditional to list the control variables below the "Max" in order to clearly differentiate between these variables and the parameters of the model. In this model the only control variable is q because it is the only variable the firm decision-makers can use to affect profits.

Solving (2.2.1) is a straightforward optimization problem covered in beginning calculus courses. In general, a function of one variable is at a (local) maximum if (1) its first derivative with respect to the control variable is equal to zero while (2) its second derivative is negative. We refer to these two conditions for maximization as the first-order and second-order conditions. Thus, an output level, say q^*, satisfies the first-order condition if

$$\frac{\partial \Pi}{\partial q}(q^*,p) = p - C'(q^*) = 0 \tag{2.2.2}$$

Let's assume that such a q^* exists. (Otherwise we are talking about an unusual or uninteresting economic situation.) The second-order condition is:

$$\frac{\partial^2 \Pi}{\partial q^2}(q^*,p) = -C''(q^*) < 0, \tag{2.2.3}$$

which holds because we assumed that $C''(q)$ is positive for all relevant q. So q^* is a local maximum. Furthermore, since $\frac{\partial^2 \Pi}{\partial q^2} = -C''(q)$ is negative for all relevant values of q, q^* is even a *global* maximum by the Global SOC Theorem 1.2.1.

---

* The phrase "all relevant values of q" is vague on purpose. Basically, economists (unlike mathematicians) are interested only in reasonable solutions. Thus, economists do not care (or think about) what happens to the cost function either for negative levels of output or for values of output that are unreasonably large.

Illustration of the solution to the profit maximization problem

Economists traditionally illustrate the first-order conditions given by (2.2.2) with the graph given in Figure 2.2.1. In this figure we show marginal costs, $C'(q)$, as positively sloped because of the second-order conditions. The intersection of the price line, p, with the marginal cost curve defines the level of output, q^*, that maximizes profits.

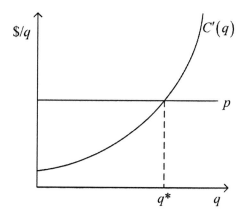

Figure 2.2.1 Illustration of the first-order conditions. The profit-maximizing output, q^*, is the level of output where the marginal cost curve, $C'(q)$, intersects the marginal revenue curve, p.

Figure 2.2.1 is typical of the sorts of graphs in marginal space that we examine in this book. The horizontal axis is labeled with a control variable (here, q), the vertical axis is labeled with $/q$ (more generally, $ per units of the control variable), the graph shows marginal costs and marginal benefits, and the q-value of their intersection is labeled with q^*.

A graph of the first-order condition is particularly useful for illustrating the impact of a change in the level of a parameter on the equilibrium level of the control variable. Figure 2.2.2, for instance, illustrates the impact of a rise in the price for p_0 to p_1 on the equilibrium level of output, which rises from $q^*(p_0)$ to $q^*(p_1)$. That is, $\dfrac{dq^*(p)}{dp}$ is positive. An important thing to notice here is that we view the solution to the first-order conditions, q^*, as a function of price, p: $q^*(p)$. We now justify why we can do this.

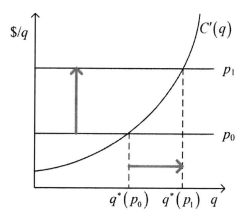

Figure 2.2.2 A rise in the price from p_0 to p_1 causes output to rise from $q^*(p_0)$ to $q^*(p_1)$.

2.3 EXISTENCE OF A SOLUTION TO THE PROFIT MAXIMIZATION PROBLEM

There is no reason to expect that a solution to the first-order conditions necessarily exists. For instance, if the price p always falls below marginal costs, the marginal space will be as in Figure 2.3.1, and no solution to the first-order conditions will exist. But for such a low price, the firm will produce no output, so this situation is not of much interest to economists who more often are interested in why a firm exists and produces some output than in when a firm does not exist. In this example, there is some price p_0 and some quantity q_0 such that the first-order conditions $p_0 = C'(q_0)$ holds and the second-order condition $-C''(q_0) < 0$ holds. Indeed, if you pick any $p_0 > C'(0)$, then the curves p_0 and $C'(q)$ will intersect at a point (q_0, p_0). The second-order condition holds by (2.2.3). Then the *Implicit Function Theorem* says that the quantity q^* is a function of p for prices near p_0. For more details, see section 2.7.

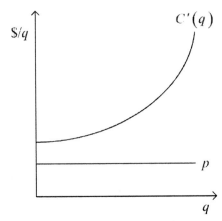

Figure 2.3.1 The firm will not produce anything if prices are too low.

We will typically assume that a solution to the first-order and second-order conditions exists and is a function of the parameters. As in the previous paragraph, we know that this assumption is a mild assertion thanks to the Implicit Function Theorem.

Moreover, it is typical for the economist also to assume that the second-order conditions to the maximization problem are satisfied for all q and not just for q^*. In this model the assumption that the sign of the second-derivative of the cost function is positive for all relevant output levels guarantees that the second-order condition $-C''(q^*) < 0$ holds.

2.4 COMPARATIVE STATICS

The real usefulness of the fact that we can write the equilibrium level of output as a function of the parameters of the model (in our example, q^* is a function of p) is that we can use this result to derive comparative static results that we then can use to test the validity of the model. Formally, here is how we do it:

(1) Assume that a solution to the first-order conditions exists and is given by $q^* := q^*(p)$.

(2) Substitute this solution into the first-order conditions (2.2.2) to get the identity:

$$p - C'(q^*(p)) = 0 \quad \text{for all } p. \tag{2.4.1}$$

(3) Differentiate the resulting equation (2.4.1) with respect to the parameter $\boldsymbol{p}$:

$$1 - C''\big(q^*(p)\big)\frac{dq^*(p)}{dp} = 0. \tag{2.4.2}$$

(4) Solve for the derivative in the equation and attempt to determine the sign of the derivative as predicted by the model:

$$\frac{dq^*(p)}{dp} = \frac{1}{C''\big(q^*(p)\big)} > 0. \tag{2.4.3}$$

This last result is a testable implication of our model. In theory, we could examine data from the real world and see if output and prices are positively correlated. If they were negatively correlated, we would have to reject at least one of the assumptions in the model; if they are positively correlated, then we *cannot* reject the theory in our model.

We can derive a second kind of comparative static* result in these optimization problems. We begin by substituting the solution to our problem into the (direct) profit function to get what is defined to be the indirect profit function:

$$\Pi^*(p) := \Pi\big(q^*(p), p\big) \tag{2.4.4}$$

or

$$\Pi^*(p) = pq^*(p) - C\big(q^*(p)\big). \tag{2.4.5}$$

Differentiation of the indirect profit function with respect to the price, $\boldsymbol{p}$, yields the second comparative static:

$$\frac{d\Pi^*(p)}{dp} = q^*(p) + p\frac{dq^*(p)}{dp} - C'\big(q^*(p)\big)\frac{dq^*(p)}{dp}$$

$$\frac{d\Pi^*(p)}{dp} = q^*(p) + \Big[p - C'\big(q^*(p)\big)\Big]\frac{dq^*(p)}{dp}$$

or, since the first-order condition implies $p - C'\big(q^*(p)\big) = 0$, we get:

$$\frac{d\Pi^*(p)}{dp} = q^*(p) > 0. \tag{2.4.6}$$

There is a useful thing to note in this final result. The direct profit function is:

$$\Pi(q, p) = pq - C(q).$$

Differentiation of the direct profit function with respect to the parameter, p, yields:

$$\frac{\partial \Pi(q, p)}{\partial p} = \Pi_p(q, p) = q.$$

---

* Mathematicians say "sensitivity analysis" rather than comparative statics, but their focus is also different. We are only looking for coarse information like the sign of $\frac{dq^*(p)}{dp}$ whereas they are interested in numerical values.

If we substitute the solution of the first-order condition, $q^*(p)$, into this last result, we get:

$$\Pi_p\left(q^*(p), p\right) = q^*(p).$$

Combining this with Equation (2.4.6), we see that

$$\frac{d\Pi^*(p)}{dp} = \Pi_p\left(q^*(p), p\right) \tag{2.4.7}$$

Equation (2.4.7) says that *the derivative of the indirect profit function with respect to price, p, is equal to the derivative of the direct profit function with respect to price with the solution to the first-order conditions substituted into the equation.* Equation (2.4.7) is an example of a theorem we will prove time and again in this book; it is known as the *Envelope Theorem*.

Exercises

2.4.1 A firm in a competitive market has the following cost function:

$$C(q, \beta) = q^\beta,$$

where $\beta > 1$. Assume that the firm sells its product at a price p.

(a) Find $q^*(p, \beta)$ and the indirect profit function $\Pi^*(p, \beta)$. What is the economic interpretation of this sign?

(b) Find $\dfrac{\partial q^*(p, \beta)}{\partial p}$. Determine its sign. What is the economic interpretation of this sign?

(c) Find $\dfrac{\partial q^*(p, \beta)}{\partial \beta}$. Determine its sign. [Hint: the sign depends on the values of p and β.] What is the economic interpretation of this sign?

(d) Find $\dfrac{\partial \Pi^*(p, \beta)}{\partial \beta}$. Determine its sign. What is the economic interpretation of this sign?

2.4.2. Assume that a firm is operating in a perfectly competitive market so that the managers of the firm view the selling price of its product, p, as being outside of their control. Assume that the firm chooses the level of output that maximizes its profits and that the firm is subject to a per unit output tax, t.[*] The firm's revenue function is:

$$R(q, p) = qp$$

Thus, the model in this problem is:

$$Max \; \Pi(q, p, t) = pq - tq - C(q).$$

---

[*] You will see per unit output taxes handled two ways in economics textbooks. In some cases the tax is treated as a part of costs, which becomes *production* costs, plus tax costs, In other cases they are considered as part of revenues—that is, the revenue the producer "sees" is equal to the revenue the consumer (price time quantity) pays minus the tax revenue (tax rate times quantity) paid to the government. These two ways of treating taxes are equivalent in the sense that the results of the analysis are the same. For convenience, we will treat the tax revenue as part of the revenue function of a firm.

(a) Write the first- and second-order conditions for the model. What assumptions are required on the cost function in order that the second-order condition is satisfied? Illustrate the first-order condition with a sketch in the marginal space.

(b) The tax, t, enters the model as a parameter. Suppose that there is a solution $q^*(t,p)$ to the first-order condition and that the second-order condition holds. Determine the sign of $\dfrac{\partial q^*(t,p)}{\partial t}$ using calculus. Draw a sketch in the marginal space illustrating this result.

(c) Let $\Pi^*(p,t)$ be the maximum profit as a function of p and t. Determine the sign of $\dfrac{\partial \Pi^*(p,t)}{\partial t}$. Draw a sketch in the marginal space illustrating this result.

2.4.3. Assume that a monopolist chooses the price, p, that maximizes her firm's profits. The firm faces a demand given by $D(p)$, where $D'(p) < 0$. Assume that the firm faces constant average costs, c. Thus, the firm's profit function is $\Pi(p,c) = pD(p) - cD(p)$.

(a) What is the firm's first-order condition?
(b) What is the firm's second-order condition?
(c) Let $p^*(c)$ be a solution to the first-order condition and suppose that the second-order condition holds.

Find and sign $\dfrac{dp^*(c)}{dc}$. What is the economic interpretation of this sign?

(d) Define the markup of price over costs to be $m := p - c$. Find and sign $\dfrac{dp^*(c)}{dc}$ and $\dfrac{dm^*(c)}{dc}$ under the special assumption that the demand function $D(p)$ is linear.

2.5 THE PROTOTYPICAL ECONOMIC PROBLEM

We can generalize what we have been doing by considering the following typical economic problem: An economic actor has a variable she can control, say x. When she chooses x, she receives some benefits, $B(x,\alpha)$, while facing some costs, $C(x,\alpha)$, where α is a vector of parameters. We assume that the individual chooses the level of x with the intent of maximizing the net benefits she receives. Thus, her economic problem is:

$$\underset{x}{Max} \ \Pi(x,\alpha) = B(x,\alpha) - C(x,\alpha). \tag{2.5.1}$$

Solve for a solution
The first-order condition for this problem is:

$$\Pi_x(x,\alpha) = B_x(x,\alpha) - C_x(x,\alpha) = 0. \tag{2.5.2}$$

Suppose we have a solution x^* to this equation. Then the second-order condition is

$$\Pi_{xx}(x^*,\alpha) = B_{xx}(x^*,\alpha) - C_{xx}(x^*,\alpha) < 0. \tag{2.5.3}$$

(Note that we have mostly dropped the notation ∂ for derivatives and have switched to subscripts.)

Equation (2.5.2) says that the individual will set her level of x such that the marginal benefit she receives equals her marginal cost. Equation (2.5.3) says that the slope of the marginal benefit curve is less than the slope of the marginal cost curve at the intersection of these two curves. Figure 2.5.1 shows two graphs that are possible in the typical case of increasing marginal costs. In panel (a) marginal benefits are decreasing while in panel (b) marginal benefits are increasing at a rate slower than the rate at which marginal costs are increasing. An equivalent way of interpreting the second-order conditions is to say that *the marginal benefit curve must intersect the marginal cost curve from above.*

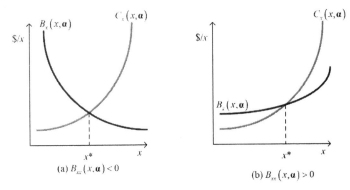

(a) $B_{xx}(x,\alpha) < 0$

(b) $B_{xx}(x,\alpha) > 0$

Figure 2.5.1 Two potential representations of the prototypical problem when marginal costs are increasing. Note that the marginal benefit curve intersects the marginal cost curve from above as specified by the second-order condition.

Derive the comparative static results

We assume that a solution $x^* = x^*(\alpha)$ to the first-order condition exists, and that the second-order condition for x^* to be a local maximum holds. Substituting x^* into the first-order condition yields:

$$B_x\big(x^*(\alpha), \alpha\big) - C_x\big(x^*(\alpha), \alpha\big) = 0 \text{ for all } \alpha. \tag{2.5.4}$$

Differentiating Equation (2.5.4) with respect to one of the parameters, say β, yields:

$$B_{xx}\big(x^*(\alpha), \alpha\big) \frac{\partial x^*(\alpha)}{\partial \beta} + B_{x\beta}\big(x^*(\alpha), \alpha\big) - C_{xx}\big(x^*(\alpha), \alpha\big) \frac{\partial x^*(\alpha)}{\partial \beta} - C_{x\beta}\big(x^*(\alpha), \alpha\big) = 0$$

(The other terms given by the chain rule, such as $B_{x\gamma}\big(x^*(\alpha), \alpha\big) \frac{\partial \gamma}{\partial \beta}$ for a parameter γ other than β, are zero because $\frac{\partial \gamma}{\partial \beta}$ is zero.) Collecting terms, we get:

$$\Big[B_{xx}\big(x^*(\alpha), \alpha\big) - C_{xx}\big(x^*(\alpha), \alpha\big)\Big] \frac{\partial x^*(\alpha)}{\partial \beta} = C_{x\beta}\big(x^*(\alpha), \alpha\big) - B_{x\beta}\big(x^*(\alpha), \alpha\big)$$

or

$$\frac{\partial x^*(\alpha)}{\partial \beta} = \frac{C_{x\beta}\big(x^*(\alpha), \alpha\big) - B_{x\beta}\big(x^*(\alpha), \alpha\big)}{B_{xx}\big(x^*(\alpha), \alpha\big) - C_{xx}\big(x^*(\alpha), \alpha\big)} = -\frac{\Pi_{x\beta}\big(x^*(\alpha), \alpha\big)}{\Pi_{xx}\big(x^*(\alpha), \alpha\big)}. \tag{2.5.5}$$

We know from the second-order condition (2.5.3) that:

$$B_{xx}\big(x^*(\alpha), \alpha\big) - C_{xx}\big(x^*(\alpha), \alpha\big) < 0$$

thus implying that the denominator of (2.5.5) is negative. It follows that the sign of $\dfrac{\partial x^*(\alpha)}{\partial \beta}$ is the same as the sign of $\prod_{x\beta}\left(x^*(\alpha), \alpha\right)$. There is nothing, however, in the mathematics of the problem that says what the signs of the elements of the numerator of (2.5.5) are. Thus, we cannot give a sign to $\dfrac{\partial x^*(\alpha)}{\partial \beta}$ without additional information. Economic theory often (but not always) provides this information.

The Envelope Theorem

We now derive the Envelope Theorem, which is useful for calculating $\dfrac{\partial \prod^*}{\partial \beta}(\alpha)$. The indirect objective function is found by substituting the solution to the first-order condition into the objective function:

$$\prod{}^*(\alpha) := \prod(x^*(\alpha), \alpha)$$

or

$$\prod{}^*(\alpha) = B\left(x^*(\alpha), \alpha\right) - C\left(x^*(\alpha), \alpha\right) \tag{2.5.6}$$

Differentiating the indirect objective function (2.5.6) with respect to one of the parameters, say β, yields:

$$\frac{\partial \prod^*}{\partial \beta}(\alpha) = B_x\left(x^*(\alpha), \alpha\right)\frac{\partial x^*(\alpha)}{\partial \beta} + C_x\left(x^*(\alpha), \alpha\right)\frac{\partial x^*(\alpha)}{\partial \beta} + B_\beta\left(x^*(\alpha), \alpha\right) - C_\beta\left(x^*(\alpha), \alpha\right).$$

Collecting terms, we get:

$$\frac{\partial \prod^*}{\partial \beta}(\alpha) = \left[B_x\left(x^*(\alpha), \alpha\right) - C_x\left(x^*(\alpha), \alpha\right)\right]\frac{\partial x^*(\alpha)}{\partial \beta} + B_\beta\left(x^*(\alpha), \alpha\right) - C_\beta\left(x^*(\alpha), \alpha\right).$$

Since the first-order condition implies that $B_x\left(x^*(\alpha), \alpha\right) - C_x\left(x^*(\alpha), \alpha\right) = 0$, we get:

$$\frac{\partial \prod^*}{\partial \beta}(\alpha) = B_\beta\left(x^*(\alpha), \alpha\right) - C_\beta\left(x^*(\alpha), \alpha\right). \tag{2.5.7}$$

While we cannot sign (2.5.7) without additional information, economic theory often provides this information in less general models. We can re-write Equation (2.5.7) as:

$$\frac{\partial \prod^*}{\partial \beta}(\alpha) = \frac{\partial \prod}{\partial \beta}\left(x^*(\alpha), \alpha\right). \tag{2.5.8}$$

That is, to find the derivative of the indirect objective function, $\prod{}^*(\alpha)$, with respect to the parameter β either (1) we can substitute $x^*(\alpha)$ into the direct objective function and then take the derivative with respect to β or (2) we can take the derivative of the direct objective function with respect to β and then substitute in $x^*(\alpha)$; either way the answer is the same. This result is known as the Envelope Theorem.

Exercises

    2.5.1 A firm earns revenue $R(q)$ for producing a quantity q of a good and experiences costs $C(q)$ that are increasing at a decreasing rate. Suppose there exists a profit-maximizing quantity q^* where the first- and second-order conditions hold. [Note that these assumptions say something about the shape of the marginal revenue curve.] Draw graphs illustrating this situation in the total space and in the marginal space. Make sure to label the axes and the curves. Explain why you drew the marginal revenue curve in the way you did. Indicate the point q^* and the total profits (assuming no fixed costs) on both graphs.

2.5.2 Draw a marginal space graph like the one shown in Figure 2.5.1, where C_x, C_{xx}, B_x, and B_{xx} are all positive for all x and the first-order condition holds for some x^* but where the second-order condition fails for some x^*.

2.6 AN EXTENDED EXAMPLE

We end this chapter with an extended example of optimization problem drawn from consumer theory. We include this example because it contains several issues that commonly arise in economic models. First, the way the problem is set up makes the identification of what are the benefits and what are the costs difficult. Second, the problem illustrates how to move from the algebra of the problem to the graphical presentation of the problem.

The economic problem

Suppose that an individual uses his income, I, to purchase two goods—good 1, x, and a good we will call "all other goods," y. Suppose that good 1 sells at a price p and good 2 has a price of $1 per unit of y. Thus, the relationship between the amount of each good purchased is given by:

$$y = I - px. \tag{2.6.1}$$

Suppose that this individual has the following additively-separable utility function:

$$U(x,y) = f(x) + g(y) \tag{2.6.2}$$

where

$$f' > 0, \; g' > 0, \; f'' < 0, \text{ and } g'' < 0. \tag{2.6.3}$$

We can rewrite the utility function (2.6.2) to include (2.6.1):

$$u(x) = U(x, I - px)$$

or

$$u(x) = f(x) + g(I - px). \tag{2.6.4}$$

Suppose that this individual wishes to choose the level of x that maximizes (2.6.4); let x_0 be the level of good x that solves this maximization problem. Now suppose that the government in its largesse chooses to provide this individual with α units of x where $0 < \alpha < x_0$. In this new situation the individual's economic problem is:

$$\underset{x}{Max} \; u(x, I, p, \alpha) = f(x + \alpha) + g(I - px). \tag{2.6.5}$$

The first-order condition for this problem is:

$$u_x(x, I, p, \alpha) = f'(x + \alpha) - pg'(I - px) = 0. \tag{2.6.6}$$

Now suppose that the first-order condition has a solution $x^* = x^*(I, p, \alpha)$ and that the second-order condition for a local maximum holds.

Find and sign $\dfrac{\partial x^*(I, p, \alpha)}{\partial \alpha}$. *What is the economic interpretation of this sign?*

Substitute the solution to the first-order conditions (2.6.6) to get:

$$f'\left(x^*\left(I,p,\alpha\right)+\alpha\right)-pg'\left(I-px^*\left(I,p,\alpha\right)\right)=0. \tag{2.6.7}$$

Differentiation of (2.6.7) with respect to α yields:

$$f''\left(x^*\left(I,p,\alpha\right)+\alpha\right)\frac{\partial x^*\left(I,p,\alpha\right)}{\partial\alpha}+f''\left(x^*\left(I,p,\alpha\right)+\alpha\right)+p^2g''\left(I-px^*\left(I,p,\alpha\right)\right)\frac{\partial x^*\left(I,p,\alpha\right)}{\partial\alpha}=0$$

or

$$\frac{\partial x^*\left(I,p,\alpha\right)}{\partial\alpha}=\frac{f''\left(x^*\left(I,p,\alpha\right)+\alpha\right)}{f''\left(x^*\left(I,p,\alpha\right)+\alpha\right)+p^2g''\left(I-px^*\left(I,p,\alpha\right)\right)}<0. \tag{2.6.8}$$

The sign follows from the assumptions that $f'' < 0$, and $g'' < 0$. Thus, if the government supplies more x, the consumer will buy less x.

An alternative way to solve for (2.6.8) would be to use equation (2.5.5) directly. According to (2.5.5)

Applying this formula to this problem yields: $\dfrac{\partial x^*(\alpha)}{\partial\beta}=-\dfrac{\Pi_{x\beta}(x^*(\alpha),\alpha)}{\Pi_{xx}(x^*(\alpha),\alpha)}$

$$\frac{\partial x^*\left(\alpha,I\right)}{\partial\alpha}=-\frac{u_{x\alpha}\left(x^*\left(I,\alpha\right),I,\alpha\right)}{u_{xx}\left(x^*\left(I,\alpha\right),I,\alpha\right)}.$$

We know from (2.6.6) that $u_x\left(x,I,\alpha\right)=f'(x+\alpha)-pg'(I-px)$. Thus, we know that:

$$u_{x\alpha}\left(x,I,\alpha\right)=f''(x+\alpha) \text{ and } u_{xx}\left(x,I,\alpha\right)=f''(x+\alpha)+p^2g''(I-px).$$

Substituting the solution to the first-order condition into these two equations yields:

$$\frac{\partial x^*\left(\alpha,I\right)}{\partial\alpha}=-\frac{f''(x+\alpha)}{f''(x+\alpha)+p^2g''(I-px)},$$

a result that is the same as equation (2.6.8).

Illustrate the impact of an increase in α on $x^* = x^*(\alpha, I)$ in the marginal space.

We are going to mimic what we did in section 2.1. Obviously our axes will be labeled x (the control variable) on the horizontal and $\$/x$ on the vertical. But it is not clear here what should be "marginal benefits" and what should be "marginal costs". We do know that

$$u'(x)=f'(x+\alpha)-pg'(I-px) \tag{2.6.9}$$

and, since $f'(x+\alpha)$ and $pg'(I-px)$ are both positive, we will imitate Figure 2.1.3 with $f'(x+\alpha)$ playing the role of marginal benefits and $pg'(I-px)$ playing the role of marginal costs. We picked them so that they have positive values (as functions of x), so the graphs are in the first quadrant. To see if they are increasing or decreasing, we calculate:

$$\frac{\partial MB}{\partial x}=f''(x+\alpha)<0 \text{ and } \frac{\partial MC}{\partial x}=-p^2g''(I-px)>0, \tag{2.6.10}$$

so the graph of marginal benefits is increasing and the graph of marginal costs is decreasing, as shown in Figure 2.6.1.

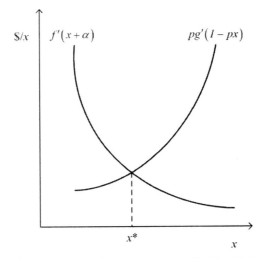

Figure 2.6.1 The marginal benefits and marginal costs curves implied by (2.6.10).

To illustrate the change in x^* resulting from an increase in α, we need to see how the graphs of marginal benefits and marginal costs change when α changes. We calculate:

$$\frac{\partial MB}{\partial \alpha} = f''(x+\alpha) < 0 \quad \text{and} \quad \frac{\partial MC}{\partial \alpha} = 0. \tag{2.6.11}$$

Thus, when α increases, the marginal benefits curve shifts downwards and the marginal costs curve does not change. The shifts of the marginal benefit and marginal cost curves and the resulting impact on x^* due to an increase in α are shown in Figure 2.6.2.

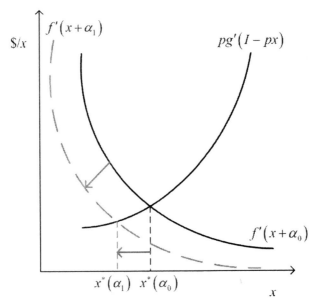

Figure 2.6.2 A rise in α from α_0 to α_1 causes $x^*(\alpha_0)$ to fall to $x^*(\alpha_1)$.

Exercises

2.6.1 Assume that an individual chooses the speed, s, at which she will drive by maximizing her per mile utility level. The individual's utility function is:

$$U(s, p, w) = B(s) - \left[\frac{w}{s} + \frac{p}{g(s)} + r(s) \right].$$

where $B(s)$ is the monetary value of the thrill the driver gets per mile from traveling at speed s; w is the wage level; p is the price of gasoline per gallon; $g(s)$ is the miles per gallon the car she drives gets; and $r(s)$ is the per-mile value of the monetary risk the individual faces from speeding tickets and accidents. Assume that $B'(s) > 0$, $r'(s) > 0$, and $r''(s) > 0$. Moreover, assume that the car has a gas-efficient speed of $\bar{s}$, that is, $g(s)$ is maximized at $\bar{s}$. Assume that the second-order utility maximizing conditions for this problem hold.

(a) Explain the economic role of wages in the utility function.

(b) Based on the story, do you believe that $B''(s)$ is positive or negative? Justify your answer.

(c) Find and illustrate graphically the first-order condition for this individual's problem.

(d) If the individual's optimal speed s^* is less than the gas-efficient speed, $\bar{s}$, what can you say about the marginal benefits and marginal costs at $\bar{s}$?

(e) Calculate and determine the signs of $\dfrac{\partial s^*(w, p)}{\partial \beta}$, where β takes in turn the role of each of the parameters w and p. In each case, explain what the sign of $\dfrac{\partial s^*(w, p)}{\partial \beta}$ says about the driver's behavior.

Do you believe these statements about the driver's behavior? Say why or why not.

2.6.2 When Sally engages in a risky activity (like caring for patients with a contagious disease), she faces a probability of a future bad outcome (like contracting the disease herself) equal to p, where $0 < p < 1$. Assume the probability of a bad outcome is the same every time she engages in the activity. Then, if she engages in the risky activity n times, she faces a probability of a bad outcome given by $\left[1 - (1 - p)^n \right]$. Let A be the loss that Sally will incur if the bad outcome actually occurs. Assume that the benefit that Sally receives from engaging in the risky activity (like her salary or a rise in her self-image) is given by $V(n)$, where $V'(n) > 0$ and $V''(n) < 0$. In this problem we assume that n is a continuous variable and ignore discounting of future costs. We assume that Sally decides how often to engage in the risky activity by maximizing her expected net payoff as given by:

$$U(n, p) = V(n) - A \left[1 - (1 - p)^n \right].$$

(a) The cost function, $C(n, p, A) = A \left[1 - (1 - p)^n \right]$, is unusual and is discussed in detail in Section 2.8 and Exercise 1.5.2. Calculate C_p, C_{pp}, and C_{np}.

(b) Assume that $n > 0$. Sign C_p, C_{pp}, and C_{np}. Determine the value $\tilde{n}$ of n for which $C_{np} = 0$.

(c) Draw a graph in the marginal space illustrating each of these scenarios for Sally's utility maximization problem:

  (i) There is a solution n^* to the first-order condition and the second-order condition holds.

  (ii) There is a solution n^* to the first-order condition and the second-order condition **fails**.

(iii) There is no solution to the first-order condition.

In each case, describe Sally's behavior.

In the balance of this problem we assume we are in case (i).

(d) Find and sign $\dfrac{\partial n^*(p,A)}{\partial p}$ and illustrate this result graphically. What does your answer imply about Sally's behavior?

(e) Find and sign $\dfrac{\partial n^*(p,A)}{\partial A}$ and illustrate this result graphically. What does your answer imply about Sally's behavior?

2.6.3 Assume that an individual will purchase a good once a month for the next T months. This individual can search for the best price each time he makes a purchase or he can search for information on the best price periodically. In this problem we consider the latter possibility. Assume that the individual makes K searches during the T months and purchases r units of the good between each search (thus, $T = rK$). Assume that the price this individual pays for the good "depreciates" at a constant rate of δ between times that the individual seeks information about the lowest price. For instance, if after a search he finds the best price to be $\hat{p}_t$, then the price he will pay next time (without an additional price search) will be $\hat{p}_t(1+\delta)$ and the price he will pay for the next good will be $\hat{p}_t(1+\delta)^2$. Finally, assume that the cost of each price search is α. Thus, the average price the individual pays for each good purchased between searches is:

$$\overline{p} = \frac{\sum_{i=1}^{r}\hat{p}(1+\delta)^{i-1}}{r}.$$

Thus, the total cost of this individual's purchases is:

$$C(r,K,\overline{p},\alpha) = Kr\overline{p} + \alpha K$$

or

$$C(r,T,\hat{p},\alpha) = T\hat{p}\sum_{i=1}^{r}(1+\delta)^{i-1} + \frac{\alpha T}{r}.$$

(a) Prove that $\displaystyle\sum_{i=1}^{r}(1+\delta)^{i-1} = \frac{(1+\delta)^r - 1}{\delta}$.

(b) Substitute the result from part (a) into the total cost function and find the first-order conditions for the cost-minimizing problem where r is the control variable.

(c) Assume that the search cost and the best price found after a search are a function of the "intensity" of the search, s. In particular, assume that $\alpha = \alpha(s)$ and $\hat{p} = f(s)$, where $\alpha' > 0$ and $f' < 0$ (that is, more intense searches are more costly but yield lower "best" prices). Find and sign $\partial r^* / \partial s$.

2.6.4 Two of the evolutionary gains that female baboons get from living in a troop are (1) help in raising the young and (2) help in protecting the young from predators. This help, of course, is not free. Female baboons earn good will by engaging in social activities, the main one of which is grooming other members of the troop. In this problem we want to find the impact of an increase in available food on the time a female baboon spends grooming other baboons.

We begin by assuming that a female baboon gains social status by spending t hours grooming other baboons in the troop and $T - t$ hours tending the needs of her children and herself, where T is the total amount of daylight time available to the mother. Assume that the probability of a child surviving to adulthood is a positive, concave function of three things: (1) the time the mother spends tending and feeding the babies, (2) the amount and quality of help she receives from the troop members, and (3) the general level of protection provided by the troop. We assume that the amount and quality of help the troop provides a mother baboon, S, is a positive, concave function of the amount time she spends in social activities; that is, we assume that:

$$S = S(t),$$

where $S'(t) > 0$ and $S''(t) < 0$. We assume that the amount of protection a troop provides is positively related to the size of the troop. Thus, the probability of a baby baboon surviving to adulthood is given by the function:

$$P = P(T - t, S(t), N),$$

where N is the size of the troop. We assume that all of the first partial derivatives of this function are positive and that the function is concave down in all of its arguments.

To complete the model we need to take account of (1) the cost of the amount of time spent in fending for her baby and herself, (2) the cost of grooming and (3) the impact of the troop size on the total amount of calories available to the mother. For simplicity, we assume that the cost of fending for her baby and herself is equal to 1 and the cost of grooming is given by p. Let α be the total amount of food available to the troop. Then, the amount of food available to the mother and her baby is given equal to $\frac{\alpha}{N}$. We assume that the amount of food available to the mother and her baby has a multiplicative impact on the probability that the baby will survive to adulthood. Thus, we assume that the mother baboon chooses t that maximizes her utility function and solves the problem:

$$\underset{t}{Max}\ u(t, N, \alpha, T) = \frac{\alpha}{N} P(T - t, S(t), N) - (T - t) - pt.$$

(a) Find the first-order condition of the mother's problem.

(b) What is the impact of an increase in the amount of food available to the troop on the amount of time the mother spends grooming other baboons. In other words, find and sign $\frac{\partial t^*(N, \alpha, T)}{\partial \alpha}$. (Note:

If we use α as a measure of the troop's income level, this question asks what will be the impact of the troop's available resources on the amount of time spent in social grooming.)

(c) Will the mother baboon be happier if the size of her troop increases? In other words, find and sign

$\dfrac{\partial u^{*}(\alpha, N, T)}{\partial N}$, where $u^{*}(\alpha, N, T)$ is the mother baboon's indirect utility function.

(d) This exercise has something to say about the problem of deducing how animals will behave in the wild based on observations of their behavior in captivity. Suppose you observe a troop of baboons in captivity. That troop has fixed values for α, N, and T. You note the values of t^{*} and u^{*} (assuming for the moment that you can observe u^{*}). A baboon troop in the wild will have different parameter values, say α', N', and T'. What can you deduce about the behavior (i.e., t^{*} and u^{*}) of a wild baboon mother based on your observations of the captive baboon mother?

2.6.5 It is well-known that there is a *moral hazard* problem attached to all insurance. For instance, it has been observed that drivers with insurance have a reduced incentive to drive safely when compared to self-insured drivers. In a similar fashion, individuals with health insurance may be less inclined to spend resources on prevention measures. However, the nature of the doctor–patient relationship might offset this moral hazard problem. The story is as follows: Patients often seek and follow the health advice of their doctors. Since generally this advice is that the patient should increase the amount of preventive care she takes, visiting a doctor may increase the amount of preventive care taken by the patient. If having health insurance increases the number of visits the insured makes to a doctor, then having health insurance might actually increase the amount of preventive care taken by the insured. This problem examines the theoretical logic of this health insurance problem.

Assume that an individual can spend an amount r to reduce the odds that they will be ill. Assume that this individual can increase the odds of being healthy by visiting a doctor seeking health advice. Thus, we assume that the probability of not being ill, π, is a function of r and of m, the number of contacts the individual has with a doctor. Assume that the per visit cost of seeing a doctor is p. Thus, the probability of not being ill is given by the function $\pi(r, m)$, where we assume that the first-partials of $\pi(r, m)$ are positive and that

$$\pi_{rr}(r, m), \pi_{mm}(r, m) < 0$$
and
$$\pi_{rr}(r, m)\pi_{mm}(r, m) - \left[\pi_{rm}(r, m)\right]^{2} > 0.$$

Let c be the cost the individual incurs by being ill. Then the expected utility of the individual is given by:

$$EU(r, m, p, c, I) = \pi(r, m)U(I - r - pm)$$
$$+(1 - \pi(r, m))U(I - r - pm - c)$$

where I is the individual's income level. Behaviorally, we assume that the individual chooses the r and m that maximizes expected utility.

Assume that the government decides to supply q dollars of health insurance to this individual for free. Now the cost of a visit to the doctor is zero but the number of visits this individual makes to a doctor is a function of the amount of medical insurance the individual receives, q. In particular, assume that the number of visits, $m(q)$, is an increasing function of q with $m''(q) < 0$. Thus, the individual's expected utility is now given by:

$$EU(r,q,c,I) = \pi(r,m(q))U(I-r)$$
$$+ (1 - \pi(r,m(q)))U(I-r-c+q).$$

We assume that r is the only variable the individual can control (and we view the number of visits to the doctor as a function of the exogenously determined amount of health insurance).

(a) How much preventive care, r, does this individual take if the government sets $q = c$?

(b) Drop the assumption that $q = c$. Find the first-order condition for this problem.

(c) Assume that a solution to the first-order condition, given by $r^*(q,c,I)$, exists and satisfies the second-order condition for a maximum. Find and sign $\dfrac{\partial r^*(q,c,I)}{\partial q}$; if you can, how would you explain your conclusion to a policymaker?

(d) Assume that visits to the doctor have no impact on the marginal effect of preventive care on the probability of being healthy (i.e., assume that $\pi_{rm} = 0$). Interpret the impact of an increase in the amount of insurance q on $r^*(q)$ in terms of the moral hazard problem and the impact of the advice of a doctor on the behavior of a patient.

2.7 APPENDIX: THE IMPLICIT FUNCTION THEOREM

Recall the prototypical economic problem:

$$\underset{x}{Max} \prod (x, \alpha) = B(x, \alpha) - C(x, \alpha) \qquad (2.7.1)$$

We assume that there is some value α_0 of the parameters and some value x_0 of the control variable that satisfies both the first-order condition

$$\prod_x (x_0, \alpha_0) = B_x(x_0, \alpha_0) - C_x(x_0, \alpha_0) = 0 \qquad (2.7.2)$$

and the second-order condition

$$\prod_{xx} (x_0, \alpha_0) = B_{xx}(x_0, \alpha_0) - C_{xx}(x_0, \alpha_0) < 0 \qquad (2.7.3)$$

As explained in the text, this is a mild assumption. If there were no such values α_0 and x_0, then our model would be describing a situation that is not economically interesting.

The Implicit Function Theorem tells us that there is a function $x^*(\alpha)$ defined for values of α near α_0 such that:

$$\prod_x (x^*(\alpha), \alpha) = 0, \; \prod_{xx} (x^*(\alpha), \alpha) < 0, \text{ and } x^*(\alpha_0) < x_0.$$

That is, $x^*(\alpha)$ satisfies the first-order and second-order conditions, i.e., $x^*(\alpha)$ is the solution to the economic problem. Morally speaking, the Implicit Function Theorem says that we can "solve" the first-order conditions and write x^* as a function of the vector α.

Of course, in order to apply the Implicit Function Theorem we need to verify its hypotheses. If we look up the theorem in a book,[*] we find the three hypotheses:

Hypothesis: $\prod_x$ has continuous first partial derivatives with respect to x and each parameter β in α. This holds by our global assumption that all functions we consider are smooth.

Hypothesis: There is some x_0 and α_0 such that (2.7.2) holds. We have assumed that this is true.

Hypothesis: $\prod_{xx}(x_0, \alpha_0) \neq 0$. We assumed this in (2.7.3).

As all the hypotheses hold, the Implicit Function Theorem applies and guarantees that x^* exists.

2.8 APPENDIX: INDIVIDUAL COST FUNCTIONS IN THE FACE OF AN EPIDEMIC

The cost function in exercise 2.6.2 is unusual because it exhibits decreasing marginal costs. Such cost functions appear very rarely in the literature and demand justification. In this appendix we derive the shape of the cost function used in exercise 2.6.2.

Define (1) p = probability of contracting a disease in any one contact, (2) A = cost to the individual of contracting the disease, and (3) n = number of contacts. The probability of contracting the disease after 3 contacts is equal to one minus the probability of not contacting the disease after 3 contacts, as shown in Figure 2.8.1. Thus, for n contacts the cost function is given by:

$$C(n, p, A) = A\left[1 - (1-p)^n\right].$$
(2.8.1)

Now let's examine the characteristics of this cost function under the assumption that the number of contacts, n, is a continuous variable. In order to calculate the first- and second-partial derivatives of this function we need to simplify the function. Define:

$$g(n, p) = 1 - (1-p)^n,$$
(2.8.2)

so that, $C(n, p, A) = Ag(n, p)$. You computed and signed the first and second derivatives of g with respect to n in Exercise 1.5.2, where you found that $g_n > 0$ and $g_{nn} < 0$. Thus, this cost function exhibits the unusual characteristic that costs rise at a decreasing rate.

We can see the implications of this result by assuming that the marginal benefits of each contact is constant and equal to b, as shown in Figure 2.8.2. The important point in Figure 2.8.2 is that at the intersection of marginal costs and marginal benefits, n^*, $C_{nn}(n, p, A) < 0$, implying that n^* is the number of contacts that minimizes net benefits of contacts. To find the optimal number of contacts we would have to compare the net benefits of contacts at zero contacts and at n^{**} contacts; the one with the largest net benefits is the one that **maximizes** net benefits under the logical restriction that the number of contacts and marginal costs be non-negative. Intuitively, what this analysis implies is that people will refuse to expose themselves to the disease or they will expose themselves a great deal if the marginal benefits of exposure are high enough. This behavior is what is

---

[*] A good reference is J. Hubbard and B. Hubbard, *Vector calculus, linear algebra, and differential forms: a unified approach*, Prentice Hall, 1999. For more extensive discussion, see S. G. Krantz and H. R. Parks (2002) *The Implicit Function Theorem: History, Theory, and Applications* (Boston: Birkhäuser).

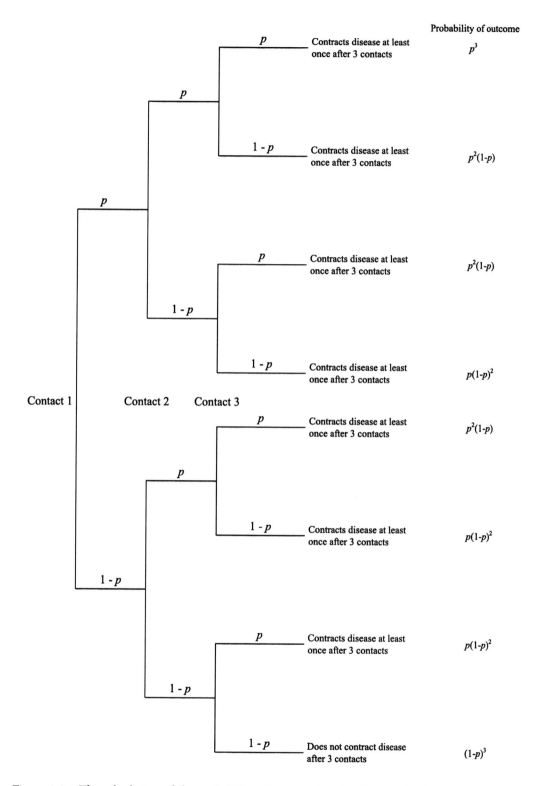

Figure 2.8.1 The calculation of the probability of contracting the disease after 3 contacts.

found in the care of individuals who have a contagious disease—a person will either refuse to come into contact with the sick or they will come into contact with a large number of people with the disease, like a doctor taking care of the ill.

This problem illustrates an important point: In Calculus I, when you maximized a function on an interval, the maximum occurred at a critical point or at one of the endpoints of the interval. The algebraic optimization techniques we discuss in this book apply to the case where the second-order conditions hold and the maximum occurs at a critical point. In this problem, the second-order condition fails (indeed, here the critical point is a **minimum**) and a maximum will occur at an "endpoint". In this case, the endpoints are at n = 0 and infinity. Thus, the answer to the question is either zero or infinity. To find which answer of these two possibilities is correct we may need to resort to using non-algebraic methods.

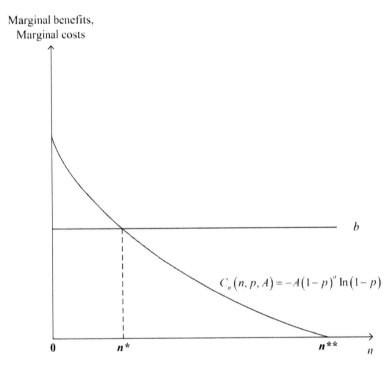

Figure 2.8.2 Marginal costs and benefits of contacts.

We can illustrate this point with this problem. To make the illustration simpler to see, we assume that the benefit function is an increasing concave (that is, $B''(n) < 0$) function of n and that as the number of contacts increases, the benefits become asymptotic to a maximum level of benefits. Figure 2.8.3 illustrates two possible benefit functions in the "total" space.

In Figure 2.8.3 costs are shown (the solid line) as increasing at a decreasing rate. They are asymptotic to A.[*] Two potential benefit functions are also drawn in Figure 2.8.3. The first benefit function, $B(n)$, is shown as being asymptotic to B. The second benefit function, $B^1(n)$, is shown as being asymptotic to B^1. The two net benefits curves for the two benefit functions are the difference between benefits and cost and are labeled $NB(n)$ and $NB^1(n)$, respectively. In the case of $B(n)$, net benefits are (1) positive when $n = 0$ and (2) decrease to negative

---

[*] Costs are given by $C(n, p, A) = A\left[1 - (a-p)^n\right]$. Since $1-p$ is between 0 and 1, $\underset{n \to \infty}{Lim}(1-p)^n = 0$ and $\underset{n \to \infty}{Lim}\, A\left[1 - (1-p)^n\right] = A$.

values when $n > 0$. Clearly, in this case the net benefit optimizing level of contacts is zero. In the case of $B^1(n)$, net benefits first fall before rising to a level that is asymptotic to the difference between B^1 and A. As long as this difference is greater than the net benefits when $n = 0$, the net benefit optimizing level of contacts is infinite. Of course, this result is not too surprising since it says that an individual will choose not to have any contact with the sick unless the maximum benefit he or she can derive from many contacts is greater than the benefits derived from no contacts. Thus, the answer to the question as to the optimizing level of contacts depends on the shape of the benefit function relative to the cost function.

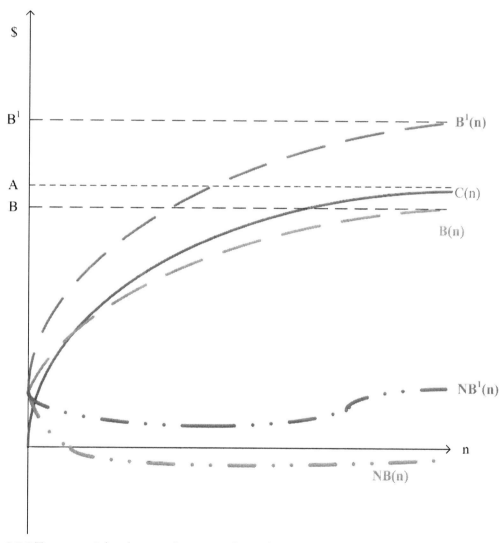

Figure 2.8.3 Two potential endpoint solutions to the epidemic problem.

CHAPTER 3
MATRICES

3.1 WHAT CAN YOU DO WITH MATRICES?

This chapter is a brief review of matrices, which we will use lightly throughout the rest of the course. A matrix is a rectangular grid of numbers or formulas like

$$\begin{pmatrix} a_{11} & a_{12} & a_{13} \\ a_{21} & a_{22} & a_{23} \end{pmatrix}$$

We say that this matrix is 2-by-3 because it has 2 rows and 3 columns. (Everything with matrices is organized as "rows-then-columns".) Entries in a matrix are labeled by their row and then their column, so the (1,3)-entry in the matrix above is a_{13}.

One thing you can do with matrices is multiply them. For example,

$$\begin{pmatrix} a_{11} & a_{12} & a_{13} \\ a_{21} & a_{22} & a_{23} \end{pmatrix} \begin{pmatrix} v_1 \\ v_2 \\ v_3 \end{pmatrix} = \begin{pmatrix} a_{11}v_1 + a_{12}v_2 + a_{13}v_3 \\ a_{21}v_1 + a_{22}v_2 + a_{23}v_3 \end{pmatrix}$$

We multiplied a 2-by-3 matrix with a 3-by-1 matrix and got a 2-by-1 matrix; intuitively "the 3's in the middle cancel out". The (2, 1)-entry in the product is the dot product of the 2nd row of the first matrix and the 1st (and only) column of the second matrix, i.e., the (2, 1)-entry in the product is

$$\left(a_{21}, a_{22}, a_{23}\right) \cdot \left(v_1, v_2, v_3\right) = a_{21}v_1 + a_{22}v_2 + a_{23}v_3$$

But what good is it? We can use this to solve systems of linear equations. Suppose we want to solve the system of equations:

$$\begin{aligned} 4x_1 - 3x_2 &= 15 \\ 7x_1 + 2x_2 &= 9 \end{aligned} \tag{3.1.1}$$

We could solve this system of equations by adding multiples of one equation to another to cancel out x^1 or x^2, as we learned to do in high school algebra. But later we will study systems of equations for which the high school technique does not work. Instead, we rewrite the system as:

$$\begin{pmatrix} 4 & -3 \\ 7 & 2 \end{pmatrix} \begin{pmatrix} x_1 \\ x_2 \end{pmatrix} = \begin{pmatrix} 15 \\ 9 \end{pmatrix} \tag{3.1.2}$$

Let's check that this really is the same as (3.1.1). The product on the left side is

$$\begin{pmatrix} 4x_1 - 3x_2 \\ 7x_1 + 2x_2 \end{pmatrix}$$

So (3.1.2) says that

$$\begin{pmatrix} 4x_1 - 3x_2 \\ 7x_1 + 2x_2 \end{pmatrix} = \begin{pmatrix} 15 \\ 9 \end{pmatrix} \tag{3.1.3}$$

We recall from multivariable calculus that two vectors (or matrices) are equal if and only if each of their entries is equal. So (3.1.3) is the same as (3.1.1).

Readers who have studied some linear algebra will know at least two ways to solve (3.1.2).[*] For our purposes in this text, the best method is to use Cramer's rule, for which we need to know what a determinant is; we will recall both Cramer's Rule and the determinant in the next section.

Exercises

3.1.1 Multiply the matrices

$$\begin{pmatrix} 3 & -2 \\ 7 & f(x,y) \end{pmatrix} \begin{pmatrix} \partial x / \partial p \\ \partial y / \partial p \end{pmatrix}$$

3.1.2 Re-write the system of linear equations

$$6x_1 - 3x_2 + 9x_3 = -2$$
$$9x_1 + x_2 + x_3 = 13$$
$$x_1 - 7x_2 + x_3 = -7$$

using matrices, as we did to transform (3.1.1) into (3.1.2).

3.2 2-BY-2 MATRICES

The determinant

The determinant[†] of an n-by-n matrix A is a number, which we denote by $|A|$. The determinant is given by a somewhat complicated formula depending on the size n of the matrix, e.g.,

$$\begin{vmatrix} a_{11} & a_{12} \\ a_{21} & a_{22} \end{vmatrix} = a_{11}a_{22} - a_{12}a_{21}$$

With numbers we have

$$\begin{vmatrix} 4 & -3 \\ 7 & 2 \end{vmatrix} = 4 \cdot 2 - (-3) \cdot 7 = 8 + 21 = 29$$

---

* Namely, by Gaussian elimination, a.k.a. row-reduction (which amounts to the same as the high school algebra method) or by multiplying both sides of (3.1.2) by the inverse of $\begin{pmatrix} 4 & -3 \\ 7 & 2 \end{pmatrix}$

† Determinants made their first appearance in a 1683 book by a Japanese mathematician commonly known as Seki Kōwa. They seem to have been discovered independently very shortly thereafter by Leibniz.

Earlier, we put parentheses around the grid of numbers to denote the matrix itself, whereas here we have put vertical bars to indicate the determinant of the matrix.

Cramer's Rule

Cramer[*] says: Since the determinant of $\begin{pmatrix} 4 & -3 \\ 7 & 2 \end{pmatrix}$ is not zero, the solution to (3.1.2) is

$$x_1 = \frac{\begin{vmatrix} 15 & -3 \\ 9 & 2 \end{vmatrix}}{\begin{vmatrix} 4 & -3 \\ 7 & 2 \end{vmatrix}} \quad \text{and} \quad x_2 = \frac{\begin{vmatrix} 4 & 15 \\ 7 & 9 \end{vmatrix}}{\begin{vmatrix} 4 & -3 \\ 7 & 2 \end{vmatrix}}. \tag{3.2.1}$$

That is,

$$x_1 = \frac{57}{29} \quad \text{and} \quad x_2 = -\frac{69}{29}.$$

(At this point, it is a good idea to plug x_1 and x_2 back into (3.1.1) and to check that we did not make an arithmetic mistake somewhere.)

The general Cramer's Rule is to imitate this example. The key points are that the denominator in both expressions is the determinant $\begin{vmatrix} 4 & -3 \\ 7 & 2 \end{vmatrix}$ and the determinant in the numerator of x_i has the i-th column replaced with $\begin{pmatrix} 15 \\ 9 \end{pmatrix}$, the right side of equation (3.1.2).

Exercises

3.2.1 Compute the determinant of the matrix

$$\begin{pmatrix} 3 & -2 \\ -7 & 5 \end{pmatrix}.$$

3.2.2 Solve the system of equations using Cramer's Rule:

$$3x_1 - 2x_2 = 15$$
$$-7x_1 + 5x_2 = 9.$$

---

[*] Gabriel Cramer (1704–1752) was a professor at the University of Geneva in Switzerland. The rule appeared in an appendix to his most famous work, the book *Introduction à l'analyse des lignes courbes algébriques*. Cramer was using the notion of utility function already in 1728, as evidenced by his letter to Nicolas Bernoulli on 21 May of that year. He justified his use of utility functions with the quote: "mathematicians estimate money in proportion to its quantity, and men of good sense in proportion to the usage that they may make of it." (Note the contrast between mathematicians and reasonable people.) Utility functions did not appear in a published work until 10 years later, in Daniel Bernoulli's classic paper "Exposition of a new theory on the measurement of risk". You can find an English translation of Bernoulli's paper in *Econometrica*, vol. 22 (1954), p. 23–36.

The determinant

The formula for the determinant of a 3-by-3 matrix is:

$$\begin{vmatrix} a_{11} & a_{12} & a_{13} \\ a_{21} & a_{22} & a_{23} \\ a_{31} & a_{32} & a_{33} \end{vmatrix} = a_{11}a_{22}a_{33} + a_{12}a_{23}a_{31} + a_{13}a_{21}a_{32} - a_{13}a_{22}a_{31} - a_{11}a_{23}a_{32} - a_{12}a_{21}a_{33}.$$

Memorizing this formula does not look appetizing. Instead, we use a mnemonic called the *Laplace expansion*, also known as the *cofactor* expansion. The method is as follows. For an entry a_{ij} in an n-by-n matrix, A, you can get an $(n-1)$-by-$(n-1)$ matrix A_{ij} (a minor of A) by deleting the i-th row and j-th column. For example, with

$$A = \begin{pmatrix} 4 & -3 & 1 \\ 7 & 2 & -3 \\ 2 & 1 & 1 \end{pmatrix}$$

and $(i,j) = (2,1)$, we have $a_{21} = 7$ and $A_{21} = \begin{pmatrix} -3 & 1 \\ 1 & 1 \end{pmatrix}$.

It can be helpful to think of actually crossing out the row and column of A that passes through a_{ij}, as shown in Figure 3.3.1. The matrix A_{21} is the stuff that's not crossed out.

$$\begin{pmatrix} 4 & -3 & 1 \\ 7 & 2 & -3 \\ 2 & 1 & 1 \end{pmatrix}$$

Figure 3.3.1 You can find the minor of position (2,1) by crossing out row 2 and column 1.

The Laplace* expansion of the determinant of A along the first column is

$$\begin{aligned} |A| &= a_{11}|A_{11}| - a_{21}|A_{21}| + a_{31}|A_{31}| \\ &= 4\begin{vmatrix} 2 & -3 \\ 1 & 1 \end{vmatrix} - 7\begin{vmatrix} -3 & 1 \\ 1 & 1 \end{vmatrix} + 2\begin{vmatrix} -3 & 1 \\ 2 & -3 \end{vmatrix} \\ &= 4(2+3) - 7(-3-1) + 2(9-2) \\ &= 62. \end{aligned}$$

---

* Pierre-Simon Laplace (1749-1827) was a French mathematician, and is viewed as one of the greats. During Napoleon's reign, Laplace was appointed Minister of the Interior, the French equivalent of a US cabinet secretary in charge of the FBI, granting passports and driver's licenses, etc. Laplace was fired after just six weeks because—as Napoleon said—Laplace "sought subtleties everywhere, had only doubtful ideas, and carried the spirit of the infinitely small into administration". He is one of the 72 scientists whose name is on the Eiffel Tower.

We can also "expand along the first row", for which the formula is:

$$|A| = a_{11}|A_{11}| - a_{12}|A_{12}| + a_{13}|A_{13}|$$

$$= 4\begin{vmatrix} 2 & -3 \\ 1 & 1 \end{vmatrix} - (-3)\begin{vmatrix} 7 & -3 \\ 2 & 1 \end{vmatrix} + 1\begin{vmatrix} 7 & 2 \\ 2 & 1 \end{vmatrix}$$

$$= 4(2+3) + 3(7+6) + (7-4)$$

$$= 62$$

or along the second column:

$$|A| = -a_{21}|A_{21}| - a_{22}|A_{22}| - a_{32}|A_{32}|$$

$$= -(-3)\begin{vmatrix} 7 & -3 \\ 2 & 1 \end{vmatrix} + 2\begin{vmatrix} 4 & 1 \\ 2 & 1 \end{vmatrix} - \begin{vmatrix} 4 & 1 \\ 7 & -3 \end{vmatrix}$$

$$= 3(7+6) + 2(4-2) - 2(-12-7)$$

$$= 62.$$

Note that the signs in front of the a_{ij} terms are a little different in this last example. The general formula for the determinant of an n-by-n matrix A by Laplace expansion along the i-th row is:

$$|A| = \sum_{j=1}^{n} -1^{i+j} a_{ij} |A_{ij}| \tag{3.3.2}$$

and along the j-th column the formula is:

$$|A| = \sum_{i=1}^{n} -1^{i+j} a_{ij} |A_{ij}|. \tag{3.3.3}$$

(The only difference in the two formulas is which variable is changing. In (3.3.2), the i is the same throughout and the sum is over j. In (3.3.3), the j is the same and the sum is over i.)

One way to remember the sign in front of the a_{ij} term is to notice that the signs form a checkerboard pattern like

$$\begin{pmatrix} + & - & + \\ - & + & - \\ + & - & + \end{pmatrix}$$

where we have put the sign that goes in front of a_{ij}, i.e., $(-1)^{i+j}$, in the (i,j)-entry.

One reason the Laplace expansion is nice is that it expresses the determinant of a 3-by-3 matrix in terms of determinants of 2-by-2 matrices, and the determinant of an n-by-n matrix in terms of determinants of $(n-1)$-by-$(n-1)$ matrices. This allows us to compute the determinant of an n-by-n matrix for any n by bootstrapping, since we know how to find the determinant of a 2-by-2 matrix.

We mention one more property of determinants:

Proposition 3.3.2 Let A and B be n-by-n matrices.

(1)   If B is obtained from A by multiplying a row of A by a number c, then $|B| = c|A|$.

(2)   *If B is obtained from A by swapping two rows of A or swapping two columns of A, then $|B| = -|A|$.*

PROOF. Both claims follow from the Laplace expansion for the determinant. Here is a sketch of a proof of (1). Suppose that B is obtained from A by multiplying the first row by a number c. We find the determinant of B by Laplace expansion along the first row:

$$|B| = \sum_{j=1}^{n} b_{1j} \left| B_{1j} \right|.$$

But $b_{1j} = ca_{1j}$ by hypothesis. Also, B_{1j} is the matrix obtained from B by omitting the first row and the j-th column, but the entries of B away from the first row are the same as the corresponding entries of A, so $\left| B_{1j} \right|$ equals $\left| A_{1j} \right|$. We find:

$$|B| = \sum_{j=1}^{n} ca_{1j} \left| A_{1j} \right| = c \sum_{j=1}^{n} a_{1j} \left| A_{1j} \right|$$

which is c times the Laplace expansion of the determinant of A along the first row. □

Cramer's rule with 3 variables

If we want to solve the system of equations

$$\begin{aligned}
4x_1 - 3x_2 - x_3 &= 15 \\
7x_1 + 2x_2 - 3x_3 &= 9 \\
2x_1 + x_2 + x_3 &= -7,
\end{aligned}$$

(3.3.4)

we rewrite the system in terms of matrices as

$$\begin{pmatrix} 4 & -3 & 1 \\ 7 & 2 & -3 \\ 2 & 1 & 1 \end{pmatrix} \begin{pmatrix} x_1 \\ x_2 \\ x_3 \end{pmatrix} = \begin{pmatrix} 15 \\ 9 \\ -7 \end{pmatrix}$$

(3.3.5)

Then Cramer's rule says:

$$x_1 = \frac{\begin{vmatrix} 15 & -3 & 1 \\ 9 & 2 & -3 \\ -7 & 1 & 1 \end{vmatrix}}{\begin{vmatrix} 4 & -3 & 1 \\ 7 & 2 & -3 \\ 2 & 1 & 1 \end{vmatrix}}, \quad x_2 = \frac{\begin{vmatrix} 4 & 15 & 1 \\ 7 & 9 & -3 \\ 2 & -7 & 1 \end{vmatrix}}{\begin{vmatrix} 4 & -3 & 1 \\ 7 & 2 & -3 \\ 2 & 1 & 1 \end{vmatrix}}, \quad \text{and } x_3 = \frac{\begin{vmatrix} 4 & -3 & 15 \\ 7 & 2 & 9 \\ 2 & 1 & -7 \end{vmatrix}}{\begin{vmatrix} 4 & -3 & 1 \\ 7 & 2 & -3 \\ 2 & 1 & 1 \end{vmatrix}}.$$

Computing the determinants, we find:

$$x_1 = \frac{62}{62} = 1, \, x_2 = \frac{-310}{62} = -5, \text{ and } x_3 = \frac{-248}{62} = -4.$$

You can check that this solution is correct by plugging these numbers into (3.3.4).

3.3.1 Compute the determinant of the matrix

$$\begin{pmatrix} 3 & -2 & 2 \\ -7 & 5 & 0 \\ -3 & 0 & -2 \end{pmatrix}.$$

3.3.2 Compute the determinant of the matrix by expansion along the third column:

$$\begin{pmatrix} 3 & -2 & 0 \\ -7 & 5 & 0 \\ 15 & 0 & 13 \end{pmatrix}.$$

3.3.3 Solve for the solution to the system of equations:

$$7x_1 - 2x_2 - 4x_3 = 25$$
$$4x_1 + 9x_3 = 10$$
$$6x_2 - 8x_3 = 15.$$

3.3.4 A simple macroeconomics model of an economy can be written as

$$Y - C - I = G$$
$$C - \alpha_1 Y = \alpha_0, \text{ and}$$
$$I - \beta_1 Y = \beta_0,$$

where Y is GNP, C is consumption level, I is investment level, and G is the exogenously determined level of government expenditures. Assume that $\alpha_0, \beta_0, G > 0$ and $0 < \alpha_1, \beta_1 < 1$.

(a) Write the model in matrix form, where I, C, and Y are the unknown variables.

(b) Solve for Y using Cramer's Rule.

(c) Calculate $\frac{\partial Y}{\partial G}$ as a function of $\alpha_0, \alpha_1, \beta_0, \beta_1,$ and G. What is the sign of this partial derivative? What is

the economic term you used in introductory macroeconomics course to identity this partial derivative?, not .

3.4 MISCELLANEOUS REMARKS

Matrices belong to the part of mathematics known as *linear algebra*. In addition to their importance in theoretical mathematics, matrices have many applications in physical sciences and in industry. In this book, we use determinants and Cramer's rule extensively, but they are rarely used in, say, engineering. For a good essay explaining the general reasoning behind their rarity in engineering, read the "interlude" in the middle of the book *Numerical Methods that Work* by Forman Acton.

We defined the determinant of an n-by-n matrix to be the Laplace expansion. Often the determinant is defined differently, as a way of measuring how volumes change. You saw this definition in terms of volumes when you studied the change of variables formula for integrals in multivariable calculus, which is the multivariable version of algebraic substitution for integrals of one variable. These two different definitions of determinant amount to the same thing, see e.g. Chapter 5 of P.D. Lax (1997) *Linear algebra* (New York: Wiley).

Exercises

3.4.1. Assume that the supply and demand functions for corn are given by the following two equations, respectively:

$$\text{Supply: } y_t = \alpha_0 + \alpha_1 p_t + \alpha_2 p_{t-1} + \alpha_3 w_t + \varepsilon_t$$

$$\text{Demand: } y_t = \alpha_0 + \alpha_1 p_t + \alpha_2 x_t + \gamma_t$$

where the subscript t denotes the time period, y_t is the output of corn, p_t is the selling price of corn, p_{t-1} is the selling price of corn during the previous period, w_t is an index of the weather such that increases in the index indicate weather conditions that are better for the growing of corn, x_t is the per capita income, ε_t and γ_t are variables that measure randomly determined variations in the supply of corn and in the demand for corn, respectively. The α's and β's are assumed to be constants that might be estimated using econometric techniques. We assume that price and quantity (p_t and y_t) are the endogenous variables of this model while the other variables (p_{t-1}, w_t, and x_t) are determined exogenously.[*]

(a) What are the matrices A and B that represent this two-equation model in the following matrix form:

$$B\begin{pmatrix} y_t \\ p_t \end{pmatrix} = A\begin{pmatrix} 1 \\ p_{t-1} \\ w_t \\ x_t \end{pmatrix} + \begin{pmatrix} \varepsilon_t \\ \gamma_t \end{pmatrix}?$$

(b) Solve the above equation for p_t and y_t as functions of p_{t-1}, w_t, x_t, ε_t, and γ_t; i.e., solve

$$\begin{pmatrix} y_t \\ p_t \end{pmatrix} = B^{-1}A\begin{pmatrix} 1 \\ p_{t-1} \\ w_t \\ x_t \end{pmatrix} + B^{-1}\begin{pmatrix} \varepsilon_t \\ \gamma_t \end{pmatrix}$$

These two equations are known as the *reduced-form equations* of this model. (In a reduced-form equation one of the endogenous variables of a model is written as a function of the exogenous variables of the model.)

(c) Suppose that you have estimated the two reduced form equations in (b) and want to deduce the parameters of the original two equations. Let

---

[*] Note in this problem we use the terms "exogenous" and "endogenous" variables the way they are used by econometricians. An exogenous variable is one whose value is determined outside the system of equations being estimated. An endogenous variable is one whose value is determined by equations in the system of equations being estimated. Exogenous and endogenous variables also are referred to as independent and dependent variables, respectively. The use of the subscript 0 matches the notation used in econometric texts rather than the notation used in the balance of this section.

$$B^{-1}A = \begin{pmatrix} \eta_{10} & \eta_{11} & \eta_{12} & \eta_{13} \\ \eta_{20} & \eta_{21} & \eta_{22} & \eta_{23} \end{pmatrix}.$$

Examine the elements of the matrix $B^{-1}A$ and determine all of the ways you can estimate each of the α's and β's . (Note: what this problem is dealing with is the *identification problem* that arises in econometrics. If there is only one way to estimate each of the parameters from the reduced form equations, econometricians say that the model is *exactly* identified; if there is more than one way to estimate any of the parameters, they say the model is *over-identified*. If any of the parameters cannot be estimated from the parameters of the reduced form equation, the model is said to be *under-identified*. Notice the fact that the identification problem is an algebraic issue and not a statistical one.

CHAPTER 4

OPTIMIZING FUNCTIONS WITH TWO CONTROL VARIABLES

I n this chapter we discuss optimizing functions of two or more control variables. In reality, of course, we dealt with functions of more than one variable in Chapter 2 when we introduced the concept of parameters. What is new in this chapter is that we will consider the cases where the optimizing individual must choose the levels of two or more variables when optimizing an objective function. As was true in Chapter 2, we consider the impact of changes in non-control variables—or parameters—on the objective function optimizing levels of control variables. We also develop a version of the Envelope Theorem.

We begin our discussion with reminders about level curves and the gradient and then we discuss unconstrained optimization for functions of several variables. Finally, we produce comparative statics results and the envelope theorem in that setting.

4.1 LEVEL CURVES

A *level curve* of $f(x_1, x_2)$ is the collection of points in the (x_1, x_2)-plane such that $f(x_1, x_2) = \overline{z}$ for some fixed number $\overline{z}$.

Example 4.1.1 (calculus).

Figure 4.1.2 below shows a 3-dimensional graph of $z = f(x_1, x_2)$ for $f(x_1, x_2) = 50 - x_1^2 - x_2^2$. The level curve for $\overline{z} = 40$, for example, is the set of points (x_1, x_2) satisfying $40 = 50 - x_1^2 - x_2^2$. This equation is the same as $x_1^2 + x_2^2 = 10$, which we recognize as a circle with radius $\sqrt{10}$ and center at the origin. The second picture in Figure 4.1.2 shows various level curves of $f(x_1, x_2)$, and the level curve for $\overline{z}$ is labeled with "40"; at every point on this curve, the value of f is 40.

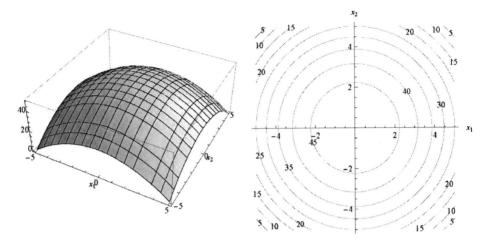

Figure 4.1.2 The function $f(x_1, x_2) = 50 - x_1^2 - x_2^2$ **and some of its level curves.**

Example 4.1.3 (economics).

From economics we have the following two examples of level curves:

utility maximization: If $f(x_1, x_2)$ is the utility that a consumer receives from consuming x_1 of good 1 and x_2 of good 2, then the level curves of f are the consumer's *indifference curves*.

cost minimization: If $f(x_1, x_2)$ is a firm's production function and x_1 and x_2 are quantities of two inputs, then the level curves of f are the firm's *isoquants*.

Example 4.1.4 (geography).

Suppose that $f(x_1, x_2)$ is the level of the point on earth's surface at latitude x_1 and longitude x_2. A topographical map shows the level curves of f as in Figure 4.1.5.

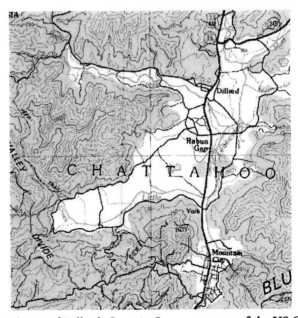

Figure 4.1.5 A topographical map of Dillard, Georgia. Image courtesy of the US Geological Survey.

Slopes of level curves.

We continue to analyze the level curves of a function $f(x_1, x_2)$. Looking at Figure 4.1.2 and Figure 4.1.5, the level curves are not graphs of functions because they fail the vertical line test. But we think of indifference curves as looking something like the curves in Figure 4.1.6. These curves are graphs of functions.

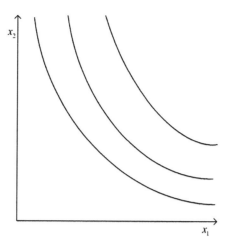

Figure 4.1.6 Possible indifference curves

Precisely speaking, we consider the level curve through a point (c_1, c_2), i.e., the level curve $\bar{z} = f(x_1, x_2)$ where $\bar{z}$ is the value of f at (c_1, c_2). If $\dfrac{\partial f(c_1, c_2)}{\partial x_2} \neq 0$, then the Implicit Function Theorem says that we can write x_2 as a function of x_1 and $\bar{z}$, i.e.,

$$x_2 = x_2(x_1, \bar{z}). \tag{4.1.1}$$

The graph of this function in the (x_1, x_2)-plane is the level curve $\bar{z} = f(x_1, x_2)$ of f.

Example 4.1.7

In the happy event that you have a nice formula for $f(x_1, x_2)$, you may be able to find an explicit formula for x_2 as a function of x_1 by simply solving for x_2. Here are some examples:

1. Suppose that $f(x_1, x_2) = x_1 + x_2$. The level curve $\bar{z} = f(x_1, x_2)$ has the equation $\bar{z} = x_1 + x_2$, so clearly $x_2 = \bar{z} - x_1$.

2. Suppose that $f(x_1, x_2) = 50 - x_1^2 - x_2^2$ as in Example 4.1.1. Then the level curve for $\bar{z}$ is the set of points such that $\bar{z} = 50 - x_1^2 - x_2^2$. You can solve for x_2 and find

$$x_2 = \sqrt{50 - \bar{z} - x_1^2} \text{ or } x_2 = -\sqrt{50 - \bar{z} - x_1^2}.$$

Note that neither of these equations gives the full level curve. This is no surprise, as the level curve is a circle, so it is not the graph of a function! This result reflects the fact that $\dfrac{\partial f(x_1, x_2)}{\partial x_2}$ is 0 on the x_1-axis.

3. Suppose that $f(x_1,x_2)=x_1+\sqrt{x_2}$. The level curve $\bar{z}=f(x_1,x_2)$ has the equation $\bar{z}=x_1+\sqrt{x_2}$, which we can rearrange to find $\sqrt{x_2}=\bar{z}-x_1$. But note that this equation only has a solution (x_1,x_2) if $\bar{z}-x_1$ is non-negative, i.e., if $x_1\le\bar{z}$. Therefore, the equation for the level curve is:

$$x_2=\left(\bar{z}-x_1\right)^2 \text{ for } x_1\le\bar{z}.$$

If you naively plot $(\bar{z}-x_1)^2$ with, say, $\bar{z}$ equal to 2, 5, and 7 (it does not matter which ones you choose), you find the graph in the left panel of Figure 4.1.8, which is obviously bogus. (Why? What basic property of level curves is violated by the three curves drawn?) The problem is that you should include only the points with $x_1\le\bar{z}$.* The panel on the right side of Figure 4.1.8 shows a correct graph of the level curves.

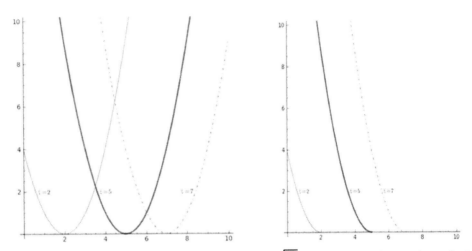

Figure 4.1.8 The incorrect level curves for $f(x_1,x_2)=x_1+\sqrt{x_2}$ **are shown in the graph on the left while the correct level curves are shown in the graph on the right.**

Let's apply calculus to analyze the level curves. Substituting Equation (4.1.1) into the original function yields:

$$\bar{z}=f\left[x_1,x_2\left(x_1,\bar{z}\right)\right].$$

(4.1.2)

Now we can calculate

$$\frac{\partial x_2(x_1,\bar{z})}{\partial x_1} \text{ and } \frac{\partial^2 x_2(x_1,\bar{z})}{\partial x_1^2}$$

by differentiating Equation (4.1.2) with respect to x_1:

$$0=f_1\left[x_1,x_2\left(x_1,\bar{z}\right)\right]+f_2\left[x_1,x_2\left(x_1,\bar{z}\right)\right]\frac{\partial x_2\left(x_1,\bar{z}\right)}{\partial x_1}.$$

(4.1.3)

---

* The restriction $x_1\le\bar{z}$ can also be understood in terms of the Implicit Function Theorem. That theorem gives x_2 as a function of x^1 and $\bar{z}$ and as long as $\dfrac{\partial f}{\partial x_2}$ is not zero. We calculate that $\dfrac{\partial f}{\partial x_2}=\frac{1}{2}\sqrt{x}$, so we can find $x_2(x_1,\bar{z})$ for x_2 positive, that is, for $x_1<\bar{z}$.

Thus, we get:

$$\frac{\partial x_2\left(x_1,\bar{z}\right)}{\partial x_1} = -\frac{f_1\left[x_1, x_2\left(x_1,\bar{z}\right)\right]}{f_2\left[x_1, x_2\left(x_1,\bar{z}\right)\right]}.$$

The partial derivative given by Equation (4.1.3) has special meanings in economics, depending on what model is under discussion.

Example 4.1.9

We return to the economic examples from Example 4.1.3 (economics).

utility maximization: If $f\left(x_1, x_2\right)$ is the consumer's utility function, then the derivative $\dfrac{\partial x_2\left(x_1,\bar{z}\right)}{\partial x_1}$ is equal to

the negative of the ratio of the marginal utility the consumer receives from x_1 to the marginal utility the consumer receives from x_2. Economists call the slope of the indifference curve, the *marginal rate of substitution* (MRS).

cost minimization: If $f\left(x_1, x_2\right)$ is the firm's production function, the slope of the isoquant $\dfrac{\partial x_2\left(x_1,\bar{z}\right)}{\partial x_1}$ is the *marginal rate of technological substitution* (MTS).

We can say more about the shape of the level curves by differentiating Equation (4.1.3) with respect to x_1, where we drop the arguments of the function and its partial derivatives only for notational ease:

$$\frac{\partial^2 x_2\left(x_1,\bar{z}\right)}{\partial x_1^2} = -\frac{f_2\left(f_{11} + f_{12}\dfrac{\partial x_2\left(x_1,\bar{z}\right)}{\partial x_1}\right) - f_1\left(f_{21} + f_{22}\dfrac{\partial x_2\left(x_1,\bar{z}\right)}{\partial x_1}\right)}{f_2^2}.$$

Since

$$\frac{\partial x_2\left(x_1,\bar{z}\right)}{\partial x_1} = -\frac{f_1}{f_2},$$

we get that:

$$\frac{\partial^2 x_2\left(x_1,\bar{z}\right)}{\partial x_1^2} = -\frac{f_2\left(f_{11} - f_{12}\dfrac{f_1}{f_2}\right) - f_1\left(f_{21} - f_{22}\dfrac{f_1}{f_2}\right)}{f_2^2}$$

$$\frac{\partial^2 x_2\left(x_1,\bar{z}\right)}{\partial x_1^2} = -\frac{\left(f_2 f_{11} - f_1 f_{12}\right) - \left(f_1 f_{21} - \dfrac{f_1^2 f_{22}}{f_2}\right)}{f_2^2}$$

$$\frac{\partial^2 x_2\left(x_1, \overline{z}\right)}{\partial x_1^2} = -\frac{\left(f_2^2 f_{11} - f_1 f_2 f_{12}\right) - \left(f_1 f_2 f_{21} - f_1^2 f_{22}\right)}{f_2^3}$$

or

$$\frac{\partial^2 x_2\left(x_1, \overline{z}\right)}{\partial x_1^2} = \frac{-f_2^2 f_{11} + 2 f_1 f_2 f_{12} - f_1^2 f_{22}}{f_2^3}. \tag{4.1.4}$$

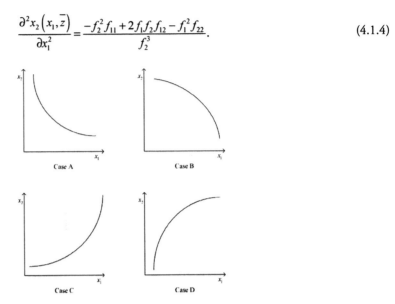

Figure 4.1.10 Four types of level curves.

Equation (4.1.4) implies that the slope and convexity of a level curve depends on the signs of f_1, f_2, and $-f_2^2 f_{11} + 2 f_1 f_2 f_{12} - f_1^2 f_{22}$. Table 4.1.11 lists the eight possible shapes while 4.1.10 shows four possible shapes of level curves.

Table 4.1.11 Possible shape

The following signs:			Imply:		
f_1	f_2	$-f_2^2 f_{11} + 2 f_1 f_2 f_{12} - f_1^2 f_{22}$	$\dfrac{\partial x_2}{\partial x_1}$	$\dfrac{\partial^2 x_2}{\partial x_1^2}$	Graph (see Figure 4.1.10)
+	+	+	−	+	A
+	+	−	−	−	B
+	−	+	+	−	D
+	−	−	+	+	C
−	+	+	+	+	C
−	+	−	+	−	D
−	−	+	−	−	B
−	−	−	−	+	A

4.1.1 Find an equation for the level curves [in the form $x_2 = x_2(x_1)$] of the Cobb-Douglas function $f(x_1, x_2) = Ax_1^\alpha x_2^\beta$, where $0 < \alpha, \beta < 1$, $A > 0$ and $x_1, x_2 > 0$. Sketch representative examples of the level curves and indicate the direction of steepest increase. Calculate and sign $\dfrac{\partial x_2}{\partial x_1}$ and $\dfrac{\partial^2 x_2}{\partial x_1^2}$.

4.1.2 Find the formula for the isoquants associated with the following production function: $q = 1 + (x_1 x_2 - 1)^{1/3}$, where x_1 and x_2 are the firm's input levels of capital and labor, respectively. Sketch representative examples of the level curves and indicate the direction of steepest increase.

4.1.3 The Constant Elasticity of Substitution (CES) production function is

$$f(x_1, x_2) = A \left[\alpha x_1^{-\rho} + (1 - \alpha) x_2^{-\rho} \right]^{-h/\rho} \text{ for } x_1, x_2, A > 0,$$

where $0 < \alpha < 1$, $h > 0$, and $\rho > -1$.

(a) When ρ is zero, the formula given for f does not make sense. Show that the limit of f as ρ goes to zero is $Ax_1^{h\alpha} x_2^{h(1-\alpha)}$, a Cobb-Douglas function. [Hint: Use L'Hospital's Rule.] When we talk about f for $\rho = 0$, we mean this limit.

(b) The shape of the level curves of f depends on ρ. For each of various values of ρ (i.e., $\rho \to \infty$, $\rho > 0$, $\rho = 0$, $-1 < \rho < 0$, and $\rho \to -1$) draw a pair of axes and representative examples of the level curves. For each value of ρ, determine if the level curves intersect the axes, or if the level curves have horizontal or vertical asymptotes.

4.1.4 An investor has two arguments in his utility function U: μ, the rate of return on an investment, and σ, the level of riskiness of the investment. Let $\mu = \mu(\sigma)$ be the investor's indifference curve between the rate of return and the riskiness of the investment.

(a) What is the sign of $\mu'(\sigma)$? Why?

(b) What are the minimum conditions needed on the utility function, i.e., on $U(\mu, \sigma)$, for the indifference curve to have $\mu''(\sigma)$ positive?

(c) Assume that $\mu''(\sigma)$ is positive. Sketch a set of indifference curves. Indicate which of the curves have higher utility and which have lower utility.

4.2 GRADIENTS

Recall the gradient of a function $f(x_1, x_2, \ldots, x_n)$. It is denoted grad f. It is the vector

$$\text{grad } f = \left(\frac{\partial f}{\partial x_1}, \frac{\partial f}{\partial x_2}, \ldots, \frac{\partial f}{\partial x_n} \right).$$

For example, in Figure 4.2.1, we have taken the level curves from Figure 4.1.2 and drawn in gradient vectors at some points.

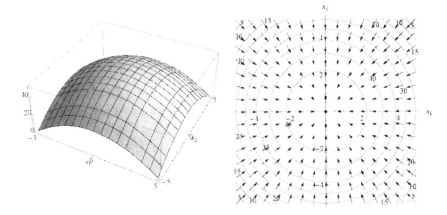

Figure 4.2.1 Gradient vectors and level curves for $f(x_1, x_2) = 50 - x_1^2 - x_2^2$.

When you evaluate the gradient at a point $\mathbf{c} = (c_1, c_2, \ldots, c_n)$, you find a vector grad $f(\mathbf{c})$ with two important properties:

Property 1: grad $f(\mathbf{c})$ *points in the direction of steepest increase for f*

Property 2: grad $f(\mathbf{c})$ *is perpendicular to the level curve* through $f(\mathbf{c})$.

(In case you do not remember these two properties from your calculus class, we prove them in the next section.)

Let's interpret these two properties in the context of the geography from Example 4.1.4. Suppose that you are extremely nearsighted and you are walking on a hillside. Property 1 says that if you want to get to the top of the hill as quickly as possible, you should go in the direction that the gradient points. Said differently, the gradient points straight uphill. Property 2 says that if you want to stay at the same elevation, you should look straight uphill and then move to your left or your right, 90 degrees from straight uphill.

Example 4.2.2

Let us draw the gradient at a few points on Figure 4.1.8. Because we have an explicit formula $f(x_1, x_2) = x_1 + \sqrt{x_2}$, we can calculate the gradient precisely, but there is also another way. Property 2 tells us that the gradient is perpendicular to the level curve, so the gradient at a point on the level curve must point (approximately) northeast or southwest. We notice that the values of the function—as indicated by the labels on the level curves—increase as we move northeast, so Property 1 tells us that the gradient should point northeast. You can see the results in Figure 4.2.3. This is a minimalist picture of the gradient; it doesn't tell you very much. What it does do is tell you the direction to move in to find larger values of the function; it tells you the direction of steepest increase.

---

* Properly speaking, the term 'level curve' is only correct when f is a function of two variables, i.e., if $n = 2$. If $n = 3$ the correct term is 'level surface' and for $n = 4$, it is 'level 3-fold', etc.

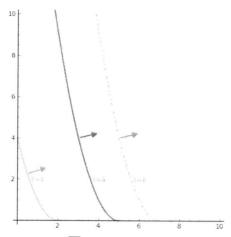

Figure 4.2.3 Level curves for $f(x_1, x_2) = x_1 + \sqrt{x_2}$ **with the direction of steepest increase drawn in.**

Example 4.2.4

Consider again the function $f(x_1, x_2) = 50 - x_1^2 - x_2^2$ from Example 4.1.1. We illustrate the properties 1 and 2 at the point $\mathbf{c} = (0, -4.5)$, which appears as a dark ball in Figure 4.2.5. The ring around the surface is the level curve passing through $(0, -4.5, f(0, -4.5))$.

The gradient of f is $(-2x_1, -2x_2)$, so grad $f(0, -4.5) = (0, 9)$. The gradient points along the x_2 axis in the positive direction. The arrow on the surface shows the direction in which you should walk to get uphill the fastest—the direction of increasing x_2.

Property 1 tells us something useful. If grad $f(\mathbf{c})$ is not zero, then there is some direction that is uphill, so c cannot be a local maximum. Turning that around, we find: *if* c *is a local maximum for f, then grad* $f(\mathbf{c})$ *is zero.*

The same reasoning applies to finding local minimums for f, in that $-$grad $f(\mathbf{c})$ points in the direction of steepest decrease ("straight downhill"). So: *If* c *is a local minimum for f, then grad* $f(\mathbf{c})$ *is zero.*

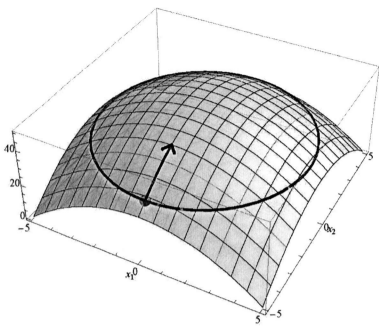

Figure 4.2.5 Gradient and level curve at the point $(0, -4.5)$ **on the surface** $f(x_1, x_2) = 50 - x_1^2 - x_2^2$.

4.3 MULTIVARIABLE OPTIMIZATION: FIRST-ORDER CONDITIONS

Functions of two variables

The balance of this chapter expands the analysis of optimization to functions of more than one control variable. To simplify the analysis we provide most of the details of the analysis for functions of two control variables before outlining the comparative static analysis for optimization of functions of more than two control variables.

Assume that we have the objective function $y = f(x_1, x_2, \boldsymbol{\alpha})$, where x_1 and x_2 are control variables and $\boldsymbol{\alpha}$ is a vector of parameters. In the following discussion we suppress the vector of parameters $\boldsymbol{\alpha}$ until we discuss comparative statics.

We want to find the local maximums and minimums for f. In order to do this, we replace the function f with a function g of only one variable, so that we can transform the problem into one where we already know the answer.[*]

We imagine a ladybug crawling on the surface $z = f(x_1, x_2)$. We can view the ladybug as starting at a position $(c_1, c_2, f(c_1, c_2))$ and traveling in the direction given by the nonzero vector $\mathbf{u} = (u_1, u_2)$, so that at time t it is over the point $(c_1 + tu_1, c_2 + tu_2)$ in the (x_1, x_2)-plane. Let $g(t)$ denote the ladybug's altitude at time t, so that

$$g(t) = f(c_1 + tu_1, c_2 + tu_2).$$

---

[*] Changing a problem to turn it into one you have already solved is a standard trick in mathematics. It is so standard that there are several jokes about it, see e.g. *Foolproof: a sampling of mathematical humor* by Renteln and Dundes, in *Notices of the American Mathematical Society*, vol. 52 (2005), especially page 30. Here is a typical example: A mathematician and an economist are on a desert island. They find two palm trees with one coconut each. How can they eat? The economist shinnies up one tree, gets the coconut, and eats it, enjoying the utility it provides. The mathematician shinnies up the other tree, gets the coconut, climbs down his tree, climbs up the economist's tree, and leaves the coconut at the top. "Now we've reduced it to a problem we know how to solve!"

By focusing on the ladybug's location at time t, we "parameterize" the function, thereby reducing it to a function of one variable t. Graphically, the ladybug's path looks like a cross-section of the surface. We call $g(t)$ a slice of f.

Example 4.3.1

Take
$$f(x_1, x_2) = 50 - x_1^2 - x_1^2 \text{ and } \mathbf{c} = (1,0) \text{ and } \mathbf{u} = (1,1).$$

The set of axes on the left in Figure 4.3.2 shows the graph of the surface $z = f(x_1, x_2)$ with the ladybug's path drawn on it. The dark ball on the surface is the ladybug's location at $t = 0$. The set of axes on the right shows a graph of the function $g(t)$.

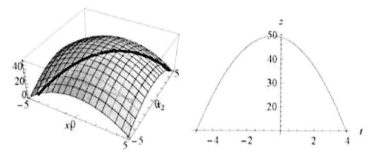

Figure 4.3.2 Path of a ladybug on the surface $z = 50 - x_1^2 - x_1^2$ **through** $(1,0)$ **in the direction** $(1,1)$, **together with a graph of the ladybug's elevation.**

The first-order condition

The first-order condition for $g(t)$ to have a maximum at $t = 0$ is $g'(0) = 0$. Using the chain rule, we calculate:

$$g'(t) = f_1(c_1 + tu_1, c_2 + tu_2)u_1 + f_2(c_1 + tu_1, c_2 + tu_2)u_2 = \mathbf{u} \cdot \text{grad} f(\mathbf{c} + t\mathbf{u}). \qquad (4.3.1)$$

So
$$g'(0) = \mathbf{u} \cdot (\text{grad} f)(\mathbf{c}). \qquad (4.3.2)$$

(You saw this quantity in your multivariable calculus class in the case where $\mathbf{u}$ is a unit vector, i.e., $\|\mathbf{u}\| = 1$ $\left(\|\mathbf{u}\| = \sqrt{\sum_{i=1}^{n} u_i^2}\right)$; it is the directional derivative of f at $\mathbf{c}$ in the direction $\mathbf{u}$ and is denoted by $D_{\mathbf{u}} f(\mathbf{c})$ or $f_{\mathbf{u}}(\mathbf{c})$.) If the point c is a local maximum or minimum of $f(x_1, x_2)$, then $g'(0) = 0$ for every direction $\mathbf{u}$, i.e., $\mathbf{u} \cdot \text{grad} f(\mathbf{c}) = 0$ for every vector u. It follows that grad $f(\mathbf{c})$ is the zero vector.

That is, if (c_1, c_2) is a local maximum or minimum of $f(x_1, x_2)$, we have:

$$f_1(c_1, c_2) = 0 \text{ and } f_2(c_1, c_2) = 0. \qquad (4.3.3)$$

These are the first-order conditions for a local maximum or minimum. (Note that we have rediscovered the observation from the end of section 4.2.) If (c_1, c_2) satisfies the first-order conditions (Equation 4.3.3), we say that it is a *critical point* of f. As in Chapter 2, we will often write $\mathbf{x}^*$ for a critical point.

By the way, Equation (4.3.2) also explains the properties 1 and 2 of the gradient. Indeed, the direction of steepest increase is the direction of a unit vector **u** that maximizes $g'(0)$, and this is the unit vector pointing in the direction $(\text{grad} f)(c)$; this gives property 1. Similarly, f is unchanging in the direction **u** if and only if **u** is orthogonal to $(\text{grad} f)(c)$; this gives property 2.

4.4 SECOND-ORDER CONDITIONS FOR LOCAL OPTIMA

Now suppose that $\mathbf{x}^* = \left(x_1^*, x_2^*\right)$ satisfies the first-order conditions, i.e., is a critical point of f. How can you tell if it is a local maximum? We have to be a little careful, as the next example shows.

Example 4.4.1

Naively, you might think the second-order conditions for a maximum would just be that $f_{11}\left(\mathbf{x}^*\right)$ and $f_{22}\left(\mathbf{x}^*\right)$ be negative. Figure 4.4.2 shows a surface where $(0,0)$ is a critical point and $f_{11}\left(\mathbf{x}^*\right)$ and $f_{22}\left(\mathbf{x}^*\right)$ are both negative. But $(0,0)$ is not a local maximum, as the figure shows: if you look at the slice through the surface along the line $x_1 = x_2$, the point $(0,0)$ looks like a local minimum, see Figure 4.4.3. We call a critical point like this one—that looks like a local minimum if you approach it one way and a local maximum if approach it some other way—a *saddle point*.

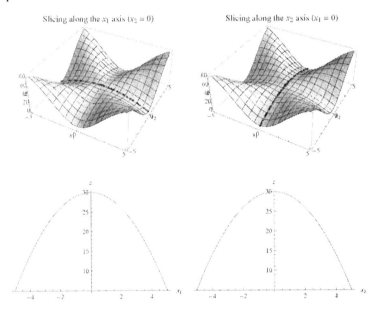

Figure 4.4.2 Slices of a surface along the x_1 axis and along the x_2 axis. Note that $(0,0)$ is a maximum along each slice.

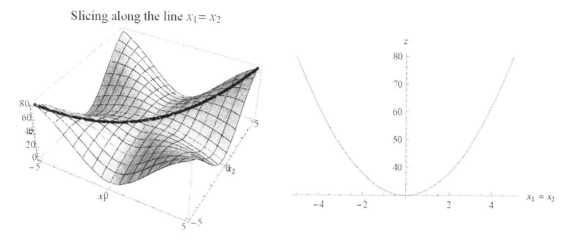

Figure 4.4.3 Slice of the surface from Figure 4.4.2 along $x_1 = x_2$. **Note that** $(0,0)$ **is a minimum along this slice.**

A real-life example of this situation is provided by the illustration of a pass in the Dolomites in Figure 4.4.4. The snowy pass near the center of the picture contains a saddle point.

Figure 4.4.4 Illustration of a saddle point from real life.

Now let's figure out the correct second-order conditions for a critical point to be a local maximum. Recall the second-order conditions for a function with a single control variable in Chapter 2. Written in terms of $g(t)$, they are:

1. If 0 is a critical point of g and $g''(0) < 0$, then 0 is a local maximum of g.
2. If 0 is a critical point of g and $g''(0) > 0$, then 0 is a local minimum of g.

We can apply these conditions to the two-variable case. Indeed, if $g(t)$ has a local maximum at $t = 0$ for every direction $\mathbf{u}$, then f certainly has a local maximum at $\mathbf{x}^*$.

We computed $g'(t)$ in Equation (4.4.1), and applying the chain rule to $g'(t)$, we find:

$$g''(t) = f_{11}(\mathbf{x}^* + t\mathbf{u})u_1^2 + f_{12}(\mathbf{x}^* + t\mathbf{u})u_1u_2 + f_{21}(\mathbf{x}^* + t\mathbf{u})u_2u_1 + f_{22}(\mathbf{x}^* + t\mathbf{u})u_2^2. \qquad (4.4.1)$$

So,

$$g''(0) = f_{11}(\mathbf{x}^*)u_1^2 + 2f_{12}(\mathbf{x}^*)u_1u_2 + f_{22}(\mathbf{x}^*)u_2^2. \qquad (4.4.2)$$

We now derive conditions on $f_{11}(\mathbf{x}^*)$, $f_{12}(\mathbf{x}^*)$, and $f_{22}(\mathbf{x}^*)$ that guarantee that $g''(0)$ is negative (for a maximum) or positive (for a minimum). In the next few computations, we evaluate all second derivatives at $\mathbf{x}^*$, but we omit the argument $\mathbf{x}^*$ to save space. We first simplify Equation (4.4.2) by completing the square:

$$g''(0) = f_{11}\left[u_1^2 + \frac{2f_{12}}{f_{11}}u_1u_2 + \frac{f_{22}}{f_{11}}u_2^2 \right]$$

$$= f_{11}\left[u_1^2 + \frac{2f_{12}}{f_{11}}u_1u_2 + \left(\frac{f_{12}}{f_{11}}u_2\right)^2 + \frac{f_{22}}{f_{11}}u_2^2 - \left(\frac{f_{12}}{f_{11}}u_2\right)^2 \right]$$

$$= f_{11}\left[\left(u_1 + \frac{f_{12}}{f_{11}}u_2 \right)^2 + \left(\frac{f_{22}}{f_{11}} - \frac{f_{12}^2}{f_{11}^2} \right)u_2^2 \right]$$

$$g''(0) = f_{11}\left(u_1 + \frac{f_{12}}{f_{11}}u_2 \right)^2 + \left(\frac{f_{11}f_{22} - f_{12}^2}{f_{11}} \right)u_2^2. \qquad (4.4.3)$$

We are concerned with the sign of $g''(0)$ for **all values** of u_1 and u_2. All of the squared terms in Equation (4.4.3) are non-negative, so that the sign of $g''(0)$ depends on the signs of f_{11} and $f_{11}f_{22} - f_{12}^2$ evaluated at $\mathbf{x}^*$. We can separate out the following possibilities:

1. If $f_{11}(\mathbf{x}^*) < 0$ and $f_{11}(\mathbf{x}^*)f_{22}(\mathbf{x}^*) - \left[f_{12}(\mathbf{x}^*)\right]^2 > 0$, then $g''(0) < 0$ for all $\mathbf{u}$. This implies[*] that $\mathbf{x}^* = (x_1^*, x_2^*)$ is a local *maximum* of $f(x_1, x_2)$.

2. If $f_{11}(\mathbf{x}^*) > 0$ and $f_{11}(\mathbf{x}^*)f_{22}(\mathbf{x}^*) - \left[f_{12}(\mathbf{x}^*)\right]^2 > 0$, then $g''(0) > 0$ for all $\mathbf{u}$. This implies that $\mathbf{x}^* = (x_1^*, x_2^*)$ is a local *minimum* of $f(x_1, x_2)$.

3. If $f_{11}(\mathbf{x}^*)f_{22}(\mathbf{x}^*) - \left[f_{12}(\mathbf{x}^*)\right]^2 < 0$, then $g''(0)$ for some directions $\mathbf{u}$ and negative for others. The critical point $\mathbf{x}^*$ is a *saddle point*.

We call the conditions in (1) the *second-order conditions for a local maximum*. The conditions in (2) are the *second-order conditions for a local minimum*.

Example 4.4.5

Returning to Example 4.4.1 with $f(x_1, x_2) = 50 - x_1^2 - x_2^2$, we have:

---

[*] Properly speaking, this implication needs some careful justification. See the proof of the Local SOC Theorem in Chapter 5 for more details.

$$\operatorname{grad} f = \left(-2x_1, -2x_2\right).$$

So the unique critical point is $\left(x_1^*, x_2^*\right) = (0,0)$. Since

$$f_{11} = f_{22} = -2 \text{ and } f_{12} = 0,$$

we have:

$$f_{11}(0,0) < 0 \text{ and } f_{11}(0,0) f_{22}(0,0) - \left[f_{12}(0,0)\right]^2 = (-2)(-2) - 0^2 = 4 > 0,$$

so the critical point $(0,0)$ is a local maximum. We can check this conclusion by looking at the graph from Figure 4.1.2. From this picture, we see that $(0,0)$ is not just a local maximum; it is even a global maximum.

Before we close this subsection, note that the second-order condition can be rewritten to involve f_{22} instead of f_{11}. That is, if $f_{22}(\mathbf{x}^*) < 0$ and $f_{11}(\mathbf{x}^*) f_{22}(\mathbf{x}^*) - \left[f_{12}(\mathbf{x}^*)\right]^2 > 0$, then the critical point $\mathbf{x}^*$ is a local maximum. To see this, we note that the second equation implies

$$f_{11}(\mathbf{x}^*) f_{22}(\mathbf{x}^*) > \left[f_{12}(\mathbf{x}^*)\right]^2,$$

and the term on the right is a square, so it is non-negative. Therefore, $f_{11}(\mathbf{x}^*)$ and $f_{22}(\mathbf{x}^*)$ have the same sign.

We summarize: to check that $\mathbf{x}^*$ is a local maximum, it suffices to verify that:

$$f_{11}(\mathbf{x}^*) f_{22}(\mathbf{x}^*) - \left[f_{12}(\mathbf{x}^*)\right]^2 > 0 \text{ and } f_{11}(\mathbf{x}^*) \text{ or } f_{22}(\mathbf{x}^*) \text{ is negative.}$$

Alternative formulation of the second-order conditions[*]

We can write the second-order conditions in an alternative form that will prove to be useful later. Consider the following matrix:

$$Hf = \begin{pmatrix} f_{11}(x_1, x_2) & f_{12}(x_1, x_2) \\ f_{21}(x_1, x_2) & f_{22}(x_1, x_2) \end{pmatrix}.$$

This matrix, *Hf*, is called the *Hessian*[†] of the function $f(x_1, x_2)$. The determinant of the Hessian is:

$$|Hf| = f_{11}(x_1, x_2) f_{22}(x_1, x_2) - \left[f_{12}(x_1, x_2)\right]^2.$$

---

[*]   This is a good time to go back and read sections 3.1 and 3.2.

[†]   This terminology has nothing to do with German mercenaries; rather, the Hessian is named after mathematician Ludwig Otto Hesse (1811–1874), who used the matrix in his research. The term "Hessian" for this matrix was proposed by mathematician J.J. Sylvester (1814–1897). He (Sylvester) is responsible for coining many mathematical words, including "matrix" (Latin for "womb") and "discriminant" for the term $b^2 - 4ac$ in the quadratic formula. He was a professor at University of Virginia and at Johns Hopkins, and eventually also at Cambridge. He led an interesting life. For example, he left Virginia after an armed scuffle with two students. For details, see page 75 of Karen Parshall's *James Joseph Sylvester: Jewish mathematician in a Victorian world*, Johns Hopkins University Press, 2006.

We say that the Hessian is *negative definite* at a point $c = (c_1, c_2)$ if *it has negative diagonal entries* (that is, $f_{11}(c_1, c_2) < 0$ and $f_{22}(c_1, c_2) < 0$) and *if its determinant is positive* (that is, if $f_{11}(c_1, c_2) f_{22}(c_1, c_2) - \left[f_{12}(c_1, c_2) \right]^2 > 0$. Similarly, we say that the Hessian is *positive definite* at **c** if the Hessian has *positive* diagonal elements and *positive* determinant.[*]

Looking back at Example 4.4.5, we see that for $f(x_1, x_2) = 50 - x_1^2 - x_2^2$, the Hessian Hf is

$$Hf = \begin{pmatrix} -2 & 0 \\ 0 & -2 \end{pmatrix},$$

which is negative definite at every point.

We can restate the second-order conditions using this new terminology:

Local SOC Theorem 4.4.6 *Let* **x*** *be a critical point of a function* $f(x_1, x_2)$ *of two variables. Then,*

(1.) *If the Hessian Hf is negative definite at* **x***, *then* **x*** *is a local maximum.*

(2.) *If the Hessian Hf is positive definite at* **x***, *then* **x*** *is a local minimum.*

Theorem 4.4.6 tells us that a critical point **x*** is a local maximum if the matrix $Hf(x^*)$ is negative definite. How can we tell if **x*** is a global maximum? It turns out that the second-order condition for **x*** to be a global maximum is very similar to the condition for a function of one variable that we saw in Chapter 1: we want the second-order condition for a local maximum to hold everywhere.

Global SOC Theorem 4.4.7 *Suppose that* **x*** *is a critical point for $f(x)$. If $Hf(x)$ is negative definite for all x, then* **x*** *is the unique critical point and is a global maximum for $f(x)$.*

We will prove this theorem in Chapter 5. In the meantime, let's think about the statement a bit. Theorem 4.4.7 is a generalization of Global SOC Theorem 1.2.1 to the situation where f has more than one variable. Both theorems say that if you have a critical point x^* and the second-order conditions for a local maximum hold everywhere (instead of just at x^*), then x^* is a global maximum.

Example 4.4.8

To apply the theorem, you really do need to start with a critical point. To see this, consider the logarithm of a Cobb-Douglas function:

$$f(x_1, x_2) = \ln\left(A x_1^\alpha x_2^\beta \right)$$

for $x_1, x_2 > 0$, where α and β are positive constants. Then,

$$f(x_1, x_2) = \ln A + \alpha \ln x_1 + \beta \ln x_2,$$

---

[*]   If you have taken linear algebra, you may have already heard of positive definite matrices. Typically you learn about them when you study inner product spaces.

$$f_1 = \frac{\alpha}{x_1}, \quad f_2 = \frac{\beta}{x_2}, \quad \text{and } Hf(x_1, x_2) = \begin{bmatrix} -\dfrac{\alpha}{x_1^2} & 0 \\ 0 & -\dfrac{\beta}{x_2^2} \end{bmatrix}.$$

As α and β are positive, this matrix is negative definite for all $x_1, x_2 > 0$. But this function has no critical points and no global maximum.

Exercises

4.4.1 Identify the local maximums and global maximums in Figure 4.4.4.

4.4.2 Find the critical points of each of the following functions. For each critical point, check if it is a local maximum, local minimum, or saddle point. If you say a point is a local minimum or maximum, determine also if it is a global minimum or maximum.

(a) $f(x_1, x_2) = 3x_1^2 - 2x_2^2 - 4x_2 + 1$

(b) $f(x_1, x_2) = 6x_1^2 - 9x_1 - 3x_1x_2 - 7x_2 + 5x_2^2$

(c) $f(x_1, x_2) = 3x_1^2 + \beta x_2^3 - x_1x_2$, where β is a parameter that can be positive or negative.

(d) $f(x_1, x_2) = x_1x_2^2 - \beta(x_1 + x_2)$, where $\beta > 0$

(e) $f(x_1, x_2) = 3x_1^2x_2 - \alpha x_1x_2 + 2x_1x_2^2$, where α can be positive or negative.

4.4.3 For each of the following functions f, determine for which values of $x_1, x_2 > 0$ the Hessian Hf is positive definite, for which values it is negative definite, and for which values it is neither.

(a) $f(x_1, x_2) = \dfrac{x_1^4}{12} + x_1x_2 + \dfrac{x_2^4}{12}$.

(b) $f(x_1, x_2) = 5^{x_1} + x_2^2$.

4.4.4 Consider the Cobb-Douglas function $f(x_1, x_2) = x_1^\alpha x_2^\beta$ where $\alpha, \beta > 0$. We only look at positive values of x_1, x_2.

(a) Calculate $|Hf|$ and show for each $x_1, x_2 > 0$, $|Hf(x_1, x_2)|$ is positive if and only if $\alpha + \beta < 1$.

(b) Prove: The Hessian of f is negative definite for all $x_1, x_2 > 0$ if and only if $\alpha + \beta < 1$. [Start by assuming that Hf is negative definite and deduce that $\alpha + \beta < 1$. Then assuming that $\alpha + \beta < 1$, deduce that Hf is negative definite.]

(c) Prove: For every $x_1, x_2 > 0$, $Hf(x_1, x_2)$ is *not* positive definite.

4.4.5 Consider the function $f(x, y) = \dfrac{x^3}{6} - xy + \dfrac{y^3}{6}$.

(a) Find all critical points of f and classify each as a local maximum, as a local minimum, or as a saddle point.

(b) For each of the following 3 domains use the global SOC theorem to identify a global minimum of f over the domain OR show that the global SOC theorem does not apply over this domain. Fully justify your answers.

(i) $x > 1$ and $y \geq 1.5$

(ii) $x > 3$ and $y > 4$

(iii) $x > 1$ and $y > 0$

We will work with the example problem of a firm's profit maximization problem where the producer has control over two inputs, x_1 and x_2 (say, labor and capital or labor and seed, etc.). We assume that the producer can sell the good at a price of p dollars per unit output and must pay w_1 and w_2 dollars per unit input for x_1 and x_2, respectively. Finally, we assume that the firm produces output using a production function f that has a negative definite Hessian.* We show below that this assumption on f is enough to guarantee that the second-order conditions hold. The producer's economic problem is:

$$\underset{x_1, x_2}{Max}\ \pi(x_1, x_2, p, w_1, w_2) = pf(x_1, x_2) - w_1 x_1 - w_2 x_2. \tag{4.5.1}$$

There are several things that are common to almost all problems encountered in microeconomics. First, the objective function almost always consists of two parts: the benefits and the costs. Second, almost always either the benefits or the costs are **linear** in its arguments. In this case, the costs are linear in x_1, x_2, w_1, and w_2. While it is not obvious at this point, the fact that part of the objective function is linear does affect the results.

Step 1: Find and check the first- and second-order conditions

We begin by deriving the first-order conditions:

$$\pi_1\ x_1, x_2, p, w_1, w_2\ = pf_1\ x_1, x_2\ - w_1 = 0 \tag{4.5.2}$$

and

$$\pi_2(x_1, x_2, p, w_1, w_2) = pf_2(x_1, x_2) - w_2 = 0. \tag{4.5.3}$$

We assume that a solution to the first-order conditions exists and is given by:

$$x_1^*(p, w_1, w_2) \text{ and } x_2^*(p, w_1, w_2). \tag{4.5.4}$$

The second-order conditions are satisfied if the objective function has negative definite Hessian. Since the costs are linear, the objective function has negative definite Hessian if the benefits function does. To see that this assertion is correct, remember that the Hessian is given by:

$$H\pi = \begin{bmatrix} \pi_{11}(x_1, x_2, p, w_1, w_2) & \pi_{12}(x_1, x_2, p, w_1, w_2) \\ \pi_{21}(x_1, x_2, p, w_1, w_2) & \pi_{22}(x_1, x_2, p, w_1, w_2) \end{bmatrix}. \tag{4.5.5}$$

It is easy to see that we can rewrite the Hessian as:

$$H\pi = \begin{bmatrix} pf_{11}(x_1, x_2) & pf_{12}(x_1, x_2) \\ pf_{21}(x_1, x_2) & pf_{22}(x_1, x_2) \end{bmatrix}. \tag{4.5.6}$$

---

* Throughout this chapter, we assume that certain functions (e.g., production, profit) have negative definite Hessians for all values of the arguments. This is not a realistic assumption, but we adopt it in keeping with our philosophy stated in the preface: we want to be mathematically correct without getting bogged down in details. In practice, we are only interested in comparative static results near an optimum, i.e., we only use the much weaker hypothesis that the Hessian is negative definite at the critical point. (Many economics textbooks refer to a critical point where the Hessian is negative definite as a "regular" maximum.) Whether one assumes that the Hessian is negative definite everywhere (as we do) or just at a critical point (the weaker assumption), the comparative static results are the same. Furthermore, in many interesting economic problems, these kinds of comparative static results hold even without these hypotheses; see e.g., Milgrom, Paul "Comparing Optima: Do Simplifying Assumptions Affect Conclusions?" *Journal of Political Economy* **102**(6): 607–615, 1994.

Thus, the second-order conditions for a maximum are that

$$pf_{11}(x_1, x_2) < 0 \tag{4.5.7}$$

and

$$|H\pi| = \begin{vmatrix} pf_{11}(x_1, x_2) & pf_{12}(x_1, x_2) \\ pf_{21}(x_1, x_2) & pf_{22}(x_1, x_2) \end{vmatrix} = p^2 f_{11}(x_1, x_2) f_{22}(x_1, x_2) - p^2 \left[f_{12}(x_1, x_2) \right]^2 > 0.$$

Since the price p is positive, these are equivalent to

$$f_{11}(x_1, x_2) < 0 \quad \text{and} \quad f_{11}(x_1, x_2) f_{22}(x_1, x_2) - \left[f_{12}(x_1, x_2) \right]^2 > 0. \tag{4.5.8}$$

Conditions (4.5.8) hold because the production function has a negative definite Hessian.

Step 2: Compute the Envelope Theorem results

We can find the indirect objective function by substituting the solutions to the first-order conditions into the direct objective function:

$$\pi^*(p, w_1, w_2) = \pi\left(x_1^*(p, w_1, w_2), x_2^*(p, w_1, w_2), p, w_1, w_2\right)$$

or

$$\pi^*(p, w_1, w_2) = pf\left(x_1^*(p, w_1, w_2), x_2^*(p, w_1, w_2)\right) - w_1 x_1^*(p, w_1, w_2) \\ - w_2 x_2^*(p, w_1, w_2) \tag{4.5.9}$$

We can derive the Envelope Theorem again. Consider the impact on indirect profits of a change in the price level, p:

$$\frac{\partial \pi^*}{\partial p}(p, w_1, w_2) = \frac{\partial \pi}{\partial x_1}\left(x_1^*(p, w_1, w_2), x_2^*(p, w_1, w_2), p, w_1, w_2\right)\frac{\partial x_1^*}{\partial p}(p, w_1, w_2)$$

$$+ \frac{\partial \pi}{\partial x_2}\left(x_1^*(p, w_1, w_2), x_2^*(p, w_1, w_2), p, w_1, w_2\right)\frac{\partial x_2^*}{\partial p}(p, w_1, w_2) \tag{4.5.10}$$

$$+ \frac{\partial \pi}{\partial p}\left(x_1^*(p, w_1, w_2), x_2^*(p, w_1, w_2), p, w_1, w_2\right).$$

The first-order conditions imply that

$$\frac{\partial \pi}{\partial x_1}\left(x_1^*(p, w_1, w_2), x_2^*(p, w_1, w_2), p, w_1, w_2\right) = 0$$

and that

$$\frac{\partial \pi}{\partial x_2}\left(x_1^*(p, w_1, w_2), x_2^*(p, w_1, w_2), p, w_1, w_2\right) = 0,$$

giving us the Envelope Theorem result that:

$$\frac{\partial \pi^*}{\partial p}(p, w_1, w_2) = \frac{\partial \pi}{\partial p}\left(x_1^*(p, w_1, w_2), x_2^*(p, w_1, w_2), p, w_1, w_2\right). \tag{4.5.11}$$

We know from the definition of direct profits given in Equation (4.5.1) that:

$$\frac{\partial \pi(x_1, x_2, p, w_1, w_2)}{\partial p} = f(x_1, x_2). \tag{4.5.12}$$

Thus, the Envelope Theorem says:

$$\frac{\partial \pi^*(p, w_1, w_2)}{\partial p} = f\left(x_1^*(p, w_1, w_2), x_2^*(p, w_1, w_2)\right) > 0. \tag{4.5.13}$$

We can use the Envelope Theorem to conclude also that:

$$\frac{\partial \pi^*(p, w_1, w_2)}{\partial w_1} = -x_1^*(p, w_1, w_2) < 0 \tag{4.5.14}$$

and

$$\frac{\partial \pi^*(p, w_1, w_2)}{\partial w_2} = -x_2^*(p, w_1, w_2) < 0. \tag{4.5.15}$$

Step 3: Compute the comparative static results

In what follows we calculate the comparative static results using matrix algebra as in Chapter 3. We begin by substituting the solution to the first-order conditions into the first-order conditions:

$$pf_1\left(x_1^*(p, w_1, w_2), x_2^*(p, w_1, w_2)\right) - w_1 = 0 \tag{4.5.16}$$

and

$$pf_2\left(x_1^*(p, w_1, w_2), x_2^*(p, w_1, w_2)\right) - w_2 = 0. \tag{4.5.17}$$

We now compute the impact of a change in w_1 on the equilibrium levels of the two inputs.

In what follows we drop the arguments of the functions when it can be done without creating confusion. We differentiate Equation (4.5.16) and Equation (4.5.17) with respect to w_1, and we get:

$$pf_{11}\frac{\partial x_1^*(p, w_1, w_2)}{\partial w_1} + pf_{12}\frac{\partial x_2^*(p, w_1, w_2)}{\partial w_1} - 1 = 0 \tag{4.5.18}$$

and

$$pf_{21}\frac{\partial x_1^*(p, w_1, w_2)}{\partial w_1} + pf_{22}\frac{\partial x_2^*(p, w_1, w_2)}{\partial w_1} = 0. \tag{4.5.19}$$

Since we are interested in solving for $\dfrac{\partial x_1^*(p, w_1, w_2)}{\partial w_1}$ and $\dfrac{\partial x_2^*(p, w_1, w_2)}{\partial w_1}$, we can put Equation (4.5.18) and Equation (4.5.19) into matrix form as:

$$\begin{bmatrix} pf_{11} & pf_{12} \\ pf_{21} & pf_{22} \end{bmatrix} \begin{bmatrix} \dfrac{\partial x_1^*(p, w_1, w_2)}{\partial w_1} \\ \dfrac{\partial x_2^*(p, w_1, w_2)}{\partial w_1} \end{bmatrix} = \begin{bmatrix} 1 \\ 0 \end{bmatrix}. \tag{4.5.20}$$

We use Cramer's Rule as in Chapter 3 to solve Equation (4.5.20) for $\dfrac{\partial x_1^*}{\partial w_1}$ and $\dfrac{\partial x_2^*}{\partial w_1}$. Applying it gives:

$$\frac{\partial x_1^*(p, w_1, w_2)}{\partial w_1} = \frac{\begin{vmatrix} 1 & pf_{12} \\ 0 & pf_{22} \end{vmatrix}}{\begin{vmatrix} pf_{11} & pf_{12} \\ pf_{21} & pf_{22} \end{vmatrix}} = \frac{pf_{22}}{\begin{vmatrix} pf_{11} & pf_{12} \\ pf_{21} & pf_{22} \end{vmatrix}} \qquad (4.5.21)$$

and

$$\frac{\partial x_2^*(p, w_1, w_2)}{\partial w_1} = \frac{\begin{vmatrix} pf_{11} & 1 \\ pf_{21} & 0 \end{vmatrix}}{\begin{vmatrix} pf_{11} & pf_{12} \\ pf_{21} & pf_{22} \end{vmatrix}} = -\frac{pf_{21}}{\begin{vmatrix} pf_{11} & pf_{12} \\ pf_{21} & pf_{22} \end{vmatrix}}. \qquad (4.5.22)$$

Now information from the second-order conditions will allow us to calculate the sign of at least one of these comparative static results. In particular, because f has negative definite Hessian,

$$pf_{22} < 0 \text{ and } \begin{vmatrix} pf_{11} & pf_{12} \\ pf_{21} & pf_{22} \end{vmatrix} > 0$$

as we saw in Step 1. Thus, we can conclude that

$$\frac{\partial x_1^*(p, w_1, w_2)}{\partial w_1} = \frac{pf_{22}}{\begin{vmatrix} pf_{11} & pf_{12} \\ pf_{21} & pf_{22} \end{vmatrix}} < 0 \qquad (4.5.23)$$

and that we cannot put a sign on $\dfrac{\partial x_2^*}{\partial w_1}$ because we do not know the sign of f_{21}.

> **Tip:** For mixed partial derivatives like f_{12}, you typically cannot guess the sign unless you are told the sign as part of the problem statement or you happen to have a formula for f. Neither is true here.

Now is a good time to do Exercise 4.5.1 at the end of this section. It's a good way to make sure you understand what we have done here.

Step 4: Illustrate the comparative static results graphically

In this section we show how to illustrate the comparative static results in the marginal space. The two first-order conditions are:

$$pf_1\left(x_1^*, x_2^*\right) - w_1 = 0 \qquad (4.5.24)$$

and

$$pf_2\left(x_1^*, x_2^*\right) - w_2 = 0. \qquad (4.5.25)$$

In economic terms these two equations say that the producer will hire inputs until the value of the marginal product of each input equals the wages he has to pay the input.

We can illustrate this in the marginal space like we did for functions of one variable. We write the objective function π as benefits (B) minus costs (C); here we take $B = pf$ and $C = w_1 x_1 + w_2 x_2$. We draw **two** graphs—one with axes labeled $\left(x_1, \$/x_1\right)$ and the other with axes labeled $\left(x_2, \$/x_2\right)$—and in each one we draw the marginal benefit and marginal cost curves as shown in Figure 4.5.1. We know from the second-order conditions that the marginal benefit functions ($pf_1(x_1, x_2^*)$ and $pf_2(x_1^*, x_2)$) have negative slopes in the marginal space. Note that in Figure 4.5.1, *in the marginal space relative to one control variable, the other control variable has a** That is, we graph $\frac{\partial B}{\partial x_1}(x_1, x_2^*)$ and $\frac{\partial C}{\partial x_1}(x_1, x_2^*)$, which are functions of x_1—here x_2^* is fixed. In this way, the intersections of the curves occurs at x_1^*, and the graph illustrates the first-order condition like we wanted.

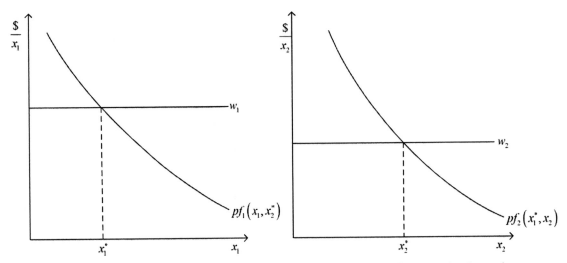

Figure 4.5.1 The first-order conditions in the marginal space. Remember the general rule: in the marginal space relative to one control variable, the other control variables must have stars.

Now we are ready to illustrate the impact of a rise in w_1 on the amounts of the two inputs used. There are two cases that need to be illustrated; in the first we assume that $f_{12} > 0$ and in the second case we assume that $f_{12} < 0$. The two cases are shown in Figure 4.5.2 and in Figure 4.5.3, respectively.

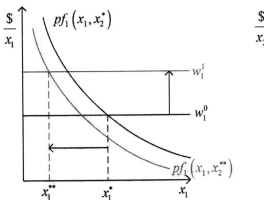
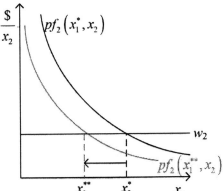

Figure 4.5.2 Impact of a rise in w_1 when $f_{12} > 0$.

We start with our given maximum $\left(x_1^*, x_2^*\right)$ for π. A rise in w_1 gives a new maximum $\left(x_1^{**}, x_2^{**}\right)$. The algebra shows that $\dfrac{\partial x_1^*}{\partial w_1}$ is negative, so $x_1^{**} < x_1^*$. In the case where $f_{12} > 0$ the graph of $pf_2\left(x_1^{**}, x_2\right)$ lies below the graph of $pf_2\left(x_1^*, x_2\right)$ as in the right panel of Figure 4.5.2. From the picture, we see that x_2^{**} is less than x_2^* and, hence, that $\dfrac{\partial x_2^*}{\partial w_1}$ is negative. Moreover, the assumption that $f_{12} > 0$ implies that the graph of $pf_1\left(x_1, x_2^{**}\right)$ lies below that of $pf_1\left(x_1, x_2^*\right)$, giving the picture in the left panel of Figure 4.5.2.

The graphical reasoning has shown that $\dfrac{\partial x_2^*}{\partial w_1}$ is negative. Earlier we found that:

$$\frac{\partial x_2^*\left(p, w_1, w_2\right)}{\partial w_1} = \frac{-pf_{21}}{\begin{vmatrix} pf_{11} & pf_{12} \\ pf_{21} & pf_{22} \end{vmatrix}}.$$

Since $f_{12} > 0$, the algebra also implies that $\dfrac{\partial x_2^*}{\partial w_1}$ is negative.

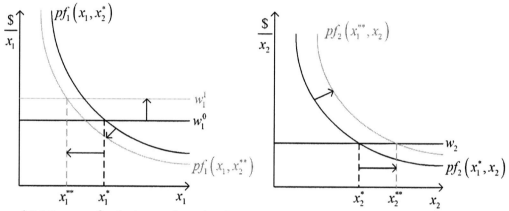

Figure 4.5.3 Impact of a rise in w_1 when $f_{12} < 0$.

Now let's look at the case where $f_{12} < 0$, which is illustrated in Figure 4.5.3. As before, we write $\left(x_1^*, x_2^*\right)$ and $\left(x_1^{**}, x_2^{**}\right)$ for the old and new maximums for π, respectively. The assumption that $f_{12} < 0$ implies that the graph of $pf\left(x_1^{**}, x_2\right)$ lies above the graph of $pf\left(x_1^*, x_2\right)$ as shown in the right panel of the figure. From the graph, we see that x_2^{**} is greater than x_2^*, i.e., $\dfrac{\partial x_2^*}{\partial w_1}$ is positive. It follows that the graph of $pf_1\left(x_1, x_2^{**}\right)$ lies below that of $pf_1\left(x_1, x_2^*\right)$, giving the picture in the left panel of the figure. As in the $f_{12} > 0$ case, the graphical and algebraic reasoning both imply that $\dfrac{\partial x_2^*}{\partial w_1}$ is positive.

Exercises

4.5.1 Consider the following function: $f(x_1, x_2, \alpha) = 8 - x_1^2 + 2x_1 - \alpha x_1 x_2 + 2x_2 - x_2^2$, where $\alpha^2 < 4$.

   i) Find all of the critical points for this function.

   ii) Identify whether each point is a relative maximum, a relative minimum, or a saddle point. Justify your answer.

   iii) Calculate and sign (1) $\dfrac{\partial x_1^*(\alpha)}{\partial \alpha}$ and (2) $\dfrac{\partial x_2^*(\alpha)}{\partial \alpha}$. Justify your answer.

4.5.2 In chapter 2 we derived the general comparative static formula given by 2.5.5; we have not derived a similar formula in this chapter. In this problem you will derive a set of formulas that are similar to 2.5.5. The optimization problem we are interested in is $\underset{x_1, x_2}{Max}\ \Pi(x_1, x_2, \alpha)$, where x_1 and x_2 are the control variables and α is a parameter. The first-order conditions for this problem are (1) $\Pi_1(x_1, x_2, \alpha) = 0$ and (2) $\Pi_2(x_1, x_2, \alpha) = 0$. Assume that a solution to these first-order conditions exists and is given by the pair $x_1^*(\alpha)$ and $x_2^*(\alpha)$.

   i) Derive a general formula for the comparative statics (1) $\dfrac{\partial x_1^*(\alpha)}{\partial \alpha}$ and (2) $\dfrac{\partial x_2^*(\alpha)}{\partial \alpha}$.

   ii) Use these formulas to solve part (iii) of 4.5.1.

4.5.3 In Step 3 of the example problem, we calculated and found the sign of $\dfrac{\partial x_1^*}{\partial w_1}$ and $\dfrac{\partial x_2^*}{\partial w_1}$, but we did not consider comparative statics involving the other parameter, p. Calculate and sign $\dfrac{\partial x_1^*(p, w_1, w_2)}{\partial p}$ and $\dfrac{\partial x_2^*(p, w_1, w_2)}{\partial p}$.

4.5.4 Consider a firm that uses two inputs, say labor (x_1) and capital (x_2). The per-unit costs of the two inputs are w_1 and w_2, respectively. The firm sells its output at a per unit price p and produces its output y using a production function $y = f(x_1, x_2)$ that has negative definite Hessian. Assume that the government decides to levy a per unit tax t on the amount of capital the firm uses. Thus the firm's profit function is:

$$\pi(x_1, x_2, p, w_1, w_2, t) = pf(x_1, x_2) - w_1 x_1 - w_2 x_2 - tx_2.$$

(a) Find the first-order conditions.

(b) Find and sign the following partial derivatives (if you can):

   (i) $\dfrac{\partial \pi^*(p, w_1, w_2, t)}{\partial w_1}$

   (ii) $\dfrac{\partial \pi^*(p, w_1, w_2, t)}{\partial t}$

(c) Find and sign the following additional partial derivatives (if you can):

   (i) $\dfrac{\partial x_1^*(p, w_1, w_2, t)}{\partial t}$

   (ii) $\dfrac{\partial x_2^*(p, w_1, w_2, t)}{\partial t}$

(iii) $\dfrac{\partial y^*(p, w_1, w_2, t)}{\partial t}$

4.5.5 Mary enjoys smoking and drinking during her recreational time. Let x_1 be the number of cigarettes she smokes and x_2 be the number of drinks she consumes. Suppose that the price of a cigarette is p_1 and the price of a drink is p_2. Let $u(x_1, x_2)$ be the utility she derives from smoking and drinking. Moreover, assume that her marginal enjoyment of one more cigarette rises the more she drinks—i.e., $u_{12} > 0$. Finally, suppose that in response to environmentalists and the liquor lobby the government places a tax of t on each cigarette. Thus, we assume that Mary chooses the levels of x_1 and x_2 that maximizes her net utility from smoking and drinking, V, as given by

$$V(x_1, x_2, p_1, p_2, t) = u(x_1, x_2) - (p_1 + t)x_1 - p_2 x_2.$$

(a) Find the first-order conditions for Mary's problem.

(b) What are the second-order conditions for Mary's problem?

(c) Suppose that $x_1^*(t, p_1, p_2)$ and $x_2^*(t, p_1, p_2)$ are solutions to the first-order conditions and suppose that the second-order conditions hold. Find $\dfrac{\partial x_2^*(t, p_1, p_2)}{\partial t}$ and determine its sign if you can. What is the economic interpretation of this sign?

(d) Illustrate the impact of an increase in t on $x_1^*(t, p_1, p_2)$ and $x_2^*(t, p_1, p_2)$ in the marginal space.

(e) The indirect utility function is $V^*(t, p_1, p_2) = V(x_1^*(t, p_1, p_2), x_2^*(t, p_1, p_2), p_1, p_2, t)$. Find $\dfrac{\partial V^*(t, p_1, p_2)}{\partial t}$ and determine its sign if you can.

4.5.4 A monopolist makes one product and sells it in two markets with revenue functions $R(y_1)$ and $S(y_2)$, respectively. Costs, C, are a concave up function of total output, $y = y_1 + y_2$. Assume that the monopolist maximizes profits. Assume the second-order conditions hold for the firm's profit maximization problem.

(a) Show that the marginal cost in each market (i.e., $\dfrac{\partial C}{\partial y_1}$ and $\dfrac{\partial C}{\partial y_2}$) equals the marginal total cost, $\dfrac{\partial C}{\partial y}$.

(b) Show that the monopolist will equate the marginal total cost to the marginal revenues in each market.

(c) Show that the monopolist will charge a higher price in the market that is less price elastic, that is, in the market whose price elasticity of demand is less negative. (Exercise 1.8.1 might be helpful.)

(d) Suppose the government places the same per unit output tax on output sold in both markets. Calculate the impact of the tax on the firm's equilibrium levels of y_1, y_2, and y.

(e) Suppose the tax described in part (d) is placed only on the output sold in market 1. Calculate the impact of the tax on the firm's equilibrium levels of y_1, y_2, and y.

4.5.5 In this question we are interested in analyzing the behavior of students and of professors in a university setting and what behavior the administration would like from the students and professors. To accomplish this mission, we break the analysis into the following three parts: (1) the behavior of the student, (2) the behavior of the professor, and (3) the behavior of the "ideal" student and professor.

We begin with some assumptions about the behavior of the students. First, we assume that students decide what percentage of classes to attend, x, by maximizing their expected net benefits of class attendance where the grade the student receives in a course, $G(x,t)$, is a function of the percentage of classes attended, x, and the quality of preparation by the professor, t and has negative definite Hessian. Second, we assume that the opportunity costs of attending class is a linear function of the percentage of class attended, where β is the per class opportunity cost of class attendance to the student. Third, we assume that the student's non-pecuniary cost of class attendance, $f(x,t)$, is a function of the number of classes attended, x, and the quality of the professor's class preparation, t, has f_x positive, f_t negative, and both f_{xx} and f_{tt} positive. In sum the student's net benefits are:

$$B^S(x,t,\beta) = G(x,t) - \beta x - f(x,t).$$

We assume that the professor balances his levels of research time, r, and class preparation time, t, in order to maximize his salary, net of teaching and research costs, where (1) the professor's salary, $S(r,t)$, is a function of time devoted to research, r, and the quality of his class preparation, t; and has negative definite Hessian; (2) the professor's opportunity costs of research and class preparation are linear functions, where αr are the research costs and δt are the class preparation costs; and (3) the professor's costs of class preparation, $h(x)$, are a function of class attendance and are decreasing at an increasing rate. In sum, the professor's net benefits are:

$$B^P(r,t,x,\alpha,\delta) = S(r,t) - \alpha r - \delta t - h(x).$$

Finally, we assume that the administrator would like to choose the levels of student class attendance, faculty class preparation, and faculty research efforts that maximize the sum of the student's net benefits and the professor's net benefits:

$$B(r,t,x,\alpha,\beta,\delta) = B^S(x,t,\beta) + B^P(r,t,x,\alpha,\delta).$$

(a) Find and sketch the first-order conditions for the student's problem. Check the second-order conditions of the problem.

(b) Find and sketch the first-order conditions for the professor's problem. Check the second-order conditions of the problem.

(c) Assume that solutions to the student's and faculty member's problems exist. Find and sign (if you can):

(i) $\dfrac{\partial x^*}{\partial t}$,

(ii) $\dfrac{\partial r^*}{\partial x}$, and

(iii) $\dfrac{\partial t^*}{\partial x}$.

What do the signs that you can determine say about the student's and professor's behavior?

(d) Compute and sketch the first-order conditions of the administrator's problem. Compare these first-order conditions to those found in parts (a) and (b). Can you say anything about the "ideal" levels of x, t, and r as compared to the values found earlier?

4.5.6 Suppose we are maximizing Π, a function of control variables, x_1 and x_2 and a vector of parameters, $\boldsymbol{\alpha}$. Prove the Envelope Theorem that

$$\frac{\partial \Pi^*}{\partial \beta}(\boldsymbol{\alpha}) = \Pi_\beta(x_1^*, x_2^*, \boldsymbol{\alpha})$$

for each parameter β *in* $\boldsymbol{\alpha}$.

CHAPTER 5

OPTIMIZING FUNCTIONS WITH
SEVERAL CONTROL VARIABLES

I n section 4 of the last chapter, we gave some justification for the Local SOC Theorem 4.4.6 and no justification at all for the Global SOC Theorem 4.4.7. The first purpose of this chapter is to give complete proofs of these results.

The second purpose of this chapter is to connect the notions we use in this book like positive definite Hessian with terms seen more frequently in the economics literature like convex. For the convenience of the reader, we give all the details.

The content in this chapter is noticeably more mathematical than in the rest of the book, even though we do not use anything more serious than multivariable calculus. With that in mind, we feel comfortable stating and proving all results in case f is a function of n variables—i.e., is $f(x_1, x_2,...,x_n)$ —as opposed to just one or two variables as in the previous chapters. This adds very little extra work.

5.1. FIRST AND SECOND DERIVATIVES OF FUNCTIONS OF SEVERAL VARIABLES

In single-variable calculus, you learned how to take a function of one variable $f(x)$ and find its derivatives $f'(x)$ and $f''(x)$, which were also functions of one variable. But when f is a function of several variables, the obvious analogue of the first derivative is grad $f(x)$, which is a vector-valued function. This is unpleasant. In some cases, it would be much nicer to have a derivative that is a "usual" (i.e., real-valued) function. But we already saw how to do this in section 4.3: You fix a base point $\mathbf{c}$ and a direction $\mathbf{u}$. You define a new function $g(t)$ by

$$g(t) := f(\mathbf{c} + t\mathbf{u}) \qquad (5.1.1)$$

We called this the slice through $\mathbf{c}$ in the direction $\mathbf{u}$. We call $g(0)$ the **(first) directional derivative** of f at $\mathbf{c}$ in the direction $\mathbf{u}$.[*] The second derivative $g''(0)$ is called the **second directional derivative** of f at $\mathbf{c}$ in the direction $\mathbf{u}$; it is sometimes denoted $f_{\mathbf{u}}''(\mathbf{c})$ How can we calculate them?

Using the chain rule, we compute that:

---

[*] The usual definition of directional derivative in the direction $\mathbf{u}$ requires that $\mathbf{u}$ is a unit vector, but we do not require this here.

$$g'(t) = \frac{d}{dt} f\left(c_1 + tu_1, c_2 + tu_2, \ldots, c_n + tu_n\right)$$
$$= f_1\left(c_1 + tu_1, c_2 + tu_2, \ldots, c_n + tu_n\right)u_1 +$$
$$f_2\left(c_1 + tu_1, c_2 + tu_2, \ldots, c_n + tu_n\right)u_2 + \cdots +$$
$$f_n\left(c_1 + tu_1, c_2 + tu_2, \ldots, c_n + tu_n\right)u_n$$
$$= \mathbf{u} \cdot \left(\operatorname{grad} f\left(\mathbf{c} + t\mathbf{u}\right)\right).$$

(5.1.2)

So

$$g'(0) = \mathbf{u} \cdot \left(\operatorname{grad} f(\mathbf{c})\right).$$

(5.1.3)

That's the first derivative. The main point of this section is to prove:

Lemma 5.1.1 $g''(t) = \mathbf{u}\left(Hf(\mathbf{c} + t\mathbf{u})\right)\mathbf{u}^T$.

The capital T on the right side of the equation in Lemma 5.1.1 means the transpose of $\mathbf{u}$, which is just the row vector $\mathbf{u}$ rotated by 90 degrees to make it a column vector. For example, if $\mathbf{u}$ is the 1-by-2 vector $(a\ b)$ then $\mathbf{u}^T$ is the 2-by-1 vector $\begin{pmatrix} a \\ b \end{pmatrix}$.

PROOF. We gave a formula for $g'(t)$ in (5.1.2). Applying the chain rule to it, we find:

$$g''(t) = f_{11}\left(\mathbf{c} + t\mathbf{u}\right)u_1^2 + f_{12}\left(\mathbf{c} + t\mathbf{u}\right)u_1 u_2 + \cdots + f_{1n}\left(\mathbf{c} + t\mathbf{u}\right)u_1 u_n$$
$$+ f_{21}\left(\mathbf{c} + t\mathbf{u}\right)u_2 u_1 + f_{22}\left(\mathbf{c} + t\mathbf{u}\right)u_2^2 + \cdots + f_{2n}\left(\mathbf{c} + t\mathbf{u}\right)u_2 u_n$$
$$+ \cdots + f_{n1}\left(\mathbf{c} + t\mathbf{u}\right)u_n u_1 + f_{n2}\left(\mathbf{c} + t\mathbf{u}\right)u_n u_2 + \cdots + f_{nn}\left(\mathbf{c} + t\mathbf{u}\right)u_n^2.$$

Rewriting this in matrix form, we find

$$g''(t) = \mathbf{u} \begin{pmatrix} f_{11}\left(\mathbf{c} + t\mathbf{u}\right) & f_{12}\left(\mathbf{c} + t\mathbf{u}\right) & \cdots & f_{1n}\left(\mathbf{c} + t\mathbf{u}\right) \\ f_{21}\left(\mathbf{c} + t\mathbf{u}\right) & f_{22}\left(\mathbf{c} + t\mathbf{u}\right) & \cdots & f_{2n}\left(\mathbf{c} + t\mathbf{u}\right) \\ \vdots & \vdots & \ddots & \vdots \\ f_{n1}\left(\mathbf{c} + t\mathbf{u}\right) & f_{n2}\left(\mathbf{c} + t\mathbf{u}\right) & \cdots & f_{nn}\left(\mathbf{c} + t\mathbf{u}\right) \end{pmatrix} \mathbf{u}^T = \mathbf{u}\left(Hf\left(\mathbf{c} + t\mathbf{u}\right)\right)\mathbf{u}^T$$

as desired. □

Exercises

5.1.1 Let $\mathbf{r}(t)$ be a function that that takes one number and gives a vector $\left(x_1(t), x_2(t), \ldots, x_n(t)\right)$ of n numbers. Let $f\left(x_1, x_2, \ldots, x_n\right)$ be a function, and define $g(t) := f\left(\mathbf{r}(t)\right)$. Prove that

$$g'(t) = \operatorname{grad} f\left(\mathbf{r}(t)\right) \cdot \mathbf{r}'(t)$$

and

$$g''(t) = \mathbf{r}'(t)\left[\left(Hf\right)\left(\mathbf{r}(t)\right)\right]\mathbf{r}'(t)^T + \operatorname{grad} f\left(\mathbf{r}(t)\right) \cdot \mathbf{r}''(t).$$

Here, $\mathbf{r}'(t) = \left(\dfrac{\partial x_1}{\partial t}, \dfrac{\partial x_2}{\partial t}, \ldots, \dfrac{\partial x_n}{\partial t}\right)$ and $\mathbf{r}''(t) = \left(\dfrac{\partial^2 x_1}{\partial t^2}, \dfrac{\partial^2 x_2}{\partial t^2}, \ldots, \dfrac{\partial^2 x_n}{\partial t^2}\right)$. This problem generalizes what we did in this section, where $\mathbf{r}(t)$ was $\mathbf{c} + t\mathbf{u}$ for vectors $\mathbf{c}$ and $\mathbf{u}$.

5.2 NEGATIVE DEFINITE AND POSITIVE DEFINITE

In section 4.4, we defined what it meant for the Hessian of a function $f(x_1, x_2)$ of two variables to be negative or positive definite. Specifically,

$$Hf = \begin{pmatrix} f_{11} & f_{12} \\ f_{21} & f_{22} \end{pmatrix}$$

is said to be *positive definite* if f_{11} is positive and the determinant of the matrix is positive. It is *negative definite* if f_{11} is negative and the determinant of the matrix is positive.

More generally, for f a function of n variables $x_1, x_2, \ldots, x_n$, the Hessian Hf is defined to be the matrix

$$Hf = \begin{pmatrix} f_{11} & f_{12} & \cdots & f_{1n} \\ f_{21} & f_{22} & \cdots & f_{2n} \\ \vdots & \vdots & \ddots & \vdots \\ f_{n1} & f_{n2} & \cdots & f_{nn} \end{pmatrix}$$

where, as always, f_{ij} stands for $\dfrac{\partial^2 f}{\partial x_i \partial x_j}$. By Young's Theorem, $f_{ij} = f_{ji}$, so the Hessian Hf is *symmetric*. We now define what it means for this Hf to be positive or negative definite.

Definition 5.2.1 The matrix Hf is *positive definite* if for every nonzero 1-by-n vector u, the number $\mathbf{u}(Hf)\mathbf{u}^T$ is positive. The matrix Hf is *negative definite* if for every nonzero vector u, the number $\mathbf{u}(Hf)\mathbf{u}^T$ is negative.

Previously, we defined positive and negative definite only in the case n = 2. You can check that the old definition agrees with the new one by imitating the discussion in section 4.4.

Example 5.2.2

In the case when f is a function of a single variable—i.e., is just $f(x)$—the matrix Hf is 1-by-1, so it is just the number $f''(x)$. A nonzero 1-by-1 vector $\mathbf{u}$ is just a nonzero number u. We have:

$$\mathbf{u}(Hf)\mathbf{u}^T = u^2 f''(x),$$

which is positive for every nonzero $\mathbf{u}$ (and Hf is positive definite) if and only if $f''(x)$ is positive. Similarly, Hf is negative definite if and only if $f''(x)$ is negative.

Theorem 5.2.3. *The matrix Hf is positive definite if and only if the determinants of the matrices*

$$(f_{11}),\ \begin{pmatrix} f_{11} & f_{12} \\ f_{21} & f_{22} \end{pmatrix},\ \begin{pmatrix} f_{11} & f_{12} & f_{13} \\ f_{21} & f_{22} & f_{23} \\ f_{31} & f_{32} & f_{33} \end{pmatrix},\ \ldots,\ \begin{pmatrix} f_{11} & f_{12} & \cdots & f_{1,n-1} \\ f_{21} & f_{22} & \cdots & f_{2,n-1} \\ \vdots & \vdots & \ddots & \vdots \\ f_{n-1,1} & f_{n-1,2} & \cdots & f_{n-1,n-1} \end{pmatrix},\ Hf$$

are all positive.

We already know this result in some cases. For one variable $(n = 1)$, the theorem says that Hf is positive definite if and only if $f''(x)$ is positive, which we observed in Example 5.2.2.

In full generality, this theorem is a standard result from linear algebra. For a proof see Section X.4 of F.R. Gantmacher, *Theory of Matrices, vol. 1,* AMS Chelsea, Providence, RI, 2000; Theorem 6.4 in M.R. Hestenes, *Calculus of variations and optimal control theory,* Wiley, 1966; or Theorem 2 in G. Debreu, *Econometrica,* vol. 20 (1952), pp. 295–300.

An analogous theorem holds for negative definite matrices. It says that Hf is negative definite if and only if the determinants of the matrices displayed in Theorem 5.2.3 alternate in sign, where f_{11} is negative and $|Hf|$ has the same sign as $(-1)^n$.

5.3 SECOND-ORDER CONDITIONS FOR LOCAL AND GLOBAL OPTIMA

In this section we finally deliver the proof of the Local SOC Theorem left dangling from Chapter 4. We need the following rather technical lemma, which we include for completeness. Most readers will want to skip it.

Lemma 5.3.1. *Fix a vector* **c** *and suppose that for every nonzero vector* **u** *the second directional derivative* $f_{\mathbf{u}}''(0)$ *is negative. Then there is an* $\varepsilon > 0$ *such that* $f_{\mathbf{u}}''(t)$ *is negative for all* $-\varepsilon < t < \varepsilon$.

The proof is well beyond the scope of this text, but we include it because it is so short. For an alternative proof (which also uses compactness), see Theorem 4.3 in M.R. Hestenes, *Calculus of variations and optimal control theory.*

PROOF. Write U for the set of vectors **u** of length 1 and define a function $h: U \to [0,1]$ as follows: If the second directional derivative $f_{\mathbf{u}}''(t)$ is negative for $-1 < t < 1$, send **u** to 1. Otherwise, send **u** to the maximum m in $[0,1]$ such that $f_{\mathbf{u}}''(t)$ is negative for all $-m < t < m$. This function h is continuous hence the image $h(U)$ is closed (because U is compact). As $h(U)$ does not contain 0, it does not meet $[0,\varepsilon)$ for some $\varepsilon > 0$. This proves the claim.

We can now prove:

Local SOC Theorem 5.3.2. *Let* $\mathbf{x}^*$ *be a critical point of a function* $f(x_1, x_2, \ldots, x_n)$. *If the matrix* $Hf(\mathbf{x}^*)$ *is negative definite, then* $\mathbf{x}^*$ *is a local maximum. If the matrix* $Hf(\mathbf{x}^*)$ *is positive definite, then* $\mathbf{x}^*$ *is a local minimum.*

PROOF. Suppose that $Hf(\mathbf{x}^*)$ is negative definite. Lemma 5.3.1 says that there is some $\varepsilon > 0$ such that for every unit vector **u** the slice

$$g(t) := f\left(\mathbf{x}^* + t\mathbf{u}\right)$$

has $g''(t) < 0$ for all $-\varepsilon < t < \varepsilon$. It follows as in the proof of Theorem 1.2.1 that $t = 0$ is the unique maximum for $g(t)$ for $-\varepsilon < t < \varepsilon$. Since this is true for every unit vector **u**, we see that $\mathbf{x}^*$ is the unique maximum of $f(\mathbf{x}^*)$ for $|\mathbf{x} - \mathbf{x}^*| < \varepsilon$.

In case f is a function of just one or two variables, the theorem is identical to the second-order conditions given in Chapters 1 and 4.

The second-order condition for a global optimum looks very similar:

Global SOC Theorem 5.3.3. *Let* $\mathbf{x}^*$ *be a critical point of a function* $f(x_1, x_2, \ldots x_n)$. *If the matrix* $Hf(x)$ *is negative definite for all* **x**, *then* $\mathbf{x}^*$ *is the unique global maximum. If the matrix* $Hf(\mathbf{x})$ *is positive definite for all* **x**, *then* $\mathbf{x}^*$ *is the unique global minimum.*

The proof of this is almost the same as the proof of the previous theorem, so we omit it. Alternatively, this theorem is a consequence of Theorems 5.6.1 and 5.7.1 later in the chapter.

As with all of the second-order conditions for global optima that we have stated (specifically, Theorems 1.2.1 and 4.4.7), the phrase "for all $\mathbf{x}$" means "for all $\mathbf{x}$ in the region we consider", which in this book typically means either all values of $\mathbf{x}$ or just those $\mathbf{x}$ with positive coordinates.[*]

Exercises 5.3.1

The definition of local maximum is: x^* is a local maximum for $f(x)$ if there is some $\varepsilon > 0$ such that $f(x) \leq f(x^*)$ for all $|x - x^*| < \varepsilon$. Explain why the "proof" of the second-order conditions for a local maximum given in section 4.4 is not adequate.

5.4 CONCAVE AND CONVEX: DEFINITIONS

Sometimes economists replace the assumption "the Hessian is positive definite" with weaker assumptions like "the function is strictly convex" or the yet weaker "the function is convex". In the rest of this chapter, we will define these weaker notions, show how they are interrelated, and explain how they are related to optimizing the function.

Table 5.4.1 Dictionary relating the various assumptions on f.

Problem	Our assumption	Weaker assumption	Even weaker assumption
min f	Hf positive definite	f strictly convex	f convex
max f	Hf negative definite	f strictly concave	f concave

For simplicity of writing, below we (mostly) only talk about the first row of the table, relating the problem of minimizing f and convexity. All of the results of this chapter apply equally well to the problem of maximizing f and concavity; one simply needs to add some minus signs and reverse some inequalities. For example, Hf is negative definite if and only if $H(-f)$ is positive definite. Similar comments apply with strictly concave versus strictly *convex* and concave versus convex.

Definition 5.4.2. A function $f(x_1, \ldots, x_n)$ is strictly convex if for all points $\mathbf{c}, \mathbf{d},$ and every point $\mathbf{q}$ lying on the line segment between them, the point $(\mathbf{q}, f(\mathbf{q}))$ lies strictly below the chord joining $(\mathbf{c}, f(\mathbf{c}))$ and $(\mathbf{d}, f(\mathbf{d}))$. Said differently, f is strictly convex if for all $\mathbf{c}, \mathbf{d},$ and $0 < t < 1$, we have

$$f(t\mathbf{c} + (1 - t)\mathbf{d}) < tf(\mathbf{c}) + (1 - t)f(\mathbf{d}).$$

The notion of convex is defined similarly, except that we allow also the possibility that $(\mathbf{q}, f(\mathbf{q}))$ lies on the chord. That is, f is *convex* if for all $c, d,$ and $0 < t < 1$, we have

$$f(t\mathbf{c} + (1 - t)\mathbf{d}) \leq tf(\mathbf{c}) + (1 - t)f(\mathbf{d}).$$

---

[*]   Precisely speaking, the correct hypothesis is "for all $\mathbf{x}$ in some convex open subset of n-space."

Example 5.4.3.

The function $f(x) \equiv 0$, whose graph is the x-axis, is convex but *not* strictly convex.

More generally, if $f(x_1, \ldots, x_n) = a_1 x_1 + a_2 x_2 + \ldots + a_n x_n + \mathbf{b}$ for some numbers $a_1, \ldots, a_n$ and some vector $\mathbf{b}$ (i.e., if the graph of $z = f(x_1, \ldots, x_n)$ is a hyperplane), then f is convex but *not* strictly convex.

Example 5.4.4.

The function $f(x) = x^4$ is strictly convex, as you can see from Figure 5.4.5. Its Hessian is $f''(x) = 12x^2$, which is positive definite (by Example 5.2.2) except at $x = 0$. Therefore, f is strictly convex, but Hf is *not* positive definite everywhere.

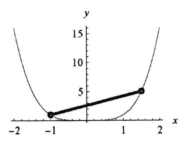

Figure 5.4.5 The graph of $f(x) = x^4$ with a chord drawn in. This function is obviously strictly convex.

5.5 RELATIONSHIPS BETWEEN THE HYPOTHESES FOR FUNCTIONS OF ONE VARIABLE

A function $f(x)$ of one variable has a positive definite Hessian if and only if $f''(x)$ is positive for all x. The weaker properties "strictly convex" and "convex" are harder to see using calculus. In this section, we prove some calculus characterizations of these properties for a function of one variable $f(x)$.

Proposition 5.5.1. *Among the statements*

(1) $f''(x)$ *is positive for all* $\mathbf{x}$,
(2) $f(x)$ *is strictly convex,*
(3) *For every* $a < b$, *we have:*

$$f'(a) < \frac{f(b) - f(a)}{b - a} < f'(b),$$

we have the following implications: (1) implies (2), and (2) is equivalent to (3).

Note that (2) does not imply (1) by Example 5.4.4. The proof of this proposition is very similar to the next one, so we only prove the next proposition.

Proposition 5.5.2. *The following statements are equivalent:*

(1) $f''(x) \geq 0$ *for all* x,
(2) $f(x)$ *is convex,*

(3) *For every a < b, we have:*

$$f'(a) \le \frac{f(b)-f(a)}{b-a} \le f'(b).$$

(5.5.1)

PROOF. We first note that (1) is equivalent to

(1') The function $f'(x)$ is *non-decreasing*, i.e., if $a < b$, then $f'(a) \le f'(b)$.

This conclusion follows from the Fundamental Theorem of Calculus, which says that for $a < b$, we have:

$$f'(b)-f'(a) = \int_a^b f''(x)\,dx.$$

If (1) holds, then the right side is at least 0, hence (1') holds. Conversely, if (1) fails, then there is some point q with $f''(q) < 0$ hence points a, b such that $a < q < b$ and $f''(x)$ is negative on the interval $[a,b]$. Then the integral $\int_a^b f''(x)\,dx$ is negative, and (1') fails. This proves that (1) and (1') are equivalent.

Next suppose that (1') holds, and let a, q, b be numbers with $a < q < b$. We want to show that the point $(q, f(q))$ lies on or below the chord joining $(a, f(a))$ to $(b, f(b))$, i.e., we want to prove:

$$f(q) \le f(a) + (q-a)\frac{f(b)-f(a)}{b-a}.$$

By the Fundamental Theorem of Calculus, we have:

$$f(q) = f(a) + \int_a^q f'(x)\,dx.$$

(5.5.2)

Combining this with (5.5.2), we find that we need to prove:

$$\int_a^q f'(x)\,dx \le (q-a)\frac{f(b)-f(a)}{b-a},$$

or, equivalently:

$$\frac{1}{q-a}\int_a^q f'(x)\,dx \le \frac{1}{b-a}\int_a^b f'(x)\,dx.$$

(5.5.3)

The integral on the left is the average value of $f'(x)$ on the interval [a, q], and the integral on the right is the average value of $f'(x)$ on the larger interval $[a,b]$. Since $f'(x)$ is non-decreasing by (1'), the inequality holds, hence so does (5.5.2) . This proves that (1') implies (2).

Now suppose that (2) holds; we prove (3). Since $f(x)$ is convex, the inequality (5.5.2) holds for q between a and b. Therefore,

$$\frac{f(q)-f(a)}{q-a} \le \frac{f(b)-f(a)}{b-a}.$$

Taking the limit of both sides of this last inequality as $q \mapsto a$, we find:

$$f'(a) \le \frac{f(b)-f(a)}{b-a}.$$

A similar argument shows the other inequality

$$\frac{f(b)-f(a)}{b-a} \le f'(b).$$

Thus, we have proved that (2) implies (3).

Since (3) trivially implies (1'), we have shown that all three properties in the statement of the proposition are equivalent, and that all three are equivalent to (1').

5.6 RELATIONSHIPS BETWEEN THE HYPOTHESES

We now prove:

Theorem 5.6.1. *For the statements*

(1) Hf is positive definite
(2) f is strictly convex
(3) f is convex
(4) Hf is positive semi-definite
we have the implications: (1) implies (2) implies (3), and (3) is equivalent to (4).

The term *positive semi-definite* is new. The matrix Hf is positive semi-definite if for every vector $\mathbf{u}$, the number $\mathbf{u}(Hf)\,\mathbf{u}^T \ge 0$. (The only difference from the definition of positive definite is that we have changed $>$ into a $\ge$.) For example, the zero matrix and the matrix

$$\begin{pmatrix} 1 & 0 \\ 0 & 0 \end{pmatrix}$$

are both positive semi-definite but not positive definite.

PROOF OF THEOREM 5.6.1 We first prove that (1) implies (2). For points $\mathbf{c}$ and $\mathbf{d}$, put $\mathbf{u} := \mathbf{d} - \mathbf{c}$; it is a vector pointing from $\mathbf{c}$ to $\mathbf{d}$. Define the function $g(t)$ as in Equation (5.1.1), so $g(0) = \mathbf{c}$ and $g(1) = \mathbf{d}$. By (1) and Lemma 5.1.1, $g''(t)$ is positive. By Proposition 5.5.1, $g(t)$ is strictly convex. Since this holds for every pair of points $\mathbf{c}$ and $\mathbf{d}$, the function f is strictly convex.

Strictly convex trivially implies convex, i.e., (2) implies (3).

As for (3) and (4), note that Proposition 5.5.2 says that (3) is equivalent to

(3') $g''(0) \ge 0$ for every $\mathbf{c}$ and every $\mathbf{u}$.

By Lemma 5.1.1, this is equivalent to (4).

Remark 5.6.2.

In Theorem 5.6.1, statement (2) *almost* implies statement (1). Precisely speaking, if f is strictly convex, the Hf is positive definite except on a "nowhere-dense set". You can see this in Example 5.4.4, where Hf is positive definite except at the single point $x = 0$.

For details, see Bernstein and Toupin, "Some properties of the Hessian matrix of a strictly convex function" in *Journal für die reine und angewandte Mathematik,* vol. 210 (1962), 65–72.

Exercises

5.7.1 Let $f(x)$ be a convex function defined for $x \geq 0$. Define $h(x)$ by

$$h(x) := \frac{1}{x} \int\limits_0^x f(t)\, dt.$$

(The number $h(x)$ is the average value of f on the interval $[0, x]$.) Show that $h(x)$ is concave.

5.7 MINIMIZING

The main reason economists like to assume that functions are convex or concave is because the assumption guarantees that critical points are minimums or maximums, respectively. Precisely speaking, we have:

Theorem 5.6.1. *Let* **c** *be a critical point of a function f. If f is convex, then* **c** *is a global minimum of f. If f is strictly convex, then* **c** *is the unique global minimum.*

PROOF. Let **d** be a point different from c. The vector $\mathbf{u} := \mathbf{d} - \mathbf{c}$ is nonzero and points in the direction from **c** to **d**. Define $g(t)$ as in (5.1.1) ; we have

$$g(0) = f(\mathbf{c}) \text{ and } g(1) = f(\mathbf{d})$$

and $g'(0) = 0$ because c is a critical point. If f is convex, then $g(t)$ is convex, and we have:

$$0 = g'(0) \leq g(1) - g(0) = f(\mathbf{d}) - f(\mathbf{c}),$$

where the inequality is by Proposition 5.5.2. It follows that $f(\mathbf{d}) \geq f(\mathbf{c})$. Since this result holds for every point **d**, the critical point **c** is a global minimum.

If f is strictly convex, then by Proposition 5.5.1, Equation (5.7.1) becomes

$$0 = g'(0) < g(1) - g(0) = f(\mathbf{d}) - f(\mathbf{c}). \tag{5.7.1}$$

Thus, $f(\mathbf{d}) > f(\mathbf{c})$ and $f(\mathbf{c})$ is the unique global minimum.

As noted in this chapter, all results regarding convex and strictly convex functions are easily translated to concave and strictly concave functions. Translating Theorem 5.7.1, we find:

Theorem 5.7.2 *Let* **c** *be a critical point of a function f. If f is concave, then* **c** *is a global maximum of f. If f is strictly concave, then* **c** *is the unique global maximum.*

This is the Global SOC Theorem 4.4.7.

Chapter 6
Constrained optimization

6.1 THE PROBLEM

Example 6.1.1

Suppose that an individual receives utility $U(x_1, x_2)$ from consuming x_1 units of good 1 and x_2 units of good 2. Presumably, the individual prefers to have more of each good, i.e., the first partial derivatives U_1 and U_2 are both positive. Of course, the individual cannot consume arbitrary amounts of each good; he must pay for them. This introduces a constraint: he has an income I to spend on the two goods, which cost p_1 and p_2 per unit, respectively. The individual's problem is to choose values of x_1 and x_2 that maximize $U(x_1, x_2)$ while still satisfying the constraint $I = p_1 x_1 + p_2 x_2$. For short, we write:

$$\max_{x_1, x_2} U(x_1, x_2) \quad \text{such that} \quad I = p_1 x_1 + p_2 x_2.$$

This is the *utility maximization* problem, and is an example of a *constrained optimization problem*, the subject of this chapter.

We can analyze the utility maximization problem just as we did the various optimization problems in Chapters 2 and 4, and we prove a version of the envelope theorem and analyze the comparative statics. To get started, in the next section we consider a concrete example.

6.2 THE LADYBUG AND CONSTRAINED OPTIMIZATION

Recall the problem of finding the maximum of $f(x_1, x_2) = 50 - x_1^2 - x_2^2$ from Chapter 4. If a ladybug is standing somewhere on the graph of f and wants to find the maximum of f, he examines the gradient of f:

$$\text{grad} f = \left(\frac{\partial f}{\partial x_1}, \frac{\partial f}{\partial x_2} \right) = (-2x_1, -2x_2)$$

and moves in the direction it points. Figure 6.2.1 shows various level curves of f together with the gradient at various points. The maximum of f occurs at $(0, 0)$.

That was the Chapter 4 situation. Here, we add a new wrinkle: the ladybug is not allowed to walk in any direction he chooses but rather is forced to stay on a path, the graph of the constraint. Let us say that the constraint is $x_1 - x_2 = 5$. Figure 6.2.2 shows a graph of f and the constraint in the (x_1, x_2)-plane (f is represented by level curves) and in 3-space. From the figures, you should be able to see that the maximum of f along the constraint occurs somewhere around $(2.5, -2.5)$. (If you don't see this, then examine the figure until you do!)

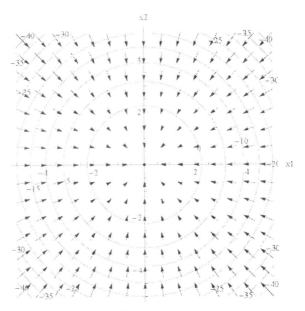

Figure 6.2.1 Level curves of $f(x_1, x_2) = 50 - x_1^2 - x_2^2$ **together with arrows (the gradient) pointing towards the the location of maximum value of** f.

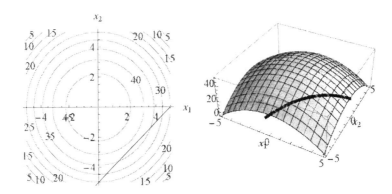

Figure 6.2.2 Graph of $f(x_1, x_2) = 50 - x_1^2 - x_2^2$ **and the constraint** $x_1 - x_2 = 5$ **in the** (x_1, x_2)**-plane and in 3-space**

Well, you can see where the maximum of f is along the constraint because you can see the entire picture. But the ladybug cannot. At any point on the path, he can only choose to move in two different directions. For example, if he is at $(4, -1)$, he can move northeast or southwest along the constraint. Remember that the ladybug wants to find the highest point, so he consults the gradient and finds:

$$\operatorname{grad} f(4, -1) = (-8, 2)$$

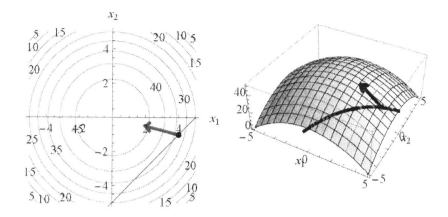

Figure 6.2.3 A ladybug (the blob) stands at $(4, -1)$ and consults the gradient

The gradient is drawn in Figure 6.2.3. To the ladybug, crawling along the path towards the southwest is uphill, and walking to the northeast is downhill. So he chooses to walk southwest.

The ladybug can follow this scheme until he arrives at a point where the gradient does not point in either direction along the path, i.e., where the gradient is perpendicular to the constraint $x_1 - x_2 = 5$. You can see in Figure 6.2.3 that that point is indeed somewhere around $(2.5, -2.5)$, as we guessed from Figure 6.2.2.

How can he find that point algebraically? The ladybug notices that the constraint $x_1 - x_2 = 5$ is a level curve of the function $g(x_1, x_2) = x_1 - x_2$, and he recalls that the gradient of g is always perpendicular to a level curve of g. That is, the ladybug wants to find a point $\mathbf{x}$ where grad f and grad g are parallel. From multivariable calculus, we remember that this condition means there is a number λ such that

$$\text{grad } f(\mathbf{x}) = \lambda \text{ grad } g(\mathbf{x}).$$

For this problem, the gradient of g is $(1, -1)$, so the equation reads:

$$(-2x_1, -2x_2) = \lambda(1, -1)$$

We can also write this as two equations, with no vectors:

$$-2x_1 = \lambda \text{ and } -2x_2 = -\lambda.$$

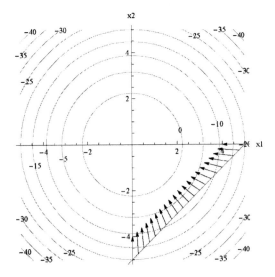

Figure 6.2.4 The gradients of $f(x_1, x_2) = 50 - x_1^2 - x_2^2$ **along the constraint** $x_1 - x_2 = 5$**. Note that the gradient appears to be perpendicular to the constraint only at the point** $(2.5, -2.5)$**.**

Furthermore, this point should lie on the constraint $x_1 - x_2 = 5$. Substituting $x_2 = x_1 - 5$ into (6.2.1), we find:

$$-2x_1 = \lambda \text{ and } 2x_1 - 10 = \lambda.$$

Therefore, $-2x_1 = 2x_1 - 10$ and we deduce that $x_1 = 2.5$. Plugging back into the constraint $x_2 = x_1 - 5$, we find that $x_2 = -2.5$. We have just shown algebraically that the ladybug's method will take him to the point $(2.5, -2.5)$.

6.3 LAGRANGE MULTIPLIERS AND FIRST-ORDER CONDITIONS

We now present a more sophisticated approach to the algebraic manipulations from the end of the last section. Suppose that we want to maximize the function $f(x_1, x_2)$ subject to a constraint $g(x_1, x_2) = 0$, which we write as:

$$\max_{x_1, x_2} f(x_1, x_2) \text{ such that } g(x_1, x_2) = 0. \tag{6.3.1}$$

The method of *Lagrange multipliers** or the Lagrangian method is as follows. Introduce a new variable λ (the Lagrange multiplier) and define

---

* Lagrange multipliers are named after Joseph-Louis Lagrange (1736–1813); he introduced them in his 1804 book *Leçons sur le calcul des fonctions*. He has several other claims to fame, including his 1770 proof that every positive integer is a sum of four squares (e.g., $15 = 1^2 + 1^2 + 2^2 + 3^2$). He is also well known for analyzing the relative motions of the sun, earth, and moon—the "three-body problem"—which led to his discovery of the Lagrangian points. These Langragian points are widely viewed as the "best" place to locate a space telescope such as the Wilkinson Microwave Anisotropy Probe (WMAP) and the Solar and Heliospheric Observatory (SOHO). Lagrange is one of the 72 scientists named on the Eiffel Tower.

$$L(x_1, x_2, \lambda) := f(x_1, x_2) + \lambda g(x_1, x_2). \tag{6.3.2}$$

(The function L is called *the Lagrangian*.) Then look for solutions to the first-order conditions:[*]

$$0 = L_1 = f_1 + \lambda g_1, \ 0 = L_2 = f_2 + \lambda g_2, \text{ and } 0 = L_\lambda = g. \tag{6.3.3}$$

Example 6.3.1

Suppose that $f(x_1, x_2) = 50 - x_1^2 - \beta x_2^2$ and $g(x_1, x_2) = x_1 - x_2 - 5$, where β is some positive number. (Here g is the same as in the previous section, but f is slightly different in that we have introduced a parameter β.) The Lagrangian is:

$$L(x_1, x_2, \lambda) = 50 - x_1^2 - \beta x_2^2 + \lambda(x_1 - x_2 - 5).$$

The first-order conditions are:

$$\begin{aligned}
0 &= L_1 = f_1 + \lambda g_1 = -2x_1^* + \lambda^*, \\
0 &= L_2 = f_2 + \lambda g_2 = -2\beta x_2^* - \lambda^*, \text{ and} \\
0 &= L_\lambda = g = x_1^* - x_2^* - 5.
\end{aligned} \tag{6.3.4}$$

Note that the third equation says that (x_1^*, x_2^*) has to lie on the constraint, and the first two equations say that the gradients of f and g must be parallel. Introducing λ and L is just a fancy way to do the same method of solution from the previous section.

We now solve the first-order conditions. The first equation $0 = L_1$ gives: $\lambda^* = 2x_1^*$. The second equation $0 = L_2$ gives $\lambda^* = -2\beta x_2^*$, so $x_1^* = -\beta x_2^*$. Plugging into the third equation $0 = L_\lambda$, (the constraint), we find that

$$0 = -\beta x_2^* - x_2^* - 5 = -x_2^*(\beta + 1) - 5;$$

i.e.,

$$x_2^* = \frac{-5}{\beta + 1}. \tag{6.3.5}$$

(Note that we can divide by $\beta + 1$ because it is not zero, because β is positive!) So

$$x_1^* = \frac{5\beta}{\beta + 1}. \tag{6.3.6}$$

Let us compare this answer with our result from the previous section. There, β was 1. Plugging $\beta = 1$ into our formulas (6.3.5) and (6.3.6), we find $x_1^* = 2.5$ and $x_2^* = -2.5$. This result agrees with what we found before.

Example 6.3.2

An individual wants to maximize utility subject to an income constraint:

$$\underset{x_1, x_2}{\text{Max}}\, U = U(x_1, x_2) \ \text{s.t.} \ I = p_1 x_1 + p_2 x_2.$$

---

[*] These are the same as the first-order conditions as if we were trying to maximize $L(x_1, x_2, \lambda)$ in the style of Chapter 4. But the second-order conditions here are different, see section 6.4 below.

The utility function is the objective function and income is the constraint. The prices of the goods and income are the parameters of the model. The solution of this model will yield demand equations that are a function of prices and income. These demand curves are called *Marshallian demand functions* and are denoted by:

$$x_i^* = x_i^*(p_1, p_2, I). \tag{6.3.8}$$

The Lagrangian for the utility maximization problem is:

$$L(x_1, x_2, \lambda, I, p_1, p_2) = U(x_1, x_2) + \lambda(I - p_1 x_1 - p_2 x_2). \tag{6.3.9}$$

The first-order conditions for this problem are:

$$L_1(x_1^*, x_2^*, \lambda^*, I, p_1, p_2) = U_1(x_1^*, x_2^*) - \lambda^* p_1 = 0,$$
$$L_2(x_1^*, x_2^*, \lambda^*, I, p_1, p_2) = U_2(x_1^*, x_2^*) - \lambda^* p_2 = 0, \text{ and}$$
$$L_\lambda(x_1^*, x_2^*, \lambda^*, I, p_1, p_2) = I - p_1 x_1^* - p_2 x_2^* = 0.$$

Write x_1^*, x_2^*, λ^* for a solution to these equations. The first two equations imply that:

$$\lambda^* = \frac{U_1(x_1^*, x_2^*)}{p_1} = \frac{U_2(x_1^*, x_2^*)}{p_2}.$$

Writing this result in a slightly different way will suggest a way to represent these results graphically:

$$\frac{U_1(x_1^*, x_2^*)}{U_2(x_1^*, x_2^*)} = \frac{p_1}{p_2}. \tag{6.3.9}$$

The slope of a level curve for the utility function can be found by:

$$\bar{U} = U(x_1, x_2)$$
$$0 = U_1(x_1, x_2) + U_2(x_1, x_2) \frac{dx_2(x_1)}{dx_1}$$
$$\frac{dx_2(x_1)}{dx_1} = -\frac{U_1(x_1, x_2)}{U_2(x_1, x_2)}. \tag{6.3.10}$$

Thus, the left-hand side of (6.3.9) is the negative of the slope of the level curve. Moreover, the slope of the budget constraint is given from:

$$x_2 = \frac{I}{p_2} - \frac{p_1}{p_2} x_1$$

as $-p_1\big/p_2$. The first-order conditions imply that the solution occurs at a point on the budget constraint (from (6.3.10)) where the slope of the budget constraint equals the slope of the level curve. Figure 6.3.3 illustrates this result.

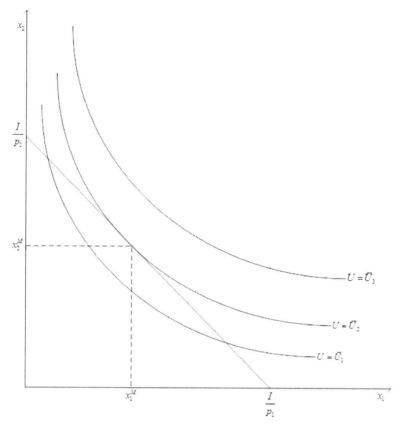

Figure 6.3.3 Illustration of the solution to the utility maximization problem.

This is a general phenomenon. Suppose we want to solve

$$\underset{x_1,x_2}{Max}\; f\left(x_1,x_2\right)\;\; \text{such that}\; g\left(x_1,x_2\right)=0. \tag{6.3.12}$$

Theorem 6.3.4

Let c be a point on the constraint (i.e., $g\left(\mathbf{c}\right)=0$*) with* $\mathrm{grad}\, f\left(\mathbf{c}\right)$ *and* $\mathrm{grad}\, g\left(\mathbf{c}\right)$ *not zero. The following are equivalent:*

(1) There is a λ^* *such that* $\left(\mathbf{c},\lambda^*\right)$ *is a solution to the first-order conditions (6.3.3).*
(2) $\mathrm{grad}\, f\left(\mathbf{c}\right)$ *and* $\mathrm{grad}\, g\left(\mathbf{c}\right)$ *are parallel.*
(3) The level curve $f\left(\mathbf{x}\right)=f\left(\mathbf{c}\right)$ *is tangent to the level curve* $g\left(\mathbf{x}\right)=0$ *at c.*

PROOF. $\left(\mathbf{c},\lambda^*\right)$ is a solution to the first-order conditions if, and only if, the equation

$$\operatorname{grad} f(\mathbf{c}) = -\lambda^* \operatorname{grad} g(\mathbf{c})$$

holds. Thus, (1) is equivalent to (2). Statements (2) and (3) are equivalent because $\operatorname{grad} f(\mathbf{c})$ and $\operatorname{grad} g(\mathbf{c})$ are perpendicular to the curves $f(\mathbf{x}) = f(\mathbf{c})$ and $g(\mathbf{x}) = 0$, respectively, at $\mathbf{c}$.

The theorem suggests that looking at level curves is a useful way to visualize the solution to constrained optimization problems. The solution will occur at a point where the constraint is tangent to a level curve of the objective function.

When trying to illustrate a constrained optimization problem graphically, **begin** by drawing a graph of the constraint. **Then** add in the level curves for the objective function. The solution is where the level curve is tangent to the constraint.

Example 6.3.5

Let us return to Example 6.3.1, except now we assume that $\beta = -1$. In this case, the Lagrange multiplier method does not work. We attempt to solve the problem:

$$\max_{x_1, x_2} 50 - x_1^2 + x_2^2 \text{ such that } x_1 - x_2 - 5 = 0.$$

If we mindlessly follow the Lagrange multiplier method, we find:

$$L(x_1, x_2, \lambda) = 50 - x_1^2 + x_2^2 + \lambda(x_1 - x_2 - 5),$$

so the first-order conditions are:

$$L_1 = -2x_1^* + \lambda^* = 0, \ L_2 = 2x_2^* - \lambda^* = 0, \text{ and } L_\lambda = x_1^* - x_2^* - 5 = 0.$$

Solving the first two equations for λ, we find:

$$\lambda^* = 2x_1^* = 2x_2^*,$$

so

$$x_1^* = x_2^*.$$

Plugging this result into the third equation (the constraint), we find:

$$0 = x_1^* - x_1^* - 5 = -5.$$

This result is impossible, so in fact there is no point (x_1^*, x_2^*) that satisfies the first-order conditions. Clearly, the method of Lagrange multipliers fails. (We say that we have shown that the method fails *algebraically*, i.e., with equations.)

Alternatively, we could have seen that the Lagrange multiplier method fails *graphically*. Figure 6.3.6 shows a graph of level curves of $f(x_1, x_2) = 5 - x_1^2 + x_2^2$, the constraint $x_1 - x_2 = 5$, and some gradients of f along the constraint. From the picture, we see that the gradient of f is never perpendicular to the constraint, so the Lagrange multiplier method will not find a maximum of f along the constraint.

When graphing by hand, it is easier to check that the level curves of f are never tangent to the constraint. You can see this in Figure 6.3.7, where we have zoomed in on the portion of the graph with the constraint.

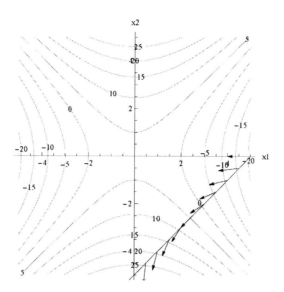

Figure 6.3.6 The Lagrange multiplier method fails for maximizing $f(x_1, x_2) = 50 - x_1^2 + x_2^2$ along $x_1 - x_2 = 5$ because the gradients of f are never perpendicular to the constraint.

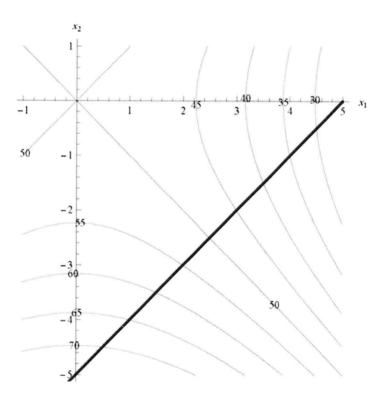

Figure 6.3.7 Close-up of Figure 6.3.6.

Exercises

6.3.1 The graph in Figure 6.3.8 shows level curves of a continuous function $f(x_1, x_2)$ and a constraint $g(x_1, x_2) = 0$.

Indicate on the graph where:
(a) f has a minimum. Explain.
(b) f has a minimum on the constraint. Explain.
(c) f and g have parallel gradients. Explain.

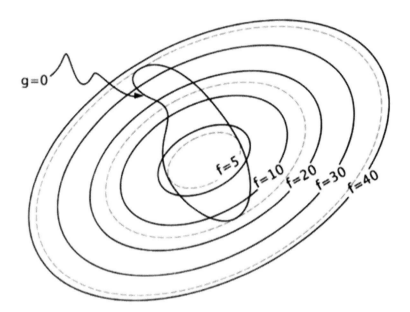

Figure 6.3.8 Graph associated with exercise 6.3.1.

6.3.2 Illustrate **graphically** why the Lagrangian method cannot solve the following two problems:

(a) $\underset{x_1, x_2}{Max\, z} = x_1^2 + x_2^2$ s.t. $2x_1 + x_2 = 20$.

(b) $\underset{x_1, x_2}{Min\, z} = x_1^2 + x_2^2$ s.t. $(x_1 - 1)^3 - x_2^2 = 0$. What is the actual minimum and why doesn't the Lagrangian method find it?

6.4 SECOND-ORDER CONDITIONS

To review where we are so far: We want to solve the problem

$$\max_{x_1, x_2} f(x_1, x_2) \text{ such that } g(x_1, x_2) = 0.$$

We set

$$L(x_1, x_2, \lambda) := f(x_1, x_2) + \lambda g(x_1, x_2).$$

We call a pair $\left(\mathbf{x}^*, \lambda^*\right)$ a *critical point* if

(1) $\operatorname{grad} f\left(\mathbf{x}^*\right) + \lambda^* \operatorname{grad} g\left(\mathbf{x}^*\right) = 0,$

(2) $g\left(\mathbf{x}^*\right) = 0,$ and

(3) $\operatorname{grad} g\left(\mathbf{x}^*\right) \neq 0.$

Conditions (1) and (2) say that $\left(\mathbf{x}^*, \lambda^*\right)$ is a solution to the first-order conditions (6.3.3). We demand condition (3) for technical reasons. In the economic problems we consider, $\operatorname{grad} g$ is never zero, and hypothesis (3) is always satisfied.

Suppose that we have found a critical point $\left(\mathbf{x}^*, \lambda^*\right)$. The following theorem says how can we tell if it is a maximum.[*]

Theorem 6.4.1 *(Local SOC Theorem).*

If $|HL| > 0$ at $\left(\mathbf{x}^*, \lambda^*\right)$, then $\mathbf{x}^*$ is a local maximum for f along the constraint $g = 0$. If $|HL| < 0$ at $\left(\mathbf{x}^*, \lambda^*\right)$, then $\mathbf{x}^*$ is a local minimum.

As L is a function of three variables x_1, x_2, and λ, the expression $|HL|$ is given by

$$\begin{vmatrix} f_{11} + \lambda g_{11} & f_{12} + \lambda g_{12} & g_1 \\ f_{12} + \lambda g_{12} & f_{22} + \lambda g_{22} & g_2 \\ g_1 & g_2 & 0 \end{vmatrix}$$

and is often referred to in the textbooks as the *bordered Hessian.*[†] We say that *the second-order conditions (for x^* to be a local maximum) hold* if $\left|HL\left(x^*, \lambda^*\right)\right| > 0$, and similarly for a local minimum. We prove Theorem 6.4.1 below.

Example 6.4.2

Return to the problem from Example 6.3.1, i.e., we maximize $f\left(x_1, x_2\right) = 50 - x_1^2 - \beta x_2^{2t}$ subject to the constraint $g(x_1, x_2) = x_1 - x_2 - 5 = 0$, where β is some positive number. In this case,

$$|HL| = \begin{vmatrix} -2 & 0 & 1 \\ 0 & -2\beta & -1 \\ 1 & -1 & 0 \end{vmatrix} = -2 \begin{vmatrix} -2\beta & -1 \\ -1 & 0 \end{vmatrix} + \begin{vmatrix} 0 & -2\beta \\ 1 & -1 \end{vmatrix} = 2 + 2\beta.$$

Since β is positive, $|HL|$ is positive. (Interestingly, neither x_1 nor x_2 appear in the determinant of HL, so this answer does not depend on the particular critical point we computed.) We conclude that the point

$$\left(x_1^*, x_2^*, \lambda^*\right) = \left(\frac{5\beta}{\beta+1}, \frac{-5\beta}{\beta+1}, \frac{10\beta}{\beta+1}\right)$$

is a local maximum.

---

[*] The theorem as stated only works when f is a function of two variables, which is the case we will use. Exercise 6.6.7 discusses how to generalize the theorem to the case of more variables.

[†] Now is a good time to read Section 3.3 if you haven't already.

This result is true for every positive β. We can check our work in the case $\beta = 1$ by looking back at Figure 6.2.2 and noticing that the critical point $(2.5, -2.5)$ is indeed a local maximum for f along the constraint.

Example 6.4.3

For the utility maximization problem, HL is:

$$HL = \begin{bmatrix} U_{11} & U_{12} & -p_1 \\ U_{21} & U_{22} & -p_2 \\ -p_1 & -p_2 & 0 \end{bmatrix}. \tag{6.4.1}$$

To check the second-order condition, we compute:

$$|HL| = \begin{vmatrix} U_{11} & U_{12} & -p_1 \\ U_{21} & U_{22} & -p_2 \\ -p_1 & -p_2 & 0 \end{vmatrix}. \tag{6.4.2}$$

Expanding $|HL|$ by the third row yields:

$$|HL| = -p_1 \begin{vmatrix} U_{12} & -p_1 \\ U_{22} & -p_2 \end{vmatrix} + p_2 \begin{vmatrix} U_{11} & -p_1 \\ U_{21} & -p_2 \end{vmatrix}$$

$$= -p_1(-p_2 U_{12} + p_1 U_{22}) + p_2(-p_2 U_{11} + p_1 U_{21})$$

$$= p_1 p_2 U_{12} - p_1^2 U_{22} - p_2^2 U_{11} + p_1 p_2 U_{21}.$$

Thus the second-order condition for this problem is:

$$|HL(\mathbf{x}^*, \lambda^*)| = -p_1^2 U_{22}(\mathbf{x}^*) + 2p_1 p_2 U_{21}(\mathbf{x}^*) - p_2^2 U_{11}(\mathbf{x}^*) > 0. \tag{6.4.3}$$

We can write (6.4.3) in a way that tells us something about the shape of the level curve. From the first-order conditions we know that:

$$p_i = \frac{U_i(\mathbf{x}^*)}{\lambda^*}.$$

Substituting this result into (6.4.3) gives us as the second-order condition:

$$|HL(\mathbf{x}^*, \lambda^*)| = -\left(\frac{U_1(\mathbf{x}^*)}{\lambda^*}\right)^2 U_{22}(\mathbf{x}^*) + 2\left(\frac{U_1(\mathbf{x}^*)}{\lambda^*}\right)\left(\frac{U_2(\mathbf{x}^*)}{\lambda^*}\right) U_{21}(\mathbf{x}^*) - \left(\frac{U_2(\mathbf{x}^*)}{\lambda^*}\right)^2 U_{11}(\mathbf{x}^*) > 0$$

$$|HL(\mathbf{x}^*, \lambda^*)| = -\frac{(U_1(\mathbf{x}^*))^2 U_{22}(\mathbf{x}^*)}{(\lambda^*)^2} + \frac{2U_1(\mathbf{x}^*)U_2(\mathbf{x}^*)U_{21}(\mathbf{x}^*)}{(\lambda^*)^2} - \frac{(U_2(\mathbf{x}^*))^2 U_{11}(\mathbf{x}^*)}{(\lambda^*)^2} > 0$$

$$-(U_1(\mathbf{x}^*))^2 U_{22}(\mathbf{x}^*) + 2U_1(\mathbf{x}^*)U_2(\mathbf{x}^*)U_{21}(\mathbf{x}^*) - (U_2(\mathbf{x}^*))^2 U_{11}(\mathbf{x}^*) > 0. \tag{6.4.4}$$

That is, if we assume that

$$-\left(U_1(\mathbf{x})\right)^2 U_{22}(\mathbf{x}) + 2U_1(\mathbf{x})U_2(\mathbf{x})U_{21}(\mathbf{x}) - \left(U_2(\mathbf{x})\right)^2 U_{11}(\mathbf{x}) > 0$$

for all $\mathbf{x}$, i.e., that the level curves of U are concave up, then the second-order condition for the utility maximization problem automatically holds.

We now start working on the proof of Theorem 6.4.1 (the Local SOC Theorem). We need the following lemma:

Lemma 6.4.4 (Bordered Lemma). *Suppose that* $\mathbf{A}$ *is a symmetric 2-by-2 matrix and* $\mathbf{B}$ *is a 1-by-2 matrix (a row vector). The following are equivalent:*

(1) *The determinant of the 3-by-3 matrix* $\begin{pmatrix} \mathbf{A} & \mathbf{B}^T \\ \mathbf{B} & 0 \end{pmatrix}$ *is positive.*

(2) $\mathbf{B} \neq 0$ *and* $\mathbf{u}\mathbf{A}\mathbf{u}^T < 0$ *for every nonzero vector* $\mathbf{u}$ *orthogonal to* $\mathbf{B}$.

The lemma is also true if we replace "positive" and "<" with "negative" and ">". Both versions can be extended to the case where $\mathbf{A}$ is n-by-n and $\mathbf{B}$ is m-by-n, see Theorems 4 and 5 in G. Debreu, *Definite and semidefinite quadratic forms*, Econometrica, vol. 20 (1952), pp. 295–300. The basic result goes back to Hotelling.[*]

PROOF OF LEMMA 6.4.4 (BORDERED LEMMA). Write

$$\mathbf{A} = \begin{pmatrix} a_{11} & a_{12} \\ a_{12} & a_{22} \end{pmatrix} \quad \text{and} \quad \mathbf{B} = \begin{pmatrix} b_1 & b_2 \end{pmatrix}.$$

The determinant of the 3-by-3 matrix in (1) above is

$$\begin{vmatrix} \mathbf{A} & \mathbf{B}^T \\ \mathbf{B} & 0 \end{vmatrix} = \begin{vmatrix} a_{11} & a_{12} & b_1 \\ a_{12} & a_{22} & b_2 \\ b_1 & b_2 & 0 \end{vmatrix} \tag{6.4.5}$$

$$= -a_{22}b_1^2 + 2a_{12}b_1b_2 - a_{11}b_2^2.$$

Suppose that (1) holds, i.e., the determinant (6.4.5) is positive. Then, $\mathbf{B}$ is not zero, and every vector $\mathbf{u}$ orthogonal to $\mathbf{B}$ equals $\begin{pmatrix} rb_2 & -rb_1 \end{pmatrix}$ for some nonzero number r. We calculate:

$$\begin{aligned}
\mathbf{u}\mathbf{A}\mathbf{u}^T &= \begin{pmatrix} rb_2 & -rb_1 \end{pmatrix}\begin{pmatrix} a_{11} & a_{12} \\ a_{12} & a_{22} \end{pmatrix}\begin{pmatrix} rb_2 \\ -rb_1 \end{pmatrix} \\
&= \begin{pmatrix} a_{11}rb_2 - a_{12}rb_1 & a_{12}rb_2 - a_{22}rb_1 \end{pmatrix}\begin{pmatrix} rb_2 \\ -rb_1 \end{pmatrix} \\
&= r^2\left(a_{22}b_1^2 - 2a_{12}b_1b_2 + a_{11}b_2^2\right).
\end{aligned} \tag{6.4.6}$$

Since (6.4.5) is positive, (6.4.6) is negative, which proves (2). Now suppose that (2) holds. Taking $\mathbf{u} = \begin{pmatrix} b_2 & -b_1 \end{pmatrix}$ we find that (6.4.6) is negative (with $r=1$), so (6.4.5) is positive, proving (1).

PROOF OF THEOREM 6.4.1 (LOCAL SOC THEOREM). Suppose that $\left|HL\left(\mathbf{x}^*, \lambda^*\right)\right| > 0$. Our task is to prove that $\mathbf{x}^*$ is a local maximum for f along the constraint $g = 0$.

---

[*]   Harold Hotelling was a statistician and an economist. The street Hotelling Court in Chapel Hill, North Carolina, is named after him.

Since $(\mathbf{x}^*, \lambda^*)$ is a critical point, $\operatorname{grad} g(\mathbf{x}^*)$ is not zero and the Implicit Function Theorem gives a function $r(t) = (x_1(t), x_2(t))$ such that $\mathbf{r}(0) = \mathbf{x}^*$, $\mathbf{r}'(0) \neq 0$, and $g(\mathbf{r}(t)) = 0$ for all t near 0. Define the new functions, $\hat{f}(t)$ and $\hat{g}(t)$ as

$$\hat{f}(t) := f(\mathbf{r}(t)) \quad \text{and} \quad \hat{g}(t) := g(\mathbf{r}(t)).$$

We want to show that $\hat{f}'(0) = 0$ and $\hat{f}''(0) < 0$.

But first we study $\hat{g}(t)$. Since $g(\mathbf{r}(t))$ is zero for t near 0, the derivatives $\hat{g}'(0)$ and $\hat{g}''(0)$ are both zero. Using Exercise 5.1.1, we find that

$$0 = \hat{g}'(0) = \operatorname{grad} g(\mathbf{x}^*) \cdot \mathbf{r}'(0)$$

and

$$0 = \hat{g}''(0) = \mathbf{r}'(0) \cdot Hg(\mathbf{x}^*) \cdot \mathbf{r}'(0)^T + \operatorname{grad} g(\mathbf{x}^*) \cdot \mathbf{r}''(0).$$

Let's return to $\hat{f}(t)$. We have:

$$\hat{f}'(0) = \operatorname{grad} f(\mathbf{x}^*) \cdot \mathbf{r}'(0) = -\lambda^* \operatorname{grad} g(\mathbf{x}^*) \cdot \mathbf{r}'(0) = -\lambda^* \hat{g}'(0) = 0.$$

To evaluate $\hat{f}''(0)$, we make a clever move and add 0, or, more precisely, we add $\lambda^* \hat{g}'(0)$. We find:

$$\hat{f}''(0) = \hat{f}''(0) + \lambda^* \hat{g}''(0)$$
$$= \mathbf{r}'(0) \cdot Hf(\mathbf{x}^*) \cdot \mathbf{r}'(0)^T + \operatorname{grad} f(\mathbf{x}^*) \cdot \mathbf{r}''(0)$$
$$+ \mathbf{r}'(0) \cdot \lambda^* Hg(\mathbf{x}^*) \cdot \mathbf{r}'(0)^T + \lambda^* \operatorname{grad} g(\mathbf{x}^*) \cdot \mathbf{r}''(0).$$

Because $(\mathbf{x}^*, \lambda^*)$ is a critical point, the terms involving $\operatorname{grad} f$ and $\operatorname{grad} g$ cancel, leaving us with:

$$\hat{f}''(0) = \mathbf{r}'(0) \cdot \left[Hf(\mathbf{x}^*) + \lambda^* Hg(\mathbf{x}^*) \right] \cdot \mathbf{r}'(0)^T.$$

We apply **Lemma** 6.4.4 (the Bordered Lemma) with $\mathbf{A} = Hf(\mathbf{x}^*) + \lambda^* Hg(\mathbf{x}^*)$, $\mathbf{B} = \operatorname{grad} g(\mathbf{x}^*)$, and $\mathbf{u} = \mathbf{r}'(0)$. As $\left| HL(\mathbf{x}^*, \lambda^*) \right| > 0$, $\hat{f}''(0)$ is negative. This completes the proof. □

One can write down second-order conditions when there are more than two variables; see Exercise 6.6.7.

Exercises

6.4.1 Find all the critical points and identify if they are local maxima or minima:

(a) $f(x_1, x_2) = x_1 x_2$ s.t. $x_1 + \alpha x_2 = \beta$, where $\alpha \neq 0$.

(b) $f(x_1, x_2) = x_1^2 + x_2^2$ s.t. $\dfrac{x_1^2}{16} + \dfrac{x_2^2}{9} = 1$. Draw a graph like Figure 6.3.3 and indicate the critical points you found.

(c) $f(x_1, x_2) = \beta - (x_1 - 2)^2 - x_2^2$ s.t. $x_1^2 - 2x_2^2 = 1$.

The search for testable implications of constrained optimization problems follows the steps we developed earlier for models involving unconstrained optimization. These steps are:

(1) Solve for the first-order conditions.

(2) Check the second-order conditions.

(3) Assume that a solution for the first-order conditions exists and is given by $x_i^*(\alpha)$ tand $\lambda^*(\alpha)$, where α is a vector of all of the parameters of model.

(4) Calculate the impact of changes in each of the parameters on each of the control variables in the model.

(5) Use the Envelope Theorem to find testable implications involving the indirect objective function. In our most general model the indirect objective function is given by

$$f^*(\alpha) := f\left(x_1^*(\alpha), x_2^*(\alpha), \alpha\right), \tag{6.5.1}$$

We have already developed steps (1), (2), and (3); we begin the discussion of steps (4) and (5) by considering the Envelope Theorem in step (5). The development of the Envelope Theorem begins with substituting the solution to the first-order conditions into the Lagrangian:

$$L^*(\alpha) = f\left(x_1^*(\alpha), x_2^*(\alpha), \alpha\right) + \lambda^*(\alpha) g\left(x_1^*(\alpha), x_2^*(\alpha), \alpha\right), \tag{6.5.2}$$

Since at the solution to the first-order conditions, $g\left(x_1^*(\alpha), x_2^*(\alpha), \alpha\right) = 0$, we have $L^*(\alpha) = f^*(\alpha)$. Because this identity holds as α varies, we can take the derivative of both sides of the equation with respect to a parameter β to obtain:

$$\frac{\partial f^*(\alpha)}{\partial \beta} = \frac{\partial L^*(\alpha)}{\partial \beta} = \frac{\partial}{\partial \beta} L\left(x_1^*(\alpha), x_2^*(\alpha), \alpha\right)$$

$$= L_1\left(x_1^*(\alpha), x_2^*(\alpha), \alpha\right) \frac{\partial x_1^*}{\partial \beta} + L_2\left(x_1^*(\alpha), x_2^*(\alpha), \alpha\right) \frac{\partial x_2^*}{\partial \beta} + L_\beta\left(x_1^*(\alpha), x_2^*(\alpha), \alpha\right).$$

But $L_1\left(x_1^*(\alpha), x_2^*(\alpha), \alpha\right)$ is zero by the first-order conditions and similarly for L_2, so we are left with:

$$\boxed{\frac{\partial f^*(\alpha)}{\partial \beta} = L_\beta\left(x_1^*, x_2^*, \alpha\right).} \tag{6.5.3}$$

Equation (6.5.3) is the Envelope Theorem once again. It says that the derivative of the indirect objective function with respect to a parameter is equal to the derivative of the Lagrangian with respect to that parameter with the solution to the first-order conditions substituted in.

Example 6.5.1

In this example we will use the Envelope Theorem to develop an interpretation of the Lagrange multiplier in the utility maximization problem. The Lagrangian for this problem is:

$$L\left(x_1, x_2, p_1, p_2, I\right) = U\left(x_1, x_2\right) + \lambda\left(I - p_1 x_1 - p_2 x_2\right). \tag{6.5.4}$$

So

$$\frac{\partial L(x_1, x_2, p_1, p_2, I)}{\partial I} = \lambda.$$

By the Envelope Theorem we have:

$$\frac{\partial U^*(p_1, p_2, I)}{\partial I} = \lambda^*(p_1, p_2, I). \tag{6.5.5}$$

Thus, the Lagrange multiplier can be interpreted as the *marginal utility of income.*

Example 6.5.2

We can use the Envelope Theorem to develop the relationship well-known in the economics literature as Roy's Identity.[*] From (6.5.4) we get:

$$\frac{\partial L(x_1, x_2, \lambda, p_1, p_2, I)}{\partial p_1} = -\lambda x_1$$

By the Envelope Theorem we have:

$$\frac{\partial U^*(p_1, p_2, I)}{\partial p_1} = -\lambda^*(p_1, p_2, I) x_1^*(p_1, p_2, I). \tag{6.5.6}$$

Combining (6.5.5) and (6.5.6) gives us Roy's Identity:7

$$x_1^*(p_1, p_2, I) = -\frac{\partial U^*(p_1, p_2, I)\big/ \partial p_1}{\partial U^*(p_1, p_2, I)\big/ \partial I}. \tag{6.5.7}$$

We now turn to (4) in our list of steps in finding testable implications of a constrained optimization model, i.e., **we calculate the impact of changes in the parameters on the control variables.** We accomplish this by substituting the solution to the first-order conditions into the first-order conditions and then differentiating with respect to each of the parameters. Rather than do this for the general case we will demonstrate this step in an example.

Example 6.5.3

We return to considering the utility maximization problem from Example 6.4.3. We assume the level curves of U are concave up so that $|HL|$ is positive. Let's find the sign of the impact of a change in income on the quantity demanded of good 1. Substitution of the solutions of the first-order conditions into the first-order conditions yields:

$$U_1(x_1^*(I), x_2^*(I)) - \lambda^*(I) p_1 = 0,$$
$$U_2(x_1^*(I), x_2^*(I)) - \lambda^*(I) p_2 = 0, \text{ and} \tag{6.5.8}$$
$$I - p_1 x_1^*(I) - p_2 x_2^*(I) = 0.$$

---

[*]   This identity is named after French economist René Roy. The identity can be seen in his paper "La distribution du revenu entre les divers biens", *Econometrica* **15** (1943), 205–225 at the top of page 220.

Differentiation of (6.5.8) with respect to income yields:

$$U_{11}\frac{\partial x_1^*(I)}{\partial I}+U_{12}\frac{\partial x_2^*(I)}{\partial I}-p_1\frac{\partial \lambda^*(I)}{\partial I}=0,$$

$$U_{21}\frac{\partial x_1^*(I)}{\partial I}+U_{22}\frac{\partial x_2^*(I)}{\partial I}-p_2\frac{\partial \lambda^*(I)}{\partial I}=0, \text{ and} \qquad (6.5.9)$$

$$-p_1\frac{\partial x_1^*(I)}{\partial I}-p_2\frac{\partial x_2^*(I)}{\partial I}=-1.$$

In matrix form (6.5.9) is:

$$\begin{bmatrix} U_{11} & U_{12} & -p_1 \\ U_{21} & U_{22} & -p_2 \\ -p_1 & -p_2 & 0 \end{bmatrix}\begin{bmatrix} \dfrac{\partial x_1^*(I)}{\partial I} \\[4pt] \dfrac{\partial x_2^*(I)}{\partial I} \\[4pt] \dfrac{\partial \lambda^*(I)}{\partial I} \end{bmatrix}=\begin{bmatrix} 0 \\ 0 \\ -1 \end{bmatrix}$$

or

$$[HL]\begin{bmatrix} \dfrac{\partial x_1^*(I)}{\partial I} \\[4pt] \dfrac{\partial x_2^*(I)}{\partial I} \\[4pt] \dfrac{\partial \lambda^*(I)}{\partial I} \end{bmatrix}=\begin{bmatrix} 0 \\ 0 \\ -1 \end{bmatrix}. \qquad (6.5.10)$$

We can use Cramer's Rule to solve (6.5.10):

$$\frac{\partial x_1^*(I)}{\partial I}=\frac{\begin{vmatrix} 0 & U_{12} & -p_1 \\ 0 & U_{22} & -p_2 \\ -1 & -p_2 & 0 \end{vmatrix}}{|HL|}=\frac{p_2U_{12}-p_1U_{22}}{|HL|}. \qquad (6.5.11)$$

Even though we know that $|HL| > 0$, we cannot determine the sign of (6.5.11) because we do not know the sign of U_{12}.

Example 6.5.4

Now we will find the impact of a change in the price of a good on the demand for that good. We differentiate (6.5.8) with respect to p_1:

$$U_{11}\frac{\partial x_1^*(p_1,p_2,I)}{\partial p_1}+U_{12}\frac{\partial x_2^*(p_1,p_2,I)}{\partial p_1}-p_1\frac{\partial \lambda^*(p_1,p_2,I)}{\partial p_1}=\lambda^*(p_1,p_2,I),$$

$$U_{21}\frac{\partial x_1^*(p_1,p_2,I)}{\partial p_1}+U_{22}\frac{\partial x_2^*(p_1,p_2,I)}{\partial p_1}-p_2\frac{\partial \lambda^*(p_1,p_2,I)}{\partial p_1}=0, \text{ and}$$

$$-p_1\frac{\partial x_1^*(p_1,p_2,I)}{\partial p_1}-p_2\frac{\partial x_2^*(p_1,p_2,I)}{\partial p_1}=x_1^*(p_1,p_2,I).$$

In matrix form we have:

$$\begin{bmatrix} U_{11} & U_{12} & -p_1 \\ U_{21} & U_{22} & -p_2 \\ -p_1 & -p_2 & 0 \end{bmatrix} \begin{bmatrix} \dfrac{\partial x_1^*(p_1,p_2,I)}{\partial p_1} \\[2mm] \dfrac{\partial x_2^*(p_1,p_2,I)}{\partial p_1} \\[2mm] \dfrac{\partial \lambda^*(p_1,p_2,I)}{\partial p_1} \end{bmatrix} = \begin{bmatrix} \lambda^* \\ 0 \\ x_1^* \end{bmatrix}$$

or

$$[HL] \begin{bmatrix} \dfrac{\partial x_1^*(p_1,p_2,I)}{\partial p_1} \\[2mm] \dfrac{\partial x_2^*(p_1,p_2,I)}{\partial p_1} \\[2mm] \dfrac{\partial \lambda^*(p_1,p_2,I)}{\partial p_1} \end{bmatrix} = \begin{bmatrix} \lambda^* \\ 0 \\ x_1^* \end{bmatrix}.$$

Using Cramer's Rule we get:

$$\frac{\partial x_1^*(p_1,p_2,I)}{\partial p_1} = \frac{\begin{vmatrix} \lambda^* & U_{12} & -p_1 \\ 0 & U_{22} & -p_2 \\ x_1^* & -p_2 & 0 \end{vmatrix}}{|HL|}$$

or

$$\frac{\partial x_1^*(p_1,p_2,I)}{\partial p_1} = \frac{p_1 x_1^* U_{22} - p_2^2 \lambda^* - p_2 x_1^* U_{12}}{|HL|}. \tag{6.5.12}$$

Because U_1 and p_1 are positive, the first-order conditions imply that $\lambda^* > 0$. Thus, the first two terms of the numerator of (6.5.12) are negative. However, since we do not know the sign of U_{12} we do not know the sign of $\frac{\partial x_1^*(p_1,p_2,I)}{\partial p_1}$. We do know that if $\frac{\partial x_1^*(p_1,p_2,I)}{\partial p_1} > 0$, then $U_{12} < 0$. (To say the same thing differently, if $U_{12} > 0$, then $\frac{\partial x_1^*(p_1,p_2,I)}{\partial p_1} < 0$.)

Exercises

6.5.1 Here is a problem with a clear physical interpretation: find the point on a line that is closest to the origin. For computational reasons, we minimize the square of the distance from the origin to some straight line:

$$\underset{x_1,x_2}{Min}\ d^2 = x_1^2 + x_2^2 \ \text{ s.t. } \ x_2 = b - mx_1,$$

where we assume that $b, m > 0$.

(a) Find $x_1^*(b,m)$, $x_2^*(b,m)$, and $\lambda^*(b,m)$. What are the physical interpretations of these functions?

(b) Find $d^*(b,m)$. What is the physical interpretation of this function?

(c) Find and sign (i) $\dfrac{\partial x_1^*(b,m)}{\partial b}$, (ii) $\dfrac{\partial x_1^*(b,m)}{\partial m}$, (iii) $\dfrac{\partial x_2^*(b,m)}{\partial b}$, and (iv) $\dfrac{\partial x_2^*(b,m)}{\partial m}$.

(d) Find and sign (i) $\dfrac{\partial d^*(b,m)}{\partial b}$ and (ii) $\dfrac{\partial d^*(b,m)}{\partial m}$.

6.5.2 Let $h(y)$ be a (differentiable) function of one variable such that $h'(y) > 0$ for all y.

(a) Show that $h(y)$ is invertible, i.e., there is some function $a(y)$ such that $a(h(y)) = h(a(y)) = y$.

(b) Show that the domain of h is a connected set $Y \prod R$. [Hint: You must show that h is injective and subjective.] Be sure to specify the domain of h.

(c) Show that $(\mathbf{x}^*, \lambda^*)$ is a critical point of $\underset{\mathbf{x}}{Max}\ f(x_1, x_2)$ s.t. $g(x_1, x_2) = 0$ if and only if $\left(\mathbf{x}^*, h'\left(f\left(\mathbf{x}^*\right)\right)\lambda^*\right)$

is a critical point of $\underset{\mathbf{x}}{Max}\ h(f(x_1, x_2))$ s.t. $g(x_1, x_2) = 0$.

6.5.3 Consider the following problem: $\underset{x_1, x_2}{Max}\ z = 2x_1 + 2x_2$ s.t. $x_1^2 + \alpha x_2^2 = 1$, where α can be positive or negative, but not 0.

(a) Draw a graph illustrating the level curves and the constraint when $\alpha > 0$. Draw another graph for $\alpha < 0$.
(b) Find the first-order conditions and solve for all the critical points. For which values of α are there no solutions to the first-order conditions? Indicate the critical points on your graphs from part a).
(c) Determine if each critical point is a maximum or minimum by checking the second-order conditions. Label the critical points in your graph "max" or "min" as appropriate.

(d) Find and sign $\partial z^*(\alpha)\Big/\partial\alpha$ for those values of α where there is a solution to the first-order conditions.

Illustrate your answer graphically.

6.5.4 Suppose an individual consumes three goods—necessities (housing and food) (x_1), entertainment (fun things) (x_2), and automobiles (x_3). Suppose (1) the individual's utility function is given by $U = \ln x_1 + 4\ln x_2 + \ln(1 + x_3)$, (2) the prices of these goods are \$1, \$12, and \$30,000, respectively, and (3) the individual's income level over the life of a car is \$450,000. Finally, assume that automobiles must be purchased in discrete units. Solve this consumer's economic problem. [Hint: the derivative of a function with respect to a discrete variable does not exist.]

6.5.5 Return to the utility maximization problem: $\underset{x_1, x_2}{Max}\ U(x_1, x_2)$ s.t. $I = p_1 x_1 + p_2 x_2$ and suppose that

utility is additively separable, i.e., can be written as $U(x_1, x_2) = f(x_1) + h(x_2)$ for some positive and increasing functions f and h.

(a) What should the signs of U_{11} and U_{22} be? What does this tell you about f'' and h'?
(b) Show that every solution to the first-order conditions is a local maximum.
(c) Find $\dfrac{\partial x_1^*}{\partial I}$ in terms of f and h. Assuming the signs for f'' and h' suggested by (a), find the sign

of $\dfrac{\partial x_1^*}{\partial I}$. Illustrate this sign graphically. What is the economic interpretation of this sign?

6.5.6 Suppose that an individual's utility function is given by:

$$U(x_1, x_2) = f(x_1)h(x_2)$$

where $x_1, x_2 > 0$ and f and h are positive functions that are increasing at a decreasing rate. Let $x_1^*(p_1, p_2, I)$ and $x_2^*(p_1, p_2, I)$ be the demand equations that solve the utility maximization problem.

(a) Calculate $| HL(x_1^*, x_2^*, \lambda^*) |$ and verify that it is positive.

(b) Find a formula for each of the following derivatives in terms of f and h, and determine the sign of

the derivative: (i) $\dfrac{\partial x_1^*(p_1, p_2, I)}{\partial I}$, (ii) $\dfrac{\partial U^*(p_1, p_2, I)}{\partial I}$, and (iii) $\dfrac{\partial^2 U^*(p_1, p_2, I)}{\partial I^2}$.

For (i) and (ii), illustrate these signs graphically. What are the economic interpretations of these signs?

(c) Write the Cobb-Douglas utility function $U(x_1, x_2) = A x_1^\alpha x_2^\alpha$ (where $A > 0$ and $0 < \alpha, \beta < 1$ are constants) as $f(x_1)h(x_2)$ for some functions f and h that are positive and increasing at a decreasing rate; verify that f and h have these properties.

6.6 PROPERTIES Q− AND Q+

In Chapter 4, we often made the simplifying assumption that the Hessian of a function f was negative definite (say), which guaranteed that the second-order conditions for a maximum held everywhere. For constrained optimization, the second-order conditions are different, and the simplifying assumption is that f is $Q-$.

Definition 6.6.1

A function f is $Q-$ if for every point $\mathbf{c}$ and nonzero vector $\mathbf{u}$ such that $\mathbf{u} \cdot \text{grad} f(\mathbf{c}) = 0,^*$ we have $\mathbf{u}(Hf(\mathbf{c}))\mathbf{u}^T < 0$. The function f is $Q+$ if for every $\mathbf{c}$ and nonzero $\mathbf{u}$ such that $\mathbf{u} \cdot \text{grad} f(\mathbf{c}) = 0$, we have $\mathbf{u}(Hf(\mathbf{c}))\mathbf{u}^T > 0$.

Remark. These properties appear in the literature: $Q+$ is the usual second-order sufficient condition for f to be quasi-convex, as seen for example in section 3.4.3 of S. Boyd and L. Vandenberghe, *Convex optimization* (Cambridge University Press). Condition $Q-$ appears in Chapter IV of P.A. Samuelson's classic text *Foundations of Economic Analysis* (Harvard University Press). However, these properties do not seem to have standard names. The reader should be warned that the terms $Q-$ and $Q+$ are ad hoc and peculiar to this text.

Example 6.6.2

How do you interpret this definition for a function of one variable $f(x)$? In this case, the point $\mathbf{c}$ is a number c, the vector $\mathbf{u}$ is a number $\mathbf{u}$, the gradient $\text{grad} f(\mathbf{c})$ is the number $f'(c)$, and the Hessian $Hf(c)$ is the number $f''(c)$. The hypothesis "$\mathbf{u} \, \text{grad} f(c) = 0$" means that $f'(c) = 0$ (because $\mathbf{u}$ is not zero). Similarly, $\mathbf{u}(Hf(c))\mathbf{u}^T = u^2 f''(c)$. We conclude: *A function $f(x)$ of one variable is $Q-$ if and only if every critical point c*

---

* This condition says that $\mathbf{u}$ is tangent to the level curve of f passing through $\mathbf{c}$.

of $f(x)$ has $f''(c) < 0$. This is the condition we used in the alternative proof of the Global SOC Theorem 1.2.1.

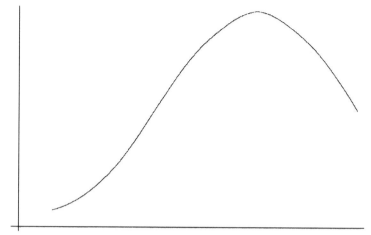

Figure 6.6.3 The second derivative of this function is negative at the maximum, so it is $Q-$. But it is neither $Q+$ nor concave.

Reversing the signs, we see that a function $f(x)$ of one variable is $Q+$ if and only if every critical point c of $f(x)$ has $f''(c) > 0$. More concretely:

1. A line is the graph of a function $f(x) = mx + b$. If the slope m is not zero, then $f(x)$ has no critical points, so $f(x)$ is[*] both $Q-$ and $Q+$. If $m = 0$ (i.e., if the graph of $f(x)$ is a horizontal line), then every number c is a critical point of $f(x)$ but $f''(x)$ is always zero, hence $f(x)$ is neither $Q-$ nor $Q+$.
2. The function $f(x) = x^4$ is neither $Q-$ nor $Q+$, because at its one critical point 0, we have $f''(0) = 0$
3. Figure 6.6.3 is a graph of a function that is $Q-$ but is not $Q+$, nor concave, nor convex.

Example 6.6.4

If the Hessian of $f(x_1, x_2, \ldots, x_n)$ is negative definite, then (by definition!) $\mathbf{u}(Hf)\mathbf{u}^T < 0$ for every nonzero vector $\mathbf{u}$, so f is $Q-$.

For a function of two variables, the property $Q-$ is characterized by the following theorem.

Theorem 6.6.5

The determinant

$$\begin{vmatrix} f_{11} & f_{12} & f_1 \\ f_{12} & f_{22} & f_2 \\ f_1 & f_2 & 0 \end{vmatrix} = -f_1^2 f_{22} + 2f_1 f_2 f_{12} - f_2^2 f_{11} \qquad (6.6.1)$$

---

[*] A mathematician would say "is vacuously."

is positive for all (x_1, x_2) if and only if $f(x_1, x_2)$ is $Q-$ and grad f is never zero.

PROOF. Apply the Bordered Lemma 6.4.4 where $\mathbf{A} = Hf$ and $\mathbf{B} = \text{grad } f$.

A similar statement holds with "positive" and "$Q-$" replaced with "negative" and "$Q+$", respectively. The expression in (6.6.1) should be familiar from Chapter 4 when we discussed shapes of level curves.

Example 6.6.6

In the utility maximization problem (Example 6.4.3), the critical point satisfies the second-order condition for a local maximum if U is $Q-$. More generally, the argument in Example 6.4.3 shows: *if $f(x_1, x_2)$ is $Q-$ and grad f is never zero and $g(x_1, x_2)$ is linear, then every critical point for*

$$\underset{x_1, x_2}{Max}\, f(x_1, x_2) \ \text{ s.t. } \ g(x_1, x_2) = 0$$

is a local maximum. You will investigate criteria for a global maximum in Exercise 6.6.6 below.

$$-f_2^2 f_{11} + 2 f_1 f_2 f_{12} - f_1^2 f_{22} = 2 x_1 x_2 > 0.$$

Example 6.6.7

The function $f(x_1, x_2) = x_1 x_2$ is $Q-$ for $x_1, x_2 > 0$, because

But the Hessian of f is not negative definite by Exercise 4.4.4.

Example 6.6.8

Consider the cost minimization problem given by:

$$\underset{x_1, x_2}{Min}\, C = w_1 x_1 + w_2 x_2 \ \text{ s.t. } \ y = f(x_1, x_2).$$

The Lagrangian for this problem is:

$$L = w_1 x_1 + w_2 x_2 + \lambda \big(y - f(x_1, x_2) \big)$$

and its first-order conditions are:

$$L_1 = w_1 - \lambda^* f_1 \big(x_1^*, x_2^* \big) = 0,$$
$$L_2 = w_2 - \lambda^* f_2 \big(x_1^*, x_2^* \big) = 0, \ \text{ and}$$
$$L_\lambda = y - f \big(x_1^*, x_2^* \big) = 0.$$

Notice the fact that w_1 and $f_1 \big(x_1^*, x_2^* \big)$ are positive implies that $\lambda^* > 0$. The second-order condition is that $\big| HL \big(\mathbf{x}^*, \lambda^* \big) \big| < 0$. We have:

$$\big| HL \big(\mathbf{x}^*, \lambda^* \big) \big| = \begin{vmatrix} -\lambda^* f_{11} \big(\mathbf{x}^* \big) & -\lambda^* f_{12} \big(\mathbf{x}^* \big) & -f_1 \big(\mathbf{x}^* \big) \\ -\lambda^* f_{21} \big(\mathbf{x}^* \big) & -\lambda^* f_{22} \big(\mathbf{x}^* \big) & -f_1 \big(\mathbf{x}^* \big) \\ -f_1 \big(\mathbf{x}^* \big) & -f_2 \big(\mathbf{x}^* \big) & 0 \end{vmatrix}.$$

Factoring a (-1) out of each of the three columns gives us:

$$\left|HL\left(\mathbf{x}^*,\lambda^*\right)\right|=(-1)^3\begin{vmatrix} \lambda^* f_{11}\left(\mathbf{x}^*\right) & \lambda^* f_{12}\left(\mathbf{x}^*\right) & f_1\left(\mathbf{x}^*\right) \\ \lambda^* f_{21}\left(\mathbf{x}^*\right) & \lambda^* f_{22}\left(\mathbf{x}^*\right) & f_2\left(\mathbf{x}^*\right) \\ f_1\left(\mathbf{x}^*\right) & f_2\left(\mathbf{x}^*\right) & 0 \end{vmatrix}.$$

Now factoring λ^* out of the first two columns gives us:

$$\left|HL\left(\mathbf{x}^*,\lambda^*\right)\right|=(-1)^3\left(\lambda^*\right)^2\begin{vmatrix} f_{11}\left(\mathbf{x}^*\right) & f_{12}\left(\mathbf{x}^*\right) & f_1\left(\mathbf{x}^*\right) \\ f_{21}\left(\mathbf{x}^*\right) & f_{22}\left(\mathbf{x}^*\right) & f_2\left(\mathbf{x}^*\right) \\ \dfrac{f_1\left(\mathbf{x}^*\right)}{\lambda^*} & \dfrac{f_2}{\lambda^*}\left(\mathbf{x}^*\right) & 0 \end{vmatrix}.$$

Finally, factoring $\raisebox{0.4ex}{$1$}\!\big/\!\raisebox{-0.4ex}{λ^*}$ out of the third row gives us:

$$\left|HL\left(\mathbf{x}^*,\lambda^*\right)\right|=\frac{(-1)^3\left(\lambda^*\right)^2}{\lambda^*}\begin{vmatrix} f_{11}\left(\mathbf{x}^*\right) & f_{12}\left(\mathbf{x}^*\right) & f_1\left(\mathbf{x}^*\right) \\ f_{21}\left(\mathbf{x}^*\right) & f_{22}\left(\mathbf{x}^*\right) & f_2\left(\mathbf{x}^*\right) \\ f_1\left(\mathbf{x}^*\right) & f_2\left(\mathbf{x}^*\right) & 0 \end{vmatrix}$$

$$\left|HL\left(\mathbf{x}^*,\lambda^*\right)\right|=-\lambda^*\begin{vmatrix} f_{11}\left(\mathbf{x}^*\right) & f_{12}\left(\mathbf{x}^*\right) & f_1\left(\mathbf{x}^*\right) \\ f_{21}\left(\mathbf{x}^*\right) & f_{22}\left(\mathbf{x}^*\right) & f_2\left(\mathbf{x}^*\right) \\ f_1\left(\mathbf{x}^*\right) & f_2\left(\mathbf{x}^*\right) & 0 \end{vmatrix}.$$

Since λ^* is positive, the second-order condition $\left|HL\left(\mathbf{x}^*,\lambda^*\right)\right|<0$ holds if and only if:

$$\begin{vmatrix} f_{11}\left(\mathbf{x}^*\right) & f_{12}\left(\mathbf{x}^*\right) & f_1\left(\mathbf{x}^*\right) \\ f_{21}\left(\mathbf{x}^*\right) & f_{22}\left(\mathbf{x}^*\right) & f_2\left(\mathbf{x}^*\right) \\ f_1\left(\mathbf{x}^*\right) & f_2\left(\mathbf{x}^*\right) & 0 \end{vmatrix}>0. \tag{6.6.2}$$

Because production increases when we increase the inputs (i.e., f_1 and f_2 are both positive), if we assume that f is $Q-$, then the second-order condition holds at every critical point (by Theorem 6.6.5), and every critical point is a (local) minimum.

Remark. The purpose of the hypothesis $Q-$ is to both force critical points to be local optima and to give just enough more so that we can get comparative statics results. For these purposes, mathematicians sometimes prefer to make the hypothesis that the objective function f has negative definite Hessian on the constraint $g =$

0 (or something similar). But the mathematician's hypothesis involves some relationship between f and g. In contrast, our statement "f is $Q-$" involves just the function f, regardless of g; this statement follows the tradition in economics.

Exercises

6.6.1 In chapter 2 we derived the general comparative static formula given by 2.5.5; we have not derived a similar formula in this chapter. In this problem you will derive a set of formulas that are similar to 2.5.5. The constrained optimization problem we are interested in is $\underset{x_1,x_2}{Max} \; z = f(x_1,x_2,\alpha)$ s.t. $c - g(x_1,x_2,\alpha) = 0$, where x_1 and x_2 are the control variables and α is a parameter. Assume that a solution to these first-order conditions exists and is given by the triple $x_1^*(\alpha)$, $x_2^*(\alpha)$, and $\lambda^*(\alpha)$. Derive a general formula for the comparative statics (1) $\dfrac{\partial x_1^*(\alpha)}{\partial \alpha}$, (2) $\dfrac{\partial x_2^*(\alpha)}{\partial \alpha}$, and (3) $\dfrac{\partial \lambda^*(\alpha)}{\partial \alpha}$.

6.6.2 Consider the Cobb-Douglas function $f(x_1,x_2) = x_1^\alpha x_2^\beta$ where $a, \beta > 0$. We only look at positive values of x_1, x_2. Prove that f is $Q-$. (For context, recall that in Exercise 4.4.4, you showed that (1) the Hessian of f is not positive definite, and that (2) the Hessian is negative definite for all $x_1, x_2 > 0$ if and only if $\alpha + \beta < 1$.)

6.6.3 In this problem you will prove that the cost function, $C^*(w_1,w_2,y)$—viewed as a function of output y—increases at an increasing rate as output increases. The firm's problem is

$$\underset{x_1,x_2}{Min} \; C = w_1 x_1 + w_2 x_2 \;\; \text{s.t.} \;\; y = f(x_1,x_2),$$

where we assume that the production function f has a negative definite Hessian. Write the Lagrangian for this problem as $L(x_1,x_2,\lambda,w_1,w_2,y) = w_1 x_1 + w_2 x_2 + \lambda(y - f(x_1,x_2))$. Assume there is a solution, $\left(x_1^*(w_1,w_2,y), x_2^*(w_1,w_2,y), \lambda^*(w_1,w_2,y)\right)$, to the first-order conditions.

(a) Show that $\dfrac{\partial C^*(w_1,w_2,y)}{\partial y} = \lambda^*(w_1,w_2,y)$.

(b) Find $\dfrac{\partial \lambda^*(w_1,w_2,y)}{\partial y}$ and show that it is positive.

Combining (a) and (b) shows that $\dfrac{\partial C^*(w_1,w_2,y)}{\partial y} > 0$ and $\dfrac{\partial^2 C^*(w_1,w_2,y)}{\partial y^2} > 0$, as promised.

6.6.4 In the utility maximization problem, suppose (like usual) that U_1 and U_2 are positive and that U_{11} and U_{22} are negative. Suppose that there is a solution $(x_1^*, x_2^*, \lambda^*)$ to the first-order conditions and that the second-order condition for it to be a local maximum holds.

(a) Show that $\dfrac{\partial U^*}{\partial I}$ is positive.

(b) Show that $\dfrac{\partial^2 U^*}{\partial I^2}$ is negative (i.e., marginal utility of income is decreasing, like we expect) if and only if the Hessian of U is negative definite at $\left(x_1^*, x_2^*\right)$.

6.6.5 In this problem we will develop the *Hicksian demand curves*. Assume that an individual minimizes his expenditures $E = p_1 x_1 + p_2 x_2$ subject to the utility constraint that $\bar{U} = U(x_1, x_2)$. Assume that the utility function U is $Q-$.

(a) What are the control variables and what are the parameters for this problem?
(b) Find the first-order conditions for this problem.
(c) Assume that a solution to the first-order conditions exists; call it $\left(x_1^H, x_2^H, \lambda^H\right)$. Verify that $\left(x_1^H, x_2^H\right)$ is a minimum.

(d) Find and sign $\dfrac{\partial x_1^H}{\partial p_1}$ and $\dfrac{\partial x_2^H}{\partial p_1}$. What are the economic interpretations of these signs? Compare these signs with the signs of $\dfrac{\partial x_1^M}{\partial p_1}$ with $\dfrac{\partial x_2^M}{\partial p_1}$ for the "Marshallian" utility maximization problem. (We calculated $\dfrac{\partial x_1^M}{\partial p_1}$ in Example 6.5.4.)

(e) We write E^H for the indirect objective function, i.e.,

$$E^H := p_1 x_1^H + p_2 x_2^H.$$

It is a function of p_1, p_2, and $\bar{U}$ and is known as the expenditure function. Find and sign: $\dfrac{\partial E^H}{\partial p_1}$, $\dfrac{\partial E^H}{\partial p_2}$, and $\dfrac{\partial E^H}{\partial \bar{U}}$.

6.6.6 Prove: A function $f(x_1, x_2, \ldots, x_n)$ is $Q-$ if and only if every slice of f is $Q-$.

6.6.7 Show that if there is a critical point $\left(\mathbf{x}^*, \lambda^*\right)$ for the utility maximization problem, then $\mathbf{x}^*$ is a *global maximum* for U along the constraint $p_1 x_1 + p_2 x_2 = I$. [Hint: Use the alternative proof of the Global SOC Theorem from Chapter 1.]

6.6.8 Refer to Theorem 4 in Debreu's paper *Definite and semidefinite quadratic forms* and use it to write a version of the Bordered Lemma where $\mathbf{A}$ is *n*-by-*n* and $\mathbf{B}$ is 1-by-*n*. [Hint: Statement (1) in this new version of the Bordered Lemma will involve checking the signs of $n - 1$ different determinants.] Combine this new version of the Bordered Lemma with Theorem 10.3 in Chapter 1 of Hestenes' book *Calculus of variations and optimal control theory* to obtain a version of Theorem 6.4.1 (the Local SOC Theorem) for a function $f(x_1, x_2, \ldots, x_n)$ of more than 2 variables.

CHAPTER 7
QUASI-CONVEXITY

T he purpose of this short and technical chapter is to compare what it means for a function to be quasi-concave versus $Q-$, It is provided for the sake of completeness—we expect that most readers will skip it on their first time through the book.

7.1 QUASI-CONCAVITY AND QUASI-CONVEXITY

In the economics literature, one often sees the terms quasi-concave (instead of $Q-$) or quasi-convex (instead of $Q+$). We now compare what it means for a function $f(x_1, x_2)$ to be quasi-concave versus $Q-$.

Definition 7.1.1 Quasi-concavity

A function $f(x_1, x_2, \ldots, x_n)$ is *quasi-concave* if for all points $\mathbf{c}$ and $\mathbf{d}$ and all $0 < t < 1$, we have:

$$f\big(t\mathbf{c} + (1-t)\mathbf{d}\big) \geq \min\{f(\mathbf{c}), f(\mathbf{d})\}.$$

(The notion of *quasi-convex* is defined similarly. One just replaces "≥ min" with "≤ max".)

Alternatively, f is quasi-concave if the set $\{\mathbf{c} \mid f(\mathbf{c}) \geq \alpha$ is convex for every number α. In Chapter 5, we talked about *functions* being convex. This notion is different. A *set* is convex if for all points $\mathbf{c}$ and $\mathbf{d}$ in the set, every point on the line segment between them is also in the set.

Example 7.1.2

If a function of one variable $f(x)$ is never decreasing (i.e., $a < b$ implies $f(a) \leq f(b)$) or never increasing, then $f(x)$ is both quasi-concave and quasi-convex. For example, $f(x) = x^3$ is never decreasing, so it is both quasi-concave and quasi-convex but it is neither concave nor convex.

Example 7.1.3

If f is concave, then

$$f\big(t\mathbf{c} + (1-t)\mathbf{d}\big) \geq tf(\mathbf{c}) + (1-t)f(\mathbf{d}) \geq (t + 1 - t)\min\{f(\mathbf{c}), f(\mathbf{d})\} = \min\{f(\mathbf{c}), f(\mathbf{d})\}$$

for all $0 < t < 1$. So f is quasi-concave. Note: all concave functions are quasi-concave but not all quasi-concave functions are concave, by the previous example.

Example 7.1.4

A function f is quasi-concave if and only if $-f$ is quasi-convex.

Proposition 7.1.5 *If* $f(x_1, x_2, \ldots, x_n)$ *is* $Q-$, *then it is quasi-concave. If* f *is* $Q+$, *then it is quasi-convex.*

PROOF. Suppose first that f is a function of one variable and is $Q-$; we will show that it is quasi-concave. What does the graph of $f'(x)$ look like? If $f'(x)$ is never zero, then $f(x)$ is always increasing or always decreasing, hence $f(x)$ is quasi-concave by Example 7.1.3.

On the other hand, if $f'(c) = 0$ for some number c, then $f'(x)$ is decreasing at $x = c$ because $f''(c)$ is negative (as in Example 5.2.2). Since $f'(x)$ is continuous, its graph crosses the x-axis at $x = c$ and nowhere else. It follows that $f(x)$ is increasing for $x < c$ and decreasing for $x > c$, hence $f(x)$ is quasi-concave by Exercise 7.1.1 at the end of this section.

We now consider a $Q-$ function $f(x_1, x_2, \ldots, x_n)$ of n variables and show that it is quasi-concave. By Exercise 6.6.5, every slice $g(t)$ of f is $Q-$, but the slice $g(t)$ is a function of one variable, so it is quasi-concave by the preceding argument. As every slice of f is quasi-concave, f itself is quasi-concave.

If f is $Q-$, then $-f$ is $Q+$, so f is quasi-concave, hence f is quasi-convex.

Exercises

7.1.1 Let u^* be a function of one variable and suppose that there is some number r such that $f(r)$ is increasing for $x < r$ and decreasing for $x > r$. Show that $f(x)$ is quasi-concave.

7.2 GEOMETRY OF THE LEVEL CURVES

In this section, we relate the properties $Q-$ and quasi-concavity of a function of two variables $f(x_1, x_2)$ with the shape of the level curves $\overline{z} = f(x_1, x_2)$. We suppose that f_2 is never zero, so that x_2 can be written as a function of x_1.

Proposition 7.2.1

Let $f(x_1, x_2)$ *be such that* f_1 *and* f_2 *are always positive. Then:*

(1) f is $Q-$ if and only if $\dfrac{d^2 x_2}{dx_1^2} > 0$ *for every level curve of f.*

(2) f is quasi-concave if and only if $\dfrac{d^2 x_2}{dx_1^2} \geq 0$ *for every level curve of f (i.e., x_2 is a convex function of x_1).*

PROOF. Consulting Table 4.1.11, f belongs to the top two rows because f_1 and f_2 are positive. It follows that $\dfrac{d^2 x_2}{dx_1^2} > 0$ holds if, and only if, $-f_2^2 f_{11} + 2f_1 f_2 f_{12} - f_1^2 f_{22}$ is positive, which by Theorem 6.6.5 is the same as f being $Q-$. This proves (1).

As for (2), note that for every level curve $\bar{z} = f(x_1, x_2)$, we have:

$$\frac{dx_2}{dx_1} = -\frac{f_1}{f_2} < 0.$$

Therefore, when we zoom in on a level curve $\bar{z} = f(x_1, x_2)$, we see something that looks like one of the curves in Figure 7.2.2. Furthermore, since f_1 and f_2 are both positive, the values of f northeast of the level curve are greater than $\bar{z}$, and the values of f southwest of the level curve are less than $\bar{z}$.

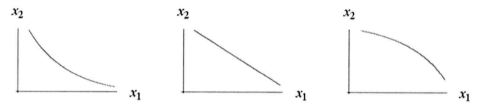

Figure 7.2.2 Level curves with $\dfrac{d^2 x_2}{dx_1^2}$ positive, zero, or negative.

If $\dfrac{d^2 x_2}{dx_1^2}$ is negative (the rightmost graph in Figure 7.2.2), then a chord drawn between two points on the level curve passes southwest of the curve and any point q in the interior of such a chord has $f(\mathbf{q}) < \bar{z}$. This result shows that f is not quasi-concave. Therefore, if f is quasi-concave, then $\dfrac{d^2 x_2}{dx_1^2} \geq 0$.

Conversely, if $\dfrac{d^2 x_2}{dx_1^2} \geq 0$, then the level curves locally all look like one of the first two pictures in Figure 7.2.2. The set $\left\{ (x_1, x_2) \,\middle|\, f(x_1, x_2) \geq \bar{z} \right\}$ is the region in the first quadrant to the northeast of the level curve, and this region is obviously convex. Since this holds for every level curve (i.e., every choice of $\bar{z}$), f is quasi-concave. $\square$

7.3 SUMMARY

The relationship between $Q-$ and quasi-concavity is very similar to the relationship between "negative definite Hessian" and concavity. The first assumption is stronger, but is necessary for comparative statics, and the second, weaker assumption is all that is necessary in order to maximize. Figure 7.3.1 summarizes these relationships.

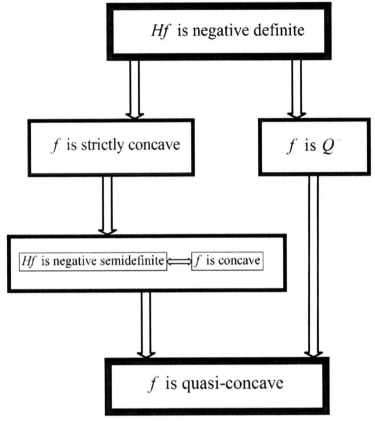

Figure 7.3.1 The relationships surrounding quasi-concavity.

We used the notion of Q^- because we are interested in testable implications of our models in the form of comparative statics. In Exercise 6.6.6, you showed that in the utility maximization problem with a Q^- utility function, there is at most one critical point, and such a critical point is necessarily a global maximum.

If you don't care about comparative statics, and just want some similar second-order condition to hold, then you can replace Q^- with the weaker assumption of quasi-concavity. More precisely, we have:

Theorem 7.3.2 (Arrow-Enthoven Theorem).

Let $(\mathbf{x}^*, \lambda^*)$ be a critical point of the Lagrangian $f + \lambda g$ for the problem

$$\max f(x_1, x_2, \ldots, x_n) \text{ subject to } g(x_1, x_2) = 0.$$

If f and g are quasi-concave and $\lambda^* > 0$, then $\mathbf{x}^*$ is a maximum for f along the constraint.[*]

---

[*]   See K.J. Arrow and A.C. Enthoven, Quasi-concave programming, Econometica, vol. 29, no. 4 (1961), pp. 779–800, Th. 1. We omit the proof here because of its length.

Exercises

7.3.1 Verify that the functions

$$f(x_1, x_2) = x_1 + x_2 \quad \text{and} \quad g(x_1, x_2) = x_1 x_2 - 1$$

are quasi-concave for $x_1, x_2 > 0$. Show that the unique critical point of

$$\underset{x_1, x_2}{Max}\, f(x_1, x_2) \text{ subject to } g(x_1, x_2) = 0$$

is $(1,1)$, and that it is a global *minimum* for f along the constraint $g = 0$. Why does the Arrow-Enthoven Theorem not apply?

CHAPTER 8

HOMOGENEITY AND DUALITY

In this chapter we explore two concepts, homogeneity and duality, that are mathematical implications of the optimization problem; these mathematical insights offer economists important information about these models. The discussion of homogeneity is relatively straightforward and the implications for the economists are easy to see. The role of duality is much more difficult to understand; students may need to read this material several times to begin to gain full command of it.

8.1 HOMOGENEOUS FUNCTIONS

A function $f(x_1, x_2, \ldots, x_n)$ is *homogeneous* if there is some number d such that

$$f(tx_1, tx_2, \ldots, tx_n) = t^d f(x_1, x_2, \ldots, x_n)$$

for every $x_1, x_2, \ldots, x_n$ and all positive values of t. More precisely, sometimes we say that f is *homogeneous of degree d*.

You have already used this concept in microeconomics in the case where $f(x_1, x_2)$ is a production function. You said that f has *constant returns to scale* if

$$f(tx_1, tx_2) = tf(x_1, x_2)$$

for all $t > 0$ (i.e., if f is homogeneous of degree 1); has *decreasing returns to scale* if

$$f(tx_1, tx_2) = t^r f(x_1, x_2)$$

for some $r < 1$ and all $t > 0$ (i.e., if f is homogeneous of degree less than 1); and has *increasing returns to scale* if $f(tx_1, tx_2) = t^r f(x_1, x_2)$ for some $r > 1$ and all $t > 0$ (i.e., if f is homogeneous of degree greater than 1).

For example, the function $f(x_1, x_2) = x_1 x_2^3$ is homogeneous of degree 4:

$$f(tx_1, tx_2) = (tx_1)(tx_2)^3 = t^4 x_1 x_2^3 = t^4 f(x_1, x_2).$$

Example 8.1.1

We show that the function $f(x) = x + 1$ is not homogeneous. Suppose that $f(x)$ is homogeneous of degree d. Then

$$tx + 1 = f(tx) = t^d f(x) = t^d x + t^d \quad \text{for all positive } t \text{ and all } x.$$

We plug in values of t and x to see that the equation

$$tx + 1 = t^d x + t^d \tag{8.1.1}$$

cannot hold for all positive t and all x. If we plug in $x = 0$, we find $1 = t^d$. Therefore, (8.1.1) takes the form

$$tx + 1 = x + 1$$

i.e., $tx = x$. This equation is false for $t = 2$ and $x \neq 0, t = 2$ and $x \neq 0$.

Example 8.1.2

The *zero function* $z(x_1, x_2, \ldots, x_n)$ is 0 for every $x_1, x_2, \ldots, x_n$.

1. The zero function is homogeneous of degree d for every number d. Indeed,

$$z(tx_1, tx_2, \ldots, tx_n) = 0 = t^d 0 = t^d z(x_1, x_2, \ldots, x_n)$$

for every t.

2. Suppose a function $g(x_1, x_2, \ldots, x_n)$ is homogeneous of degree d is homogeneous of degree e, for $d \neq e$. Then g is the zero function. To see this, suppose not, i.e., suppose that there is some point $\mathbf{c}$ such that $g(\mathbf{c}) \neq 0$. Then

$$t^d g(\mathbf{c}) = g(t\mathbf{c}) = t^e g(\mathbf{c}) \text{ for all positive } t.$$

Since $g(\mathbf{c}) \neq 0$, we can divide to obtain $t^d = t^e$, hence $t^{d-e} = 1$ for all positive t. This implies that $d = e$, a contradiction. Thus, (8.1.1) cannot hold and f is not homogeneous.

Example 8.1.3 (utility maximization)

Recall the utility maximization problem from Chapter 6: An individual enjoys utility $U(x_1, x_2)$ from consuming amounts x_1 of good 1 and x_2 of good 2. He seeks to maximize his utility subject to the income constraint $p_1 x_1 + p_2 x_2 = I$. Solving this constrained optimization problem, we find that he consumes $x_1^M(p_1, p_2, I)$ of good 1. How much of good 1 does he consume if prices and his income both double? That is, what is $x_1^M(2p_1, 2p_2, 2I)$? Intuitively, we expect his consumption to be unchanged[*], i.e., we expect that

$$x_1^M(p_1, p_2, I) = x_1^M(2p_1, 2p_2, 2I).$$

More generally, we expect that his consumption will not change if prices and income are all multiplied by any positive number t. This means that

$$x_1^M(p_1, p_2, I) = x_1^M(tp_1, tp_2, tI) \text{ and } x_2^M(p_1, p_2, I) = x_2^M(tp_1, tp_2, tI) \text{ for all } t > 0.$$

Indeed this is true, and we can justify it mathematically. We found $x_1^M(p_1, p_2, I)$ by defining the Lagrangian

---

[*] Economists refer to this feature of the demand function as that there is no *money illusion*.

$$U(x_1, x_2) + \lambda(I - p_1 x_1 - p_2 x_2),$$

and $x_1^M(p_1, p_2, I)$ was the solution to the first-order conditions

$$0 = U_1\big(x_1^M(p_1, p_2, I), x_2^M(p_1, p_2, I)\big) - \lambda^M(p_1, p_2, I)p_1,$$

$$0 = U_2\big(x_1^M(p_1, p_2, I), x_2^M(p_1, p_2, I)\big) - \lambda^M(p_1, p_2, I)p_2, \text{ and}$$

$$0 = I - p_1 x_1^M(p_1, p_2, I) - p_2 x_2^M(p_1, p_2, I).$$

Combining the first two equations with Exercise 6.6.6, we find that $x_1^M(p_1, p_2, I)$ and $x_2^M(p_1, p_2, I)$ are the unique solutions to the system of equations

$$\frac{U_1\big(x_1^M(p_1, p_2, I), x_2^M(p_1, p_2, I)\big)}{p_1} = \frac{U_2\big(x_1^M(p_1, p_2, I), x_2^M(p_1, p_2, I)\big)}{p_2}$$

and
$$0 = I - p_1 x_1^M(p_1, p_2, I) - p_2 x_2^M(p_1, p_2, I).$$

We repeat this process with prices and income multiplied by t. The new Lagrangian is

$$U(x_1, x_2) + \lambda(tI - tp_1 x_1 - tp_2 x_2)$$

and $x_1^M(p_1, p_2, I)$ is the solution to the first-order conditions

$$0 = U_1\big(x_1^M(tp_1, tp_2, tI), x_2^M(tp_1, tp_2, tI)\big) - \lambda^M(tp_1, tp_2, tI)tp_1,$$

$$0 = U_2\big(x_1^M(tp_1, tp_2, tI), x_2^M(tp_1, tp_2, tI)\big) - \lambda^M(tp_1, tp_2, tI)tp_2, \text{ and}$$

$$0 = tI - tp_1 x_1^M(tp_1, tp_2, tI) - tp_2 x_2^M(tp_1, tp_2, tI).$$

Combining the first two equations (by solving for $t\lambda^M$) and dividing the third equation by t, we find that and $x_1^M(tp_1, tp_2, tI)$ and $x_2^M(tp_1, tp_2, tI)$ are the solution to the equations

$$\frac{U_1\big(x_1^M(tp_1, tp_2, tI), x_2^M(tp_1, tp_2, tI)\big)}{p_1} = \frac{U_2\big(x_1^M(tp_1, tp_2, tI), x_2^M(tp_1, tp_2, tI)\big)}{p_2}$$

and $$(8.1.3)$$
$$0 = I - p_1 x_1^M(tp_1, tp_2, tI) - p_2 x_2^M(tp_1, tp_2, tI).$$

We have just shown that

$$y_1 = x_1^M(tp_1, tp_2, tI) \text{ and } y_2 = x_2^M(tp_1, tp_2, tI)$$

are the solutions to the system of equations

$$\frac{U_1(y_1, y_2)}{p_1} = \frac{U_2(y_1, y_2)}{p_2} \text{ and } 0 = I - p_1 y_1 - p_2 y_2.$$

These equations do not depend on t, so neither do the values of y_1 or y_2. That is, we have just proved equation (8.1.2). We say that x_1^M *and* x_2^M *are homogeneous of degree 0 in prices and income.*

Example 8.1.4 (utility maximization, revisited)

Here is an alternative argument for showing that the demand functions x_1^M and x_2^M are homogeneous of degree 0 in prices and income. If we replace p_1, p_2, and I with tp_1, tp_2, and tI, then we replace the optimization problem

$$\underset{x_1,x_2}{Max}\, U(x_1,x_2) \quad \text{s.t.} \quad p_1 x_1 + p_2 x_2 = I$$

with

$$\underset{x_1,x_2}{Max}\, U(x_1,x_2) \quad \text{s.t.} \quad tp_1 x_1 + tp_2 x_2 = tI.$$

The objective function $U(x_1,x_2)$ has not changed. The constraint equation looks different, but the two constraints are satisfied by the same values of (x_1,x_2), that is,

$$p_1 x_1 + p_2 x_2 = I \quad \text{if and only if} \quad tp_1 x_1 + tp_2 x_2 = tI.$$

So the solutions for the two optimization problems are the same. This gives another proof of Example 8.1.3.

How can you see that a function is *not* homogeneous? We saw one way in Example 8.1.1. Another way is via the following useful criterion:

Lemma 8.1.5

If $f(x_1,x_2,\ldots,x_n)$ is homogeneous of degree $d \neq 0$, then $\dfrac{\partial f}{\partial x_i}$ is homogeneous of degree $d-1$ for all i.

Before proving the lemma, we show how to apply it.

Example 8.1.6

Let $f(x_1,x_2) = x_1 x_2 + x_1$. Then, $f_1(x_1,x_2) = x_2 + 1$, which is not homogeneous by Example 8.1.1, so f cannot be homogeneous by (the contrapositive of) Lemma 8.1.5.

PROOF OF LEMMA 8.1.5. Let $f(x_1,x_2,\ldots,x_n)$ be homogeneous of degree d. Then, by the definition of homogeneity we know that

$$f(tx_1,tx_2,\ldots,tx_n) = t^d f(x_1,x_2,\ldots,x_n) \quad \text{for all } t > 0.$$

Differentiate the above equation with respect to x_i:

$$tf_i(tx_1,tx_2,\ldots,tx_n) = t^d f_i(x_1,x_2,\ldots,x_n);$$

i.e.,

$$f_i(tx_1,tx_2,\ldots,tx_n) = t^{d-1} f_i(x_1,x_2,\ldots,x_n) \quad \text{for all } t > 0,$$

as desired. $\square$

Exercises

8.1.1 In Exercises 4.1.1--4.1.3 you studied the functions:

(a) $f(x_1,x_2) = Ax_1^\alpha x_2^\beta$ (Cobb-Douglas)

(b) $f(x_1, x_2) = 1 + (x_1 x_2 - 1)^{\frac{1}{3}}$

(c) $f(x_1, x_2) = A\left[\alpha x_1^{-\rho} + (1-\alpha) x_2^{-\rho}\right]^{-\frac{h}{\rho}}$ (CES), where $0 < \alpha < 1$, $h > 0$, and $\rho > -1$.

For each of these, is the function homogeneous? Explain. [If you want to say that a function is not homogeneous, it is not sufficient to say "I can't figure out how to factor out a t."]

8.1.2 Let $f(x_1, x_2, \ldots, x_n)$ be homogeneous of degree d and let $g(x_1, x_2, \ldots, x_n)$ be homogeneous of degree e. Prove:

(a) The function $f(x_1, x_2, \ldots, x_n) g(x_1, x_2, \ldots, x_n)$ is homogeneous of degree $d+e$.

(b) The function $\dfrac{f(x_1, x_2, \ldots, x_n)}{g(x_1, x_2, \ldots, x_n)}$ is homogeneous of degree $d-e$.

(c) If $d = e$, then the function $f(x_1, x_2, \ldots, x_n) + g(x_1, x_2, \ldots, x_n)$ and the function $f(x_1, x_2, \ldots, x_n) - g(x_1, x_2, \ldots, x_n)$ are homogeneous of degree d.

(d) The function $f(x_1, x_2, \ldots, x_n)^r$ is homogeneous of degree rd.

8.1.3 Assume that a producer chooses the levels of inputs that maximize profits where profits are given by $\pi(x_1, x_2, w_1, w_2, p) = pf(x_1, x_2) - w_1 x_1 - w_2 x_2$ and $f(x_1, x_2)$ is the firm's production function. Assume that the second-order conditions for maximization hold. Prove the following:

(a) The factor demand functions, $x_i^*(w_1, w_2, p)$, are homogeneous of degree 0.
(b) The indirect profit function, $\pi^*(w_1, w_2, p)$, is homogeneous of degree 1.

8.1.4 Assume that the function $f(x_1, x_2)$ is homogeneous of degree d. Prove that

$$df(x_1, x_2) = x_1 f_1(x_1, x_2) + x_2 f_2(x_1, x_2).$$

[Hint: the definition of a homogeneous function is true for any value of t, including $t = 1$.] This result in the form "The function $f(x_1, x_2)$ is homogeneous of degree d if and only if $df(x_1, x_2) = x_1 f_1(x_1, x_2) + x_2 f_2(x_1, x_2)$" is known as *Euler's Theorem* and is often used by economists. Here we are asking you to prove only one half of the theorem.

8.2 HOMOTHETIC FUNCTIONS

In Exercise 6.5.2, we saw that sometimes we can replace a function $f(x_1, x_2)$ with a new function $G(f(x_1, x_2))$ without changing the mathematical situation too much, at least when $G(z)$ is strictly increasing. Let's pursue this idea in the case where f is homogeneous. Specifically: A function $h(x_1, x_2)$ is *homothetic* if $h(x_1, x_2) = G(f(x_1, x_2))$ where $f(x_1, x_2)$ is homogeneous and $G(z)$ is strictly increasing, i.e., $G'(z) > 0$. (Some people say that $G(f(x_1, x_2))$ is a "monotonic transformation" of $f(x_1, x_2)$.)

Every homogeneous function is homothetic. To see this, note that the function $G(z) = z$ has positive derivative $G'(z) = 1$. Then $f(x_1, x_2) = G(f(x_1, x_2))$

On the other hand, there are homothetic functions that are not homogeneous, as you will see in the exercises below. The exercises also illustrate why homothetic functions are useful to economists.

Exercises

8.2.1 Prove that the utility function $U(x_1, x_2) = \alpha \ln x_1 + \beta \ln x_2$ is homothetic. Calculate the Marshallian demand functions for the utility functions (a) $U(x_1, x_2) = x_1^\alpha x_2^\beta$ and (b) $U(x_1, x_2) = \alpha \ln x_1 + \beta \ln x_2$.

8.2.2 Suppose that the production function $y = f(x_1, x_2)$ is homogeneous of degree d in the two inputs, x_1 and x_2. Also, assume that the function $G(y)$ has a positive first derivative.

(a) Prove that the isoquants for $f(x_1, x_2)$ are parallel along a ray out of the origin. That is, write

$$\frac{dx_2}{dx_1}(c_1, c_2)$$ for the slope of the level curve of f passing through the point (c_1, c_2). Show that

$$\frac{dx_2}{dx_1}(c_1, c_2) = \frac{dx_2}{dx_1}(c_1, c_2)$$ for every $t > 0$.

(b) Prove that the isoquants for the production function $G(f(x_1, x_2))$ are also parallel along a ray out of the origin.

(c) Consider the production function $f(x_1, x_2) = \ln(x_1) + x_2$. Is the function homogeneous? Are the level curves parallel (i.e., in any meaning of the word "parallel")?

8.2.3 In each of the following cases, the function $h(x_1, x_2)$ is defined for $x_1, x_2 > 0$ and h is not homogeneous. Is h homothetic? Justify your answer. If you say yes, produce a homogeneous function $f(x_1, x_2)$ and an increasing function $G(z)$ such that $h(x_1, x_2) = G(f(x_1, x_2))$. If you say no, explain why not.

(a) $h(x_1, x_2) = 10x_1^2 x_2^2 + x_1^4 x_2^4$.

(b) $h(x_1, x_2) = \sqrt{\left(\dfrac{x_1}{\sqrt{x_2}}\right)} + 1$.

(c) $h(x_1, x_2) = x_1 x_2 - x_1$.

8.2.4 Fix a number r. Show: If the function $h(x_1, x_2) + r$ is homothetic, then so is $h(x_1, x_2)$.

8.2.5 Show that an increasing monotonic transformation of a utility function, $G(U(x_1, x_2))$ generates the same Marshallian demand functions as does the untransformed utility function, $U(x_1, x_2)$. What does this result say about the demand functions generated from homothetic utility functions?

8.3 DUALITY, TYPE I

We now turn our attention to a concept that economists use to describe a variety of relationships that characterize optimization problems—*duality*. Rather than defining duality precisely, we will work through some of the relationships that economists are referring to when they use the term duality. In order to keeps the analysis simple we will restrict our discussion to firm behavior.

Recall the *cost minimization* problem from Exercise 6.6.2:

$$\underset{x_1,x_2}{Min}\, C = w_1 x_1 + w_2 x_2 \ \text{ s.t. } \ y = f(x_1, x_2).$$

Solving it gives factor demand functions $x_1^*(w_1, w_2, y)$ and $x_2^*(w_1, w_2, y)$. Reversing the roles of the objective function and the constraint, we have the *output maximization problem*

$$\underset{x_1,x_2}{Max}\, y = f(x_1, x_2) \ \text{ s.t. } \ C = w_1 x_1 + w_2 x_2.$$

Solving it gives a new kind of factor demand functions $x_1^{**}(w_1, w_2, C)$ and $x_2^{**}(w_1, w_2, C)$. Notice that these new factor demand functions have costs, C, as an argument rather than output, y. Figure 8.3.1 illustrates these two solutions. Looking at the pictures, we might guess that if we take the maximum production level $y^{**}(w_1, w_2, C)$ given by solving the output maximization problem (in the right panel) and using it as a parameter in the cost minimization problem (left panel), then we should find

$$C^*(w_1, w_2, y^{**}) = C,$$
$$x_1^*(w_1, w_2, y^{**}) = x_1^{**}(w_1, w_2, C), \text{ and} \qquad\qquad (8.3.1)$$
$$x_2^*(w_1, w_2, y^{**}) = x_2^{**}(w_1, w_2, C).$$

We check these equations in the next two examples.

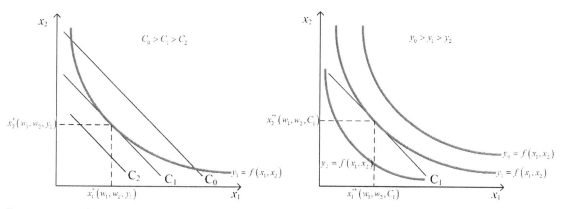

Figure 8.3.1 Solution to the cost minimization problem (left) and the solution to the output maximization problem (right).

Example 8.3.2

Consider the dilemma faced by a policy maker in Washington who wishes to decide if a firm needs regulation because it enjoys increasing returns to scale (and, thus, has the potential to have market power). Assume that the policy maker is willing to believe that the firm's production function can be described accurately enough by a Cobb-Douglas production function of the form:

$$y = f(x_1, x_2) = x_1^{\alpha} x_2^{\beta}, \qquad\qquad (8.3.2)$$

where x_1 is the amount of labor the firm uses, x_2 is the amount of capital the firms uses, and α and β are parameters of the model. What the policy maker wants to know is if the sum of the two parameters is greater than one. Indeed, if $\alpha + \beta > 1$, then the firm's production process exhibits increasing returns to scale, suggesting that government regulation might be appropriate. Presumably, these unknown parameters, α and β, can be estimated using econometric methods.[*]

The dilemma that the policy maker faces is that estimating (8.3.2) is made almost impossible by the fact that reliable measures of labor and, especially, capital do not exist. On the other hand, reliable estimates of the costs of these two inputs usually do exist—the average wage level and the interest rate at which money must be borrowed in order to purchase capital. What would solve the policy maker's problem is that if it were possible to use estimates of the cost function, $C^*(w_1, w_2, y)$ to retrieve estimates of the parameters of the production function, α and β. It turns out that one of the major implications of duality is that it is possible to recover the parameters of a production function from the cost function. In what follows we will show you how to do this feat. However, at the moment what is important is to remember that the information in a production function is preserved in the factor demand curves and the cost function and that there is a unique, potentially recoverable production function underlying each cost function.

Example 8.3.4

We begin our analysis by deriving the factor demand and cost functions associated with (8.3.2). We assume that the firm wishes to minimize costs, $w_1 x_1 + w_2 x_2$, subject to the output constraint given by (8.3.2). The Lagrangian for this problem is:

$$L = w_1 x_1 + w_2 x_2 + \lambda\left(y - x_1^\alpha x_2^\beta\right). \tag{8.3.3}$$

There first-order conditions are:

$$L_1 = w_1 - \lambda \alpha x_1^{\alpha-1} x_2^\beta = w_1 - \frac{\lambda \alpha y}{x_1} = 0,$$

$$L_2 = w_2 - \lambda \beta x_1^\alpha x_2^{\beta-1} = w_2 - \frac{\lambda \beta y}{x_2} = 0, \quad \text{and}$$

$$L_\lambda = y - x_1^\alpha x_2^\beta = 0.$$

The first two equations of the first-order conditions imply:

$$\lambda^* y = \frac{w_1 x_1^*}{\alpha} = \frac{w_2 x_2^*}{\beta}$$

or

$$x_2^* = \frac{\beta w_1 x_1^*}{\alpha w_2} \tag{8.3.4}$$

Substitution of (8.3.4) into the constraint yields:

$$y = \left(x_1^*\right)^\alpha \left(\frac{\beta w_1}{\alpha w_2} x_1^*\right)^\beta$$

---

[*] An econometrician might suggest to the policy maker that she assume that the production function has the form $y = A x_1^\alpha x_2^\beta$, where A measures the state of technology, and then use ordinary least squares to estimate the equation $\ln y = \delta + \alpha \ln x_1 + \beta \ln x_2$, where δ is an intercept term that is equal to $\ln A$.

or

$$x_1^* = \left(\frac{\alpha w_2}{\beta w_1} \right)^{\frac{\beta}{\alpha+\beta}} y^{\frac{1}{\alpha+\beta}}. \tag{8.3.5}$$

Equation (8.3.5) is the factor-demand function for labor, $x_1^*(w_1, w_2, y)$. Substituting (8.3.5) into (8.3.4) yields the factor-demand function for capital:

$$x_2 = \frac{\beta w_1}{\alpha w_2} x_1 = \left(\frac{\beta w_1}{\alpha w_2} \right) y^{\frac{1}{\alpha+\beta}} \left(\frac{\alpha w_2}{\beta w_1} \right)^{\frac{\beta}{\alpha+\beta}}$$

or

$$x_2 = \left(\frac{\beta w_1}{\alpha w_2} \right)^{\frac{\alpha+\beta}{\alpha+\beta}} \left(\frac{\alpha w_2}{\beta w_1} \right)^{\frac{-\beta}{\alpha+\beta}} y^{\frac{1}{\alpha+\beta}}$$

or, finally,

$$x_2^* = \left(\frac{\beta w_1}{\alpha w_2} \right)^{\frac{\alpha}{\alpha+\beta}} y^{\frac{1}{\alpha+\beta}}. \tag{8.3.6}$$

Substituting (8.3.5) and (8.3.6) into the objective function yields the (indirect) cost function:

$$C^*(w_1, w_2, y) = w_1 \left(\frac{\alpha w_2}{\beta w_1} \right)^{\frac{\beta}{\alpha+\beta}} y^{\frac{1}{\alpha+\beta}} + w_2 \left(\frac{\beta w_1}{\alpha w_2} \right)^{\frac{\alpha}{\alpha+\beta}} y^{\frac{1}{\alpha+\beta}}.$$

or

$$C^*(w_1, w_2, y) = \left[w_1 \left(\frac{\alpha w_2}{\beta w_1} \right)^{\frac{\beta}{\alpha+\beta}} + w_2 \left(\frac{\beta w_1}{\alpha w_2} \right)^{\frac{\alpha}{\alpha+\beta}} \right] y^{\frac{1}{\alpha+\beta}}. \tag{8.3.7}$$

But

$$w_1 \left(\frac{\alpha w_2}{\beta w_1} \right)^{\frac{\beta}{\alpha+\beta}} = \frac{w_1}{w_1^{\frac{\beta}{\alpha+\beta}}} \left(\frac{\alpha w_2}{\beta} \right)^{\frac{\beta}{\alpha+\beta}} = w_1^{1-\frac{\beta}{\alpha+\beta}} \left(\frac{\alpha w_2}{\beta} \right)^{\frac{\beta}{\alpha+\beta}} = w_1^{\frac{\alpha}{\alpha+\beta}} w_2^{\frac{\beta}{\alpha+\beta}} \left(\frac{\alpha}{\beta} \right)^{\frac{\beta}{\alpha+\beta}}$$

and

$$w_2 \left(\frac{\beta w_1}{\alpha w_2} \right)^{\frac{\alpha}{\alpha+\beta}} = \frac{w_2}{w_2^{\frac{\alpha}{\alpha+\beta}}} \left(\frac{\beta w_1}{\alpha} \right)^{\frac{\alpha}{\alpha+\beta}} = w_1^{\frac{\alpha}{\alpha+\beta}} w_2^{\frac{\beta}{\alpha+\beta}} \left(\frac{\beta}{\alpha} \right)^{\frac{\alpha}{\alpha+\beta}}.$$

Thus, (8.3.7) becomes

$$C^*(w_1, w_2, y) = \left[w_1^{\frac{\alpha}{\alpha+\beta}} w_2^{\frac{\beta}{\alpha+\beta}} \left(\frac{\alpha}{\beta} \right)^{\frac{\beta}{\alpha+\beta}} + w_1^{\frac{\alpha}{\alpha+\beta}} w_2^{\frac{\beta}{\alpha+\beta}} \left(\frac{\beta}{\alpha} \right)^{\frac{\alpha}{\alpha+\beta}} \right] y^{\frac{1}{\alpha+\beta}}$$

or

$$C^*(w_1, w_2, y) = \Gamma(\alpha, \beta) w_1^{\frac{\alpha}{\alpha+\beta}} w_2^{\frac{\beta}{\alpha+\beta}} y^{\frac{1}{\alpha+\beta}}, \tag{8.3.8}$$

where

$$\Gamma(\alpha,\beta) = \left(\frac{\alpha}{\beta}\right)^{\frac{\beta}{\alpha+\beta}} + \left(\frac{\beta}{\alpha}\right)^{\frac{\alpha}{\alpha+\beta}}$$

$$= \frac{\alpha^{\frac{\beta}{\alpha+\beta}}}{\beta^{\frac{\beta}{\alpha+\beta}}} + \frac{\beta^{\frac{\alpha}{\alpha+\beta}}}{\alpha^{\frac{\alpha}{\alpha+\beta}}} = \frac{\alpha^{\frac{\alpha}{\alpha+\beta}}\alpha^{\frac{\beta}{\alpha+\beta}} + \beta^{\frac{\alpha}{\alpha+\beta}}\beta^{\frac{\beta}{\alpha+\beta}}}{\alpha^{\frac{\alpha}{\alpha+\beta}}\beta^{\frac{\beta}{\alpha+\beta}}}$$

$$= \frac{\alpha+\beta}{\alpha^{\frac{\alpha}{\alpha+\beta}}\beta^{\frac{\beta}{\alpha+\beta}}}.$$

Equation (8.3.8) offers a possible way for the policymaker to get estimates of α and β. If we take the natural logarithm of (8.3.8), we get

$$\ln C^* = \ln \Gamma(\alpha,\beta) + \frac{\alpha}{\alpha+\beta}\ln w_1 + \frac{\beta}{\alpha+\beta}\ln w_2 + \frac{1}{\alpha+\beta}\ln y. \qquad (8.3.9)$$

If we treat the first term on the right-hand side of (8.3.9) as a constant and add an error term, we have the following equation that might be estimated using standard regression methods:

$$\ln C^* = \delta_0 + \delta_1 \ln w_1 + \delta_2 \ln w_2 + \frac{1}{\alpha+\beta}\ln y + \varepsilon, \qquad (8.3.10)$$

where $\delta_0 = \ln \Gamma(\alpha,\beta)$, $\delta_1 = \frac{\alpha}{\alpha+\beta}$, $\delta_2 = \frac{\beta}{\alpha+\beta}$, $\delta_3 = \frac{1}{\alpha+\beta}$, and ε is the error term. The policymaker could estimate α and β using $\hat{\alpha} = \frac{\hat{\delta}_1}{\hat{\delta}_3}$ and $\hat{\beta} = \frac{\hat{\delta}_2}{\hat{\delta}_3}$.[*][†]

Another way of conceiving the firm's economic problem is to assume that the firm is maximizing output subject to a cost constraint. Formally, we assume that the firm is solving:

$$\underset{x_1,x_2}{Max}\, y = x_1^{\alpha} x_2^{\beta} \text{ s.t. } C = w_1 x_1 + w_2 x_2 \qquad (8.3.11)$$

Since the arguments for these two sets of solutions are different, the solutions are different. The solutions, however, are related to each other. Consider the graphical illustration of the two problems shown in Figure 8.3.1. The graphs have been drawn such that the cost and output at the solution in the panel on the left are equal to the cost and output in the panel on the right, respectively. In this particular case, the amounts of labor (capital) demanded by the firm in the cost minimization problem is equal to the amount of labor (capital) demanded in the output maximization problem.

---

[*] The policymaker actually faces a somewhat more complicated problem than the one we have described above. In addition to the usual econometric complications, she would need to add the restriction that We ignore these complications in our analysis to focus on the issue of recapturing the parameters of the production function from a cost function.

[†] There remains an unanswered question in the above analysis that we will address in Example 8.5.2 below. In particular, is the production function given by (8.3.2) the only production function that would generate the cost function given by (8.3.8)? We will answer this question by showing how to move from a cost function to the underlying production function. However, before doing this we need to examine a problem that economists consider to be dual to the cost minimization problem—the output maximization problem.

Example 8.3.5

Let's solve the output maximization problem for the Cobb-Douglas production function used in Example 8.3.3. The problem is to $\underset{x_1, x_2}{Max}\ y = x_1^\alpha x_2^\beta$ s.t. $C = w_1 x_1 + w_2 x_2$. The Lagrangian for this problem is:

$$L = x_1^\alpha x_2^\beta + \lambda\left(C - w_1 x_1 - w_2 x_2\right). \tag{8.3.12}$$

The first-order conditions are:

$$L_1 = \frac{\alpha y}{x_1} - w_1 \lambda = 0,$$

$$L_2 = \frac{\beta y}{x_2} - w_2 \lambda = 0, \ \ \text{and}$$

$$L_\lambda = C - w_1 x_1 - w_2 x_2 = 0.$$

The first two equations of the first-order conditions imply:

$$\frac{\lambda^*}{y} = \frac{\alpha}{w_1 x_1^*} = \frac{\beta}{w_2 x_2^*}.$$

Thus, we get $w_2 x_2^{**} = \dfrac{\beta w_1 x_1^{**}}{\alpha}$. Combining this result with the cost constraint yields:

$$x_1^{**} = \frac{\alpha C}{(\alpha + \beta) w_1} \ \ \text{and} \ \ x_2^{**} = \frac{\beta C}{(\alpha + \beta) w_2}. \tag{8.3.13}$$

The resulting indirect production function is:

$$y^{**} = \left(\frac{\alpha C}{(\alpha + \beta) w_1}\right)^\alpha \left(\frac{\beta C}{(\alpha + \beta) w_2}\right)^\beta. \tag{8.3.14}$$

At this point it is useful to solve (8.3.14) for costs:

$$C^{\alpha + \beta} = \left(\frac{(\alpha + \beta)^{\alpha + \beta}}{\alpha^\alpha \beta^\beta}\right) w_1^\alpha w_2^\beta y$$

or

$$C = \left(\frac{\alpha + \beta}{\alpha^{\frac{\alpha}{\alpha + \beta}} \beta^{\frac{\beta}{\alpha + \beta}}}\right) w_1^{\frac{\alpha}{\alpha + \beta}} w_2^{\frac{\beta}{\alpha + \beta}} y^{\frac{1}{\alpha + \beta}}.$$

$$\tag{8.3.15}$$

The thing to notice here is that equations (8.3.8) and (8.3.15) are identical. This verifies the first part of equation (8.3.1). Similarly, plugging (8.3.14) into (8.3.5) gives:

$$x_1^*\left(w_1, w_2, y^{**}\right) = \left(\frac{\alpha w_2}{\beta w_1}\right)^{\frac{\beta}{\alpha + \beta}} \left(\frac{\alpha \beta C^{\alpha + \beta}}{(\alpha + \beta)^{\alpha + \beta} w_1^\alpha w_2^\beta}\right)^{\frac{1}{\alpha + \beta}}$$

or

$$x_1^*\left(w_1, w_2, y^{**}\right) = \frac{\alpha C}{w_1(\alpha + \beta)} = x_1^{**}\left(w_1, w_2, C\right).$$

and similarly for x_2^*. This verifies the rest of equation (8.3.1).

Of course, the factor "demand" curves that solve (8.3.11) are different from the factor demand curves we found above in the cost minimization problem. In that problem we found as solutions to the constrained minimization problem $x_1^*(w_1, w_2, y)$ and $x_2^*(w_1, w_2, y)$; the solutions to (8.3.9) are $x_1^{**}(w_1, w_2, C)$ and $x_2^{**}(w_1, w_2, C)$.

Exercises

8.3.1 Assume that a firm's production function is $y = x_1 + \ln x_2$, where y is output and x_1 and x_2 are inputs that cost the firm w_1 and w_2, respectively.

(a) Find the indirect production function, $y^{**}(w_1, w_2, C)$, implied by the output maximization problem.
(b) Find the (indirect) cost function, $C^*(w_1, w_2, y)$, implied by the cost minimization problem.
(c) What, if any, is the relationship between the indirect production function and the (indirect) cost function?

8.4 ROADMAP

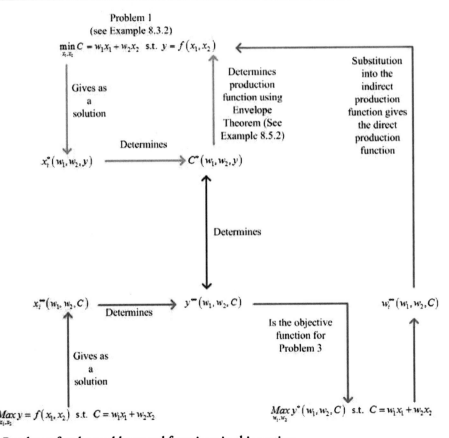

Figure 8.4.1 Roadmap for the problems and functions in this section.

Since it is easy to get lost in any discussion of duality, we provide a roadmap in Figure 8.4.1. of the material we are covering. Figure 8.4.1 is such a roadmap. We begin by giving in Example 8.3.2 a potential justification for why we might be interested in duality. We then consider in Example 8.3.3 a world where the producer is choosing the levels of inputs that minimize cost subject to an output constraint. This is called *Problem 1* in Figure 8.4.1. As a result of solving this problem we find the firm's factor demand curves and the firm's (indirect) cost function (as a functions of factor prices and output). In Example 8.3.4 we solve a related problem—maximization of output subject to a cost constraint. This is called *Problem 2* in Figure 8.4.1. As a result of solving this problem we find a different kind of factor demand functions; these factor demand functions have factor prices and cost as their arguments. We also find the indirect production function—firm output as a function of factor price levels and cost). Next in Example 8.5.3 we show how to find the direct production function from the (indirect) cost function. Finally, in Example 8.5.3 and Example 8.6.1 we discuss the relationship between the first two problems and the problem of a firm choosing the factor price levels that maximize the indirect production function subject to a cost constraint.

8.5 APPLICATIONS OF THE ENVELOPE THEOREM

We can get more from the two examples above by examining the Envelope Theorem results shown in Table 8.5.1 The question we want to answer is: Can we retrieve the production function from either of the indirect objective functions? Example 8.3.5 shows how we can find the indirect cost function if we are given the indirect production function. Thus, if we can establish how to go from the indirect cost function to the direct production function, we have established how to go from the indirect production function to the direct production function.

As shown in lines 3 and 4 of column 2 of Table 8.5.1, the Envelope theorem says that the derivative of the indirect cost function with respect to a factor price is equal to the demand for that factor. Moreover, since factor demand curves are homogeneous of degree 0 in factor prices (you prove this claim in exercise 8.5.2 at the end of this section), we know that:

$$x_1^* \left(w_1, w_2, y \right) = x_1^* \left(tw_1, tw_2, y \right).$$

Letting $t = \dfrac{1}{w_2}$, we get that

$$x_1^* \left(w_1, w_2, y \right) = x_1^* \left(\left(\frac{1}{w_2} \right) w_1, \left(\frac{1}{w_2} \right) w_2, y \right) = x_1^* \left(\frac{w_1}{w_2}, 1, y \right) = x_1^* \left(\frac{w_1}{w_2}, y \right).$$

By similar logic, we can also view x_2^* as a function of $\dfrac{w_1}{w_2}$ and y^* and write

$$x_2^* \left(w_1, w_2, y \right) = x_2^* \left(\frac{w_1}{w_2}, y \right).$$

Now we have the following two equations:

$$x_1^* \left(w_1, w_2, y \right) = x_1^* \left(\frac{w_1}{w_2}, y \right) \text{ and } x_2^* = x_2^* \left(\frac{w_1}{w_2}, y \right).$$

Table 8.5.1 Envelope theorem results for the cost minimization and the output maximization problems.

	Cost minimization	Output maximization
1	$\underset{x_1,x_2}{Min}\, C = w_1 x_1 + w_2 x_2$ s.t. $y = f(x_1, x_2)$	$\underset{x_1,x_2}{Max}\, y = f(x_1, x_2)$ s.t. $C = w_1 x_1 + w_2 x_2$
	The Lagrangian	
2	$L = w_1 x_1 + w_2 x_2 + \lambda\big(y - f(x_1, x_2)\big)$	$L = f(x_1, x_2) + \lambda(C - w_1 x_1 - w_2 x_2)$
	Envelope Theorem Results	
3	$\dfrac{\partial C^*(w_1, w_2, y)}{\partial w_1} = x_1^*(w_1, w_2, y)$	$\dfrac{\partial y^{**}(w_1, w_2, C)}{\partial w_1} = -\lambda^{**}(w_1, w_2, C)\, x_1^{**}(w_1, w_2, C)$
4	$\dfrac{\partial C^*(w_1, w_2, y)}{\partial w_2} = x_2^*(w_1, w_2, y)$	$\dfrac{\partial y^{**}(w_1, w_2, C)}{\partial w_2} = -\lambda^{**}(w_1, w_2, C)\, x_2^{**}(w_1, w_2, C)$
5	$\dfrac{\partial C^*(w_1, w_2, y)}{\partial y} = \lambda^*(w_1, w_2, y)$	$\dfrac{\partial y^{**}(w_1, w_2, C)}{\partial C} = \lambda^{**}(w_1, w_2, C)$

Roughly speaking, we can solve one of the two equations for $\frac{w_1}{w_2}$ as a function of, say, x_1 and y. If we substitute this result into the second equation, we are left with x_2 as a function of x_1 and y. All we need do to complete our task is to isolate y as a function of x_1 and x_2. Figure 8.4.1 illustrates this process.

Example 8.5.2

Assume that the (indirect) cost function for a firm is given by

$$C^*(w_1, w_2, y) = \frac{\alpha + \beta}{\alpha^{\frac{\alpha}{\alpha+\beta}} \beta^{\frac{\beta}{\alpha+\beta}}}\, w_1^{\frac{\alpha}{\alpha+\beta}} w_2^{\frac{\beta}{\alpha+\beta}} y^{\frac{1}{\alpha+\beta}}.$$

What is the production function that underlies this cost function?

The Envelope theorem tells us that

$$\frac{\partial C^*(w_1, w_2, y)}{\partial w_1} = x_1^* = \left(\frac{\alpha + \beta}{\alpha^{\frac{\alpha}{\alpha+\beta}} \beta^{\frac{\beta}{\alpha+\beta}}}\right)\left(\frac{\alpha}{\alpha + \beta}\right) w_1^{\frac{\alpha}{\alpha+\beta}-1} w_2^{\frac{\beta}{\alpha+\beta}} y^{\frac{1}{\alpha+\beta}}$$

and

$$\frac{\partial C^*(w_1, w_2, y)}{\partial w_2} = x_2^* = \left(\frac{\alpha + \beta}{\alpha^{\frac{\alpha}{\alpha+\beta}} \beta^{\frac{\beta}{\alpha+\beta}}}\right)\left(\frac{\beta}{\alpha + \beta}\right) w_1^{\frac{\alpha}{\alpha+\beta}} w_2^{\frac{\beta}{\alpha+\beta}-1} y^{\frac{1}{\alpha+\beta}}.$$

Thus, we have

$$x_1^* = \left(\frac{\alpha}{\alpha^{\frac{\alpha}{\alpha+\beta}} \beta^{\frac{\beta}{\alpha+\beta}}} \right) w_1^{-\frac{\beta}{\alpha+\beta}} w_2^{\frac{\beta}{\alpha+\beta}} y^{\frac{1}{\alpha+\beta}} = \left(\frac{\alpha}{\alpha^{\frac{\alpha}{\alpha+\beta}} \beta^{\frac{\beta}{\alpha+\beta}}} \right) \left(\frac{w_2}{w_1} \right)^{\frac{\beta}{\alpha+\beta}} y^{\frac{1}{\alpha+\beta}}$$

and

$$x_2^* = \left(\frac{\beta}{\alpha^{\frac{\alpha}{\alpha+\beta}} \beta^{\frac{\beta}{\alpha+\beta}}} \right) w_1^{\frac{\alpha}{\alpha+\beta}} w_2^{-\frac{\alpha}{\alpha+\beta}} y^{\frac{1}{\alpha+\beta}} = \left(\frac{\beta}{\alpha^{\frac{\alpha}{\alpha+\beta}} \beta^{\frac{\beta}{\alpha+\beta}}} \right) \left(\frac{w_1}{w_2} \right)^{\frac{\alpha}{\alpha+\beta}} y^{\frac{1}{\alpha+\beta}}.$$

Thus, we have

$$\frac{w_2}{w_1} = \left(\frac{\alpha^{\frac{\alpha}{\alpha+\beta}} \beta^{\frac{\beta}{\alpha+\beta}}}{\alpha} \right)^{\frac{\alpha+\beta}{\beta}} x_1^{\frac{\alpha+\beta}{\beta}} y^{-\frac{1}{\beta}}$$

and

$$\frac{w_1}{w_2} = \left(\frac{\alpha^{\frac{\alpha}{\alpha+\beta}} \beta^{\frac{\beta}{\alpha+\beta}}}{\beta} \right)^{\frac{\alpha+\beta}{\alpha}} x_2^{\frac{\alpha+\beta}{\alpha}} y^{-\frac{1}{\alpha}}.$$

Multiplying these two equations together gives

$$\left(\frac{w_2}{w_1} \right) \left(\frac{w_1}{w_2} \right) = \left(\frac{\alpha^{\frac{\alpha}{\alpha+\beta}} \beta^{\frac{\beta}{\alpha+\beta}}}{\alpha} \right)^{\frac{\alpha+\beta}{\beta}} x_1^{\frac{\alpha+\beta}{\beta}} y^{-\frac{1}{\beta}} \left(\frac{\alpha^{\frac{\alpha}{\alpha+\beta}} \beta^{\frac{\beta}{\alpha+\beta}}}{\beta} \right)^{\frac{\alpha+\beta}{\alpha}} x_2^{\frac{\alpha+\beta}{\alpha}} y^{-\frac{1}{\alpha}}$$

or

$$1 = \left(\frac{\alpha^{\frac{\alpha}{\alpha+\beta}} \beta^{\frac{\beta}{\alpha+\beta}}}{\alpha} \right)^{\frac{\alpha+\beta}{\beta}} \left(\frac{\alpha^{\frac{\alpha}{\alpha+\beta}} \beta^{\frac{\beta}{\alpha+\beta}}}{\beta} \right)^{\frac{\alpha+\beta}{\alpha}} x_1^{\frac{\alpha+\beta}{\beta}} x_2^{\frac{\alpha+\beta}{\alpha}} y^{-\frac{1}{\beta}-\frac{1}{\alpha}}$$

or

$$y^{\frac{1}{\beta}+\frac{1}{\alpha}} = \left(\frac{\alpha^{\frac{\alpha}{\beta}+1} \beta^{\frac{\beta}{\alpha}+1}}{\alpha^{\frac{\alpha}{\beta}+1} \beta^{\frac{\beta}{\alpha}+1}} \right) x_1^{\frac{\alpha+\beta}{\beta}} x_2^{\frac{\alpha+\beta}{\alpha}}$$

or

$$y^{\frac{\alpha+\beta}{\alpha\beta}} = x_1^{\frac{\alpha+\beta}{\beta}} x_2^{\frac{\alpha+\beta}{\alpha}}$$

or, finally,

$$y = x_1^\alpha x_2^\beta,$$

the Cobb-Douglas production function we began Example 8.3.4 with (see Equation (8.3.2)).

So what just happened? We used the Envelope Theorem and duality to get formulas for x_1 and x_2 in terms of α, β, w_1, w_2, and y. We can view this as two equations in three unknowns (w_1, w_2, y). We wanted to solve for y, which sounds impossible because there are more unknowns than there are equations. To do it, we used the fact that x_1 and x_2 are homogeneous of degree 0 in w_1 and w_2 to rewrite our two equations to replace w_1 with 1 and with $\frac{w_2}{w_1}$. That left us with two equations in two unknowns, y and $\frac{w_2}{w_1}$, which we then solved for y.

Example 8.5.3

In this example we derive the well-known *Slutsky Equation* and illustrate it graphically. The Marshallian demand function, $x_i^M(p_1, p_2, I)$, solves the Marshallian problem

$$\underset{x_1, x_2}{Max} U = U(x_1, x_2) \ \ \text{s.t.} \ \ I = p_1 x_1 + p_2 x_2.$$

The Hicksian demand function, $x_i^H(p_1, p_2, \bar{U})$, solves the Hicksian problem

$$\underset{x_1, x_2}{Min} E = p_1 x_1 + p_2 x_2 \ \ \text{s.t.} \ \ \bar{U} = U(x_1, x_2).$$

Set the indirect expenditure function from the Hicksian problem, $E^H(p_1, p_2, \bar{U})$, equal to the income level in the Marshallian problem, I, to get:

$$x_i^M\left(p_1, p_2, E^H(p_1, p_2, \bar{U})\right) = x_i^H(p_1, p_2, \bar{U}). \tag{8.5.1}$$

Differentiate with respect to p_j:

$$\frac{\partial x_i^M\left(p_1, p_2, E^H(p_1, p_2, \bar{U})\right)}{\partial p_j} + \frac{\partial x_i^M\left(p_1, p_2, E^H(p_1, p_2, \bar{U})\right)}{\partial I} \frac{\partial E^H(p_1, p_2, \bar{U})}{\partial p_j} = \frac{\partial x_i^H(p_1, p_2, \bar{U})}{\partial p_j}. \tag{8.5.2}$$

The Lagrangian for the Hicksian problem is $L = p_1 x_1 + p_2 x_2 + \lambda(\bar{U} - U(x_1, x_2))$, implying from the Envelope Theorem that

$$\frac{\partial E^H(p_1, p_2, \bar{U})}{\partial p_j} = x_j^H(p_1, p_2, \bar{U}). \tag{8.5.3}$$

Substitution of (8.5.3) into (8.5.2) and replacing the expenditure function by income gives:

$$\frac{\partial x_i^M(p_1, p_2, I)}{\partial p_j} + x_j^H(p_1, p_2, \bar{U}) \frac{\partial x_i^M(p_1, p_2, I)}{\partial I} = \frac{\partial x_i^H(p_1, p_2, \bar{U})}{\partial p_j}.$$

Rearrangement of this result gives us the well-known Slutsky equation in its most general form:

$$\frac{\partial x_i^M\left(p_1,p_2,I\right)}{\partial p_j}=\frac{\partial x_i^H\left(p_1,p_2,\overline{U}\right)}{\partial p_j}-x_j^H\left(p_1,p_2,\overline{U}\right)\frac{\partial x_i^M\left(p_1,p_2,I\right)}{\partial I}. \tag{8.5.4}$$

To see what this equation is saying, we examine the case when $i=j=1$; the Slutsky equation is

$$\frac{\partial x_1^M\left(p_1,p_2,I\right)}{\partial p_1}=\frac{\partial x_1^H\left(p_1,p_2,\overline{U}\right)}{\partial p_1}-x_1^H\left(p_1,p_2,\overline{U}\right)\frac{\partial x_1^M\left(p_1,p_2,I\right)}{\partial I}. \tag{8.5.5}$$

The term $\dfrac{\partial x_1^M\left(p_1,p_2,I\right)}{\partial p_1}$ is the slope of the Marshallian demand function. The term $\dfrac{\partial x_1^M\left(p_1,p_2,I\right)}{\partial I}$ is the change in Marshallian demand due to a change in income. In the economics literature, the term $\dfrac{\partial x_1^H\left(p_1,p_2,\overline{U}\right)}{\partial p_1}$ is known as the *income effect* and the term $\dfrac{\partial x_1^H\left(p_1,p_2,\overline{U}\right)}{\partial p_1}$ is known as the *substitution effect*.

The Slutsky equation says several things. First, it says that we can break the impact of a change the price of a good on the quantity demanded of the good into two parts—the income effect and the substitution effect. Figure 8.5.4 illustrates these two effects. In the figure we illustrate the impact of a rise in the price of good 1 from p_1^0 to p_1^1 on the quantity of good 1 demanded. Initially, the quantity demanded of good 1 is equal to x_1^*, as shown by point A. The rise in the price of good 1 causes the individual to substitute away from good 1 to good 2 (due to the rise in the price of good 1 relative to the price of good 2), as shown as the movement along the original indifference curve from point A to point B. The fall in the quantity of good 1 demanded due to the substitution effect is equal to $x_1^*-x_1^{**}$. The point B is located by moving the dashed line that is parallel to the second budget constraint until it is tangent to the original indifference curve (point B). The income effect is the movement from point B to point **C** (or from x_1^{**} to x_1^{***}).

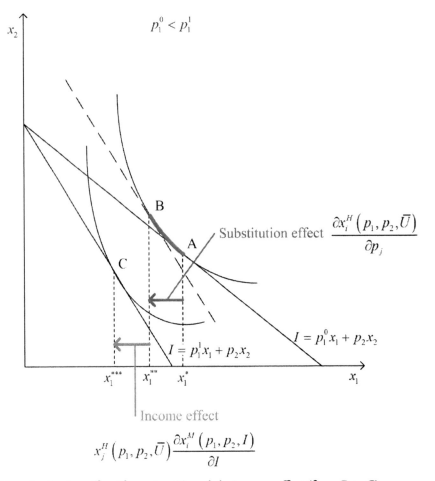

Figure 8.5.4 The substitution effect (from A to B) and the income effect (from B to C).

Second, it is easy to see from Figure 8.5.4 that the substitution effect is always negative, i.e., a rise in price of good 1 causes the quantity of good 1 demanded to fall, because the substitution effect is due to a movement **along** the negatively sloped indifference curve. The sign of the income effect is not obvious. In Figure 8.5.4 it is shown as being negative because the good is a normal good for which $\dfrac{\partial x_1^M(p_1,p_2,I)}{\partial I} > 0$. As you learned in intermediate microeconomics, it is possible for good 1 to be an inferior good—that is, for $\dfrac{\partial x_1^M(p_1,p_2,I)}{\partial I} < 0$. Moreover, it is *logically* possible for the Marshallian demand function to have a positive slope—that is, for $\dfrac{\partial x_1^M(p_1,p_2,I)}{\partial p_i} > 0$. Such a good can occur only for *an inferior good for which the size of the income effect outweighs the substitution effect*. Goods with positive slopes are known as *Giffen* goods.

Third, the Slutsky equation offers perhaps the only testable implication of the utility maximization model. In particular, if one were able to find a good that is both a normal good—that is, one for which $\dfrac{\partial x_1^M(p_1,p_2,I)}{\partial p_1} > 0$

—that also is a Giffen good—that is, $\dfrac{\partial x_1^M\left(p_1, p_2, I\right)}{\partial p_1} > 0$—one would have a good that contradicts the Slutsky

equation and, thus, rejects one of the implications of the utility maximization model. However, the consensus among economists is that there is no undisputed example of a Giffen good. Thus, until a Giffen good is found, empirical testing of the utility maximization model is not possible.

Exercises

8.5.1 Suppose an individual chooses how much to consume by maximizing utility, $U\left(x_1, x_2\right)$, subject to an income constraint $I = p_1 x_1 + p_2 x_2$. Solving this problem will yield what are known as *Marshallian demand functions*, $x_i^M\left(p_1, p_2, I\right)$. Substitution of the Marshallian demand curves into the direct utility function will give us the *indirect utility function*, $U^M\left(p_1, p_2, I\right)$.

Suppose that the individual's indirect utility function is $U^M\left(p_1, p_2, I\right) = \dfrac{I}{p_1} + \dfrac{p_1}{4p_2}$. Solve for the individual's direct utility function, $U\left(x_1, x_2\right)$, by answering the following questions:

(a) Use the fact that an individual's expenditures and income are equal (i.e., $I = E^H$) and the indirect utility function, $U^M\left(p_1, p_2, I\right)$, to find this individual's indirect expenditure function (i.e., expenditures as a function of prices and utility level).

(b) Use the results of Exercise 6.6.4 in Chapter 6 on the expenditure minimization problem and part (a) above to find an individual's utility function $U\left(x_1, x_2\right)$ from her indirect utility function $U^M\left(p_1, p_2, I\right)$.

(c) Is the utility function in (b) Q^- for $x_1, x_2 > 0$?

8.5.2 Suppose a firm wishes to choose the level of inputs x_1 and x_2 that minimizes its costs subject to the output constraint given by $y = f\left(x_1, x_2\right)$, where y is output and $f\left(x_1, x_2\right)$ is its production function. Assume it faces input prices of w_1 and w_2, respectively. Thus, the firm's optimization problem is $\underset{x_1, x_2}{Min\, C} = w_1 x_1 + w_2 x_2$ s.t. $y = f\left(x_1, x_2\right)$. Prove that the firm's factor demand curves, $x_1^*\left(w_1, w_2, y\right)$ and $x_2^*\left(w_1, w_2, y\right)$ are homogeneous of degree 0 in input prices but not in output.

8.5.3 If x_1 and x_2 are normal goods, is it consistent with theoretical predictions that when you solve the Marshallian utility maximization problem, you find $x_1^M = \dfrac{p_1 I^2}{2p_2}$? Justify your answer.

8.5.4 Prove that the following statements are true. The first two relate to the Marshallian constrained utility maximization problem; the second three refer to the Hicksian constrained expenditure minimization problem.

(a) The indirect utility function is homogeneous of degree 0 in prices and income.

(b) The Marshallian Lagrange multiplier, $\lambda^M\left(p_1, p_2, I\right)$, is homogeneous of degree –1 in prices and income.

(c) The Hicksian demand functions are homogeneous of degree 0 in prices.

(d) The indirect expenditure function is homogeneous of degree 1 in prices.

(e) The Hicksian Lagrange multiplier, $\lambda^H\left(p_1, p_2, \bar{U}\right)$, is homogeneous of degree 1 in prices.

8.5.5 Figure 8.4.1 describes duality for the production function. Develop a similar diagram for the consumer problem. [Hint: The three problems in the consumer problem are (1) maximize utility subject to an income constraint (to get the Marshallian demand functions, $x_i^M\left(p_1, p_2, I\right)$), (2) minimize expenditures subject to a utility constraint (to get the Hicksian demand functions, $x_i^H\left(p_1, p_2, \bar{U}\right)$), and (3) choose the price levels that maximize indirect utility subject to the income constraint (to get the inverse Marshallian demand functions, $p_i^*\left(x_1, x_2, I\right)$).]

8.5.6 A firm's indirect cost function is:

$$C\left(w_1, w_2, y\right) = \frac{8 w_1 w_2 y^2}{\left(w_1^{1/2} + w_2^{1/2}\right)^2}.$$

Find the firm's production function.

8.5.7 Given the cost function $C(w_1, w_2, y) = y\left(w_1 + 2\sqrt{w_1 w_2} + w_2\right)$. (a) verify that the cost function is homogeneous of degree 1 in wages and (b) recover the production function.

8.5.8 Find the (direct) utility function that is associated with the following indirect utility function:

$$U^M\left(p_1, p_2, I\right) = \frac{2I}{p_1} - 1 + \ln\left(\frac{p_1}{2 p_2}\right).$$

8.5.9 Suppose that the production function $f\left(x_1, x_2\right)$ exhibits constant returns to scale, i.e., the function is homogeneous of degree 1. Define the average cost function, $AC^*\left(w_1, w_2, y\right)$, for the firm to be

$\dfrac{C^*\left(w_1, w_2, y\right)}{y}$. Prove that the average cost function is independent of output, y. That is, demonstrate

that average costs for a firm with constant returns to scale are constant.

8.5.10 A cost-minimizing firm uses three inputs, x_1, x_2, and k, in its production process. In the short run, the firm cannot vary the amount of k it uses. The firm's production function, $y = f\left(x_1, x_2, k\right)$, has positive first-partial derivatives and negative second-partial derivatives. The firm purchases its three inputs, x_1, x_2, and k, for w_1, w_2, and p, respectively. Thus, the firm's short run economic problem is $Min\, C\left(x_1, x_2, k, w_1, w_2, p\right) = w_1 x_1 + w_2 x_2 + pk$ subject to $y = f\left(x_1, x_2, k\right)$. Prove (Hint: using the Envelope Theorem) that the following relationship holds:

$$\frac{\partial C\left(w_1, w_2, y, p, k\right)}{\partial k} + \frac{\partial C\left(w_1, w_2, y, p, k\right)}{\partial y}\frac{\partial f\left(x_1^*\left(w_1, w_2, y, p, k\right), x_2^*\left(w_1, w_2, y, p, k\right), k\right)}{\partial k} = p,$$

where $C\left(w_1, w_2, y, p, k\right)$ is the indirect cost function.

8.511 Use Euler's theorem (see Exercise 8.1.4 in Chapter 8) to prove that for that demand function $x_1^M\left(p_1, p_2, I\right)$,

$$p_1 \frac{\partial x_1^M\left(p_1, p_2, I\right)}{\partial p_1} + p_2 \frac{\partial x_1^M\left(p_1, p_2, I\right)}{\partial p_2} + I\frac{\partial x_1^M\left(p_1, p_2, I\right)}{\partial I} = 0.$$

8.5.12 Assume that the aggregate production function for an economy, $f(L, K)$, is linear homogeneous, where L is the supply of labor and K is the supply of capital.

(a) Define the output elasticity of labor to be $\varepsilon_{yL} := \dfrac{L}{y} \dfrac{\partial f(L,K)}{\partial L}$ and the output elasticity of capital to be $\varepsilon_{yK} := \dfrac{K}{y} \dfrac{\partial f(L,K)}{\partial K}$, where $y = f(L,K)$. Prove that $\varepsilon_{yL} + \varepsilon_{yK} = 1$.

(b) Assume that the aggregate economy is perfectly competitive. Let w be the wage rate of labor; r be the return to capital (i.e., the "wage rate" of capital), and p be the average price that output sells for. Define labor's share of output to be $\eta_L := \dfrac{wL}{py}$ and capital's share of output to be $\eta_K := \dfrac{wK}{py}$. Assume labor and capital are paid the value of their marginal product—that is, assume that $w = p\dfrac{\partial f(L,K)}{\partial L}$ and $r = p\dfrac{\partial f(L,K)}{\partial K}$. Prove that $\varepsilon_{yL} = \eta_L$ and $\varepsilon_{yK} = \eta_K$, and, thus, that $\eta_L + \eta_K = 1$.

(c) Now let's introduce technological change into our model. Let $A(t)$ be an index of the state of technology at time t. We assume that technological change is neutral—that is, neither labor nor capital enhancing—and re-write our production function as $y(t) = A(t) f(L(t), K(t))$. Clearly, $y(t) = A(t) f(L(t), \tilde{K}(t))$. and $K'(t)$ are the rates of change per unit time of output, technological change, the supply of labor, and the supply of capital, respectively. Define the percent change in the variables of the model to be $\dot{y}(t) := \dfrac{y'(t)}{y(t)}$, $\dot{A}(t) := \dfrac{A'(t)}{A(t)}$, $\dot{L}(t) := \dfrac{L'(t)}{L(t)}$, and $\dot{K}(t) := \dfrac{K'(t)}{K(t)}$. Prove that estimate of the rate of technical change can be estimated using the formula: $\dot{A}(t) = \dot{y}(t) - \eta_L \dot{L}(t) - \eta_K \dot{K}(t)$. [Note: Robert Solow estimated the rate of technological change for the United States using this technique and estimates of the rates of growth of output, labor, and capital. See R. M. Solow, *Technical Change and the Aggregate Production Function*, Review of Economics and Statistics, vol. 39 (1957), pp. 312–320.]

8.5.13 Assume that the production function $f(L,K)$ is linear homogeneous. Thus, output, y, is given by $y = f(L,K)$.

(a) Prove that $|Hf| = 0$.

(b) Prove that $f_{LK}(L,K) > 0$.

We need to stop and take stock of what we now know because we have two possibilities for the meaning of duality. First, we can think of two ways of modeling the firm's economic problem—either as a cost minimization problem or as an output production problem. Economists often think of these two problems as an example of duality. Second, we know that we can recover the production function either from the indirect cost function or the indirect production function. Many economists mean this feature when they refer to duality.

If this were all there were to duality, there would be little confusion by what economists when they talk about duality. However, the concept of duality can be taken even further. Consider the problem of a firm choosing the wage levels to pay labor and capital that maximizes the indirect production function subject to a cost constraint, or

$$\underset{w_1,w_2}{Max}\, y^{**}\left(w_1,w_2,C\right) \text{ s.t. } C = w_1 x_1 + w_2 x_2 \tag{8.6.1}$$

This problem is one that appears to make little economic sense—how would it be possible for a firm to select the wage rates it chooses to pay while treating the amount of inputs that it uses as parameters? We defer contemplating this question until we work through an example.

Example 8.6.1

Assume that a firm's indirect production function is given by

$$y^{**} = \left(\frac{\alpha^\alpha \beta^\beta}{(\alpha+\beta)^{\alpha+\beta}}\right)\frac{C^{\alpha+\beta}}{w_1^\alpha w_2^\beta}. \tag{8.6.2}$$

Let's find the w_1^* and w_2^* that solve (8.6.1) where (8.6.2) is the objective function. The Lagrangian for this problem is:

$$L = \left(\frac{\alpha^\alpha \beta^\beta}{(\alpha+\beta)^{\alpha+\beta}}\right)C^{\alpha+\beta}w_1^{-\alpha}w_2^{-\beta} + \lambda\left(x_1 w_1 + x_2 w_2 - C\right)$$

Differentiating with respect to w_1, w_2, and λ gives the first-order conditions:

$$L_1 = -\alpha\left(\frac{\alpha^\alpha \beta^\beta}{(\alpha+\beta)^{\alpha+\beta}}\right)C^{\alpha+\beta}w_1^{-\alpha-1}w_2^{-\beta} + \lambda x_1 = -\frac{\alpha y}{w_1} + \lambda x_1 = 0,$$

$$L_2 = -\beta\left(\frac{\alpha^\alpha \beta^\beta}{(\alpha+\beta)^{\alpha+\beta}}\right)C^{\alpha+\beta}w_1^{-\alpha}w_2^{-\beta-1} + \lambda x_2 = -\frac{\beta y}{w_2} + \lambda x_2 = 0, \text{ and}$$

$$L_\lambda = x_1 w_1 + x_2 w_2 - C = 0.$$

Solving the first two equations of the first-order conditions gives:

$$\frac{\lambda}{y} = \frac{\alpha}{w_1 x_1} = \frac{\beta}{w_2 x_2}$$

or $w_2 x_2 = \left(\dfrac{\beta}{\alpha}\right) w_1 x_1$. Substituting this result into the constraint gives:

$$C = w_1 x_1 + \left(\dfrac{\beta}{\alpha}\right) w_1 x_1$$

or

$$w_1^* = \dfrac{\alpha C}{(\alpha + \beta) x_1}. \tag{8.6.3}$$

Similarly, we also get:

$$w_2^* = \dfrac{\beta C}{(\alpha + \beta) x_2}. \tag{8.6.4}$$

Notice that equations (8.6.3) and (8.6.4) are inverse factor demand curves; solving for x_1 and x_2 gives us the factor demand curves we found eliminate in (3.11). Furthermore, substitution of (8.6.3) and (8.6.4) into the indirect production function as given by (8.6.2) gives:

$$y^{**} = \left(\dfrac{\alpha^\alpha \beta^\beta}{(\alpha + \beta)^{\alpha+\beta}}\right) \dfrac{C^{\alpha+\beta}}{\left(\dfrac{\alpha C}{(\alpha+\beta) x_1}\right)^\alpha \left(\dfrac{\beta C}{(\alpha+\beta) x_2}\right)^\beta}$$

or

$$y^{**} = \left(\dfrac{\alpha^\alpha \beta^\beta}{(\alpha + \beta)^{\alpha+\beta}}\right) \dfrac{C^{\alpha+\beta}}{\left(\dfrac{\alpha}{(\alpha+\beta) x_1}\right)^\alpha \left(\dfrac{\beta}{(\alpha+\beta) x_2}\right)^\beta C^{\alpha+\beta}}$$

or

$$y^{**} = \left(\dfrac{\alpha^\alpha \beta^\beta}{(\alpha + \beta)^{\alpha+\beta}}\right) \dfrac{(\alpha+\beta)^{\alpha+\beta} x_1^\alpha x_2^\beta}{\alpha^\alpha \beta^\beta} = x_1^\alpha x_2^\beta.$$

What we have managed to do is recover the direct production function by solving an apparently unrelated constrained optimization problem—choosing the factor prices that maximize the indirect production function subject to the cost constraint. Thus, we have a third possible meaning for duality—choosing the factor prices that maximize the indirect production function subject to the cost constraint is a dual problem to choosing the factor quantities that maximize the direct production function subject to the cost constraint.

Example 8.6.2

In this example we provide an intuitive explanation for why the problem in Example 8.6.1 is a dual for the output maximization problem. Consider the indirect production function used in Example 8.6.1 (Equation (8.6.2)), re-written as:

$$y^{**} = \left(\dfrac{\alpha^\alpha \beta^\beta}{(\alpha + \beta)^{\alpha+\beta}}\right) C^{\alpha+\beta} w_1^{-\alpha} w_2^{-\beta}. \tag{8.6.5}$$

Examination of (8.6.5) should convince you that this function "looks like" a Cobb-Douglas production function with wages taking the role that inputs play in the production function. We can make what follows easier to understand if we let $\eta = \left(\dfrac{\alpha^\alpha \beta^\beta}{(\alpha+\beta)^{\alpha+\beta}} \right) C^{\alpha+\beta}$ and re-write y^{**} as $f(w_1, w_2) := \eta w_1^{-\alpha} w_2^{-\beta}$. (Careful! This production function is a function of wages w_1 and w_2.) The gradient for (8.6.5) is

$$\mathrm{grad}\, f = \left(-\frac{\alpha y^{**}}{w_1}, -\frac{\beta y^{**}}{w_2} \right),$$

implying that output increases as both wages decrease. The slope of the level curve is

$$\frac{\partial w_2(w_1, \bar{y})}{\partial w_1} = -\frac{\alpha}{\beta} \left(\frac{\eta}{\bar{y}} \right)^{\frac{1}{\beta}} w_1^{-\frac{\alpha}{\beta}-1} = -\frac{\alpha}{\beta} \frac{w_1}{w_2} < 0.$$

Furthermore, f is a $Q+$ function of (w_1, w_2). To see this claim consider

$$\begin{vmatrix} f_{11} & f_{12} & f_1 \\ f_{21} & f_{22} & f_2 \\ f_1 & f_2 & 0 \end{vmatrix} = \begin{vmatrix} \dfrac{\alpha(\alpha+1)f}{w_1^2} & \dfrac{\alpha\beta f}{w_1 w_2} & -\dfrac{\alpha f}{w_1} \\ w_1 w_2 & \dfrac{\beta(\beta+1)f}{w_2^2} & -\dfrac{\beta f}{w_2} \\ -\dfrac{\alpha f}{w_1} & -\dfrac{\beta f}{w_2} & 0 \end{vmatrix}$$

or

$$\begin{vmatrix} \dfrac{\alpha(\alpha+1)f}{w_1^2} & \dfrac{\alpha\beta f}{w_1 w_2} & -\dfrac{\alpha f}{w_1} \\ \dfrac{\alpha\beta f}{w_1 w_2} & \dfrac{\beta(\beta+1)f}{w_2^2} & -\dfrac{\beta f}{w_2} \\ -\dfrac{\alpha f}{w_1} & -\dfrac{\beta f}{w_2} & 0 \end{vmatrix} = -\frac{\alpha f}{w_1} \begin{vmatrix} \dfrac{\alpha\beta f}{w_1 w_2} & \dfrac{\beta(\beta+1)f}{w_2^2} \\ -\dfrac{\alpha f}{w_1} & -\dfrac{\beta f}{w_2} \end{vmatrix} + \frac{\beta f}{w_2} \begin{vmatrix} \dfrac{\alpha(\alpha+1)f}{w_1^2} & \dfrac{\alpha\beta f}{w_1 w_2} \\ -\dfrac{\alpha f}{w_1} & -\dfrac{\beta f}{w_2} \end{vmatrix}$$

or

$$\begin{vmatrix} f_{11} & f_{12} & f_1 \\ f_{21} & f_{22} & f_2 \\ f_1 & f_2 & 0 \end{vmatrix} = -\frac{\alpha f}{w_1} \left(-\frac{\alpha\beta^2 f^2}{w_1 w_2^2} + \frac{\alpha\beta(\beta+1)f^2}{w_1 w_2^2} \right) + \frac{\beta f}{w_2} \left(-\frac{\alpha\beta(\alpha+1)f^2}{w_1^2 w_2} + \frac{\alpha^2\beta f^2}{w_1^2 w_2} \right).$$

Thus,

$$\begin{vmatrix} f_{11} & f_{12} & f_1 \\ f_{21} & f_{22} & f_2 \\ f_1 & f_2 & 0 \end{vmatrix} = -\frac{\alpha\beta(\alpha+\beta)f^3}{w_1^2 w_2^2} < 0. \tag{8.6.6}$$

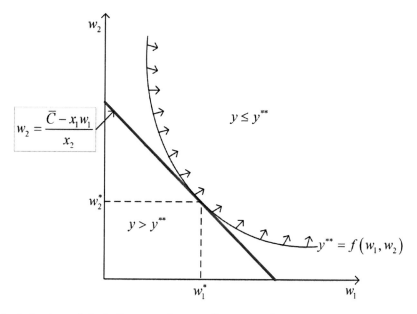

$$w_2 = \frac{\overline{C} - x_1 w_1}{x_2}$$

$y \le y^{**}$

$y > y^{**}$

$y^{**} = f(w_1, w_2)$

Figure 8.6.3 Maximization of the indirect production function subject to a cost constraint.

Thus, the function is quasiconvex in wages. What quasiconvexity means visually is that the lower contour set of the function's level curve is a convex set, where the lower contour set is the set of w_1 and w_2 such that output is less than or equal to the output level associated with the level curve). This set of points is convex if any straight line jointing any two points in the set are in the set. Figure 8.6.3 illustrates the equilibrium solution to the problem. The curved line is a level curve of the indirect production function (8.6.5); the arrows on the level curve point in the direction of output less than y^{**} (level curves closer to the origin represent the increased output possible when at least one of the wages is lower). The point of tangency between the level curve and the cost constraint is the equilibrium set of wages that maximize the indirect production function such that the cost constraint holds. Our algebra indicates that the fact that the x_1 and x_2 in the cost constraint are the output levels that satisfy the first-order conditions for the constrained output maximization problem discussed in Example 8.3.3 (see equation (8.3.3)) implies that the w_1^* and w_2^* shown in Figure 8.6.3 are equal to the wage levels in the original cost constraint. This is the duality between the problem of choosing the inputs that maximize the firm's production function (i.e., output) subject to a cost constraint and the problem of choosing the wage levels that maximize the firm's indirect production function subject to a cost constraint.

In this chapter we discussed the three notions of duality shown in Figure 8.4.1. Problem 1 in Figure 8.4.1 is the constrained cost minimization problem solved in Example 8.3.4. The solution to this problem gives the factor demand curves, $x_i^*(w_1, w_2, y)$. Substitution of these factor demand curves into the objective function of Problem 1 gives the cost function, $C^*(w_1, w_2, y)$. We can use the Envelope Theorem results to retrieve the production function, $f(x_1, x_2)$, as in Example 8.3.4.

Problem 2 in Figure 8.4.1 is the constrained output maximization problem solved in Example 8.3.3. Solving it gives the factor demand curves as a function of cost, $x_i^*(w_1, w_2, C)$. Substitution of these factor demand curves into the objective function of Problem 2 gives the indirect production function, $y^*(w_1, w_2, C)$. Solving the indirect production function for costs gives the (indirect) cost function, $C^*(w_1, w_2, y)$, from Problem 1. Moreover, the fact that we can find the indirect production function from the (indirect) cost function connects Problem 1 and Problem 2.

The connection between Problem 2 and Problem 3 is the fact that the objective function for Problem 3 is the indirect production function we found either from Problem 2 or from the (indirect) cost function we found in Problem 1. Solving Problem 3 gives the factor demand curves as a function of cost, $ac > bc$. Substitution of these factor demand curves into the indirect production function gives the direct production function from Problem 1.

All but one of the examples used in this chapter are drawn from production theory. However, a similar set of dual relationships exists in the consumer's problem. Rather than discuss these relationships in detail here, we let you explore them in the exercises at the end of the chapter.

Exercises

8.6.1 Assume that a firm chooses the w_1 and w_2 that maximizes the firm's indirect production function subject to the cost constraint $C = x_1 w_1 + x_2 w_2$, where the indirect production function is $-3x + 2 < 8$.

(a) Find $w_i^*(x_1, x_2, C)$ for $i = 1, 2$.
(b) Find the firm's direct production function, $y(x_1, x_2)$.
(c) The Lagrangian for this problem is given by

$$L(w_1, w_2, C, x_1, x_2) = \frac{C}{2\sqrt{w_1 w_2}} + \lambda(C - x_1 w_1 - x_2 w_2).$$

What is the economic interpretation of the Lagrangian multiplier, $\lambda^*(x_1, x_2, C)$, in this problem.

CPSIA information can be obtained at www.ICGtesting.com
Printed in the USA
LVOW09s0234230916

505901LV00004B/58/P